MARATHON

JEFF GALLOWAY

Library of Congress Cataloging in Publication Data

Galloway, Jeff, 1945-
Marathon!

1. Running. 2. Running-Training. 3. Fitness-Health. I. Title

ISBN: 0-9647187-3-1

First Printing: February 2000

Printed in the United States of America

Phidippides Publication
4651 Roswell Road, Suite I-802
Atlanta, GA 30342 USA

TABLE OF CONTENTS

Everyone must read this page before starting.

Why so many new people are drawn to this lifetime achievement. As we get back to our roots, we feel the satisfaction of doing something uniquely positive for body and mind. "To stick with a marathon training program for six months is to become a winner. To finish a marathon will leave you feeling like a champion."

A short history of the Greek civilization that produced the Olympics, an extensive messenger system, and a victory in 490 BC. Phidippides probably ran 260 miles but was given credit for a very important 26. The first marathon race was only 25 miles, but the ancient messenger ran 26.

This is the program for those who want to enjoy marathon satisfaction yet have a real life. You'll learn the essential components of three days of training each week, a program that allows almost anyone to complete a marathon in six months. All of the components are explained and coordinated to decrease the chance of injury and fatigue. The wall is the length of your longest run in the last three weeks.

THE LONG RUN *IS* YOUR MARATHON TRAINING PROGRAM

THE SCHEDULES

WALK BREAKS

Walk-running is what we were designed to do. How walk breaks extend capacity, erase fatigue, reduce injuries, restore resiliency, allow runners to improve time, speed recovery, and leave you feeling good enough to carry on social and family activities— even after the very long long runs. Walk breaks were part of the marathon from the very first marathon race.

The more often you take walk breaks, the better your legs feel at the end. When to take them: the earlier, the better. How fast should you walk? How fast should the running pace be between walk breaks?

While virtually eliminating slowdown at the end, they keep the legs resilient. Mentally, they break up the marathon into segments which you know you can do. How long and how often should they be taken in the marathon—when you have a time goal. How one runner improved from 3:40 to 3:25 by inserting walk breaks.

Should I change my run/walk ratio during the marathon? If I've never tried the walk breaks in training runs, would you advise taking them in the marathon? Are you saying that I can benefit from a walk break—even though I'm training for a sub-three-hour marathon? Do I have to take walk breaks at the end of my runs if my let's are tightening up? Do I need to take walk breaks during the short run during the week?

FOOD AND FAT-BURNING: FAT-BURNING AS A WAY OF LIFE

First, get yourself into the habit of regular exercise, while you teach the muscles to burn fat. Next, finish the marathon. Then turn your attention to using running and diet to burn fat if you want to.

Fat is potential energy, an unlimited supply of the very best fuel for running. How your "set point" is programmed to increase fat accumulation each year or so. Why diets don't work and how they set off the starvation reflex. Jeff Galloway's ice cream addiction.

How regular endurance exercise can move the set point down. Exercise gives you more control over your fat levels by burning up excess calories before they're deposited as fat and by training the muscle cells to burn more fat even when we're asleep. During the first 15 minutes of exercise, you burn glycogen, which produces a large waste product. From 15-45 minutes you transition into fat-burning. If you're still comfortably exercising after 45 minutes, you're in the fat-burning zone. How slow aerobic exercise with walk breaks burn more fat. Long runs are the best component for training your muscles to be fat-burners. How walk breaks effect calorie-burning. How to burn more fat by taking walk breaks. Why you don't want to lose a lot of weight and train for the marathon at the same time.

The income side of the fat ledger. Eating all day long. Small meals energize; big meals put you to sleep. Mixing carbohydrates, fat, protein, and fiber to feel good all day long. Eating a PowerBar an hour before exercise can get you motivated. How to break up your daily food into small meals. How to manage blood sugar level. Complex carbohydrates give you a discount rate, and a grace period. Galloway's lowfat foods that increase satisfaction. The reloading zone. Vitamins, minerals, alcohol, caffeine. Long-term nutritional health.

How eating during long runs improves concentration. The blood sugar challenge. Eating all day long. The starvation reflex. Managing blood sugar on long runs. Blood sugar booster foods.

24 hours before and 24 hours after. Train your stomach for the marathon. Eliminating problem foods. Jeff Galloway's eating countdown. Drink until you hear sloshing. Sports drinks. Follow the diet that got you here. Eating during the marathon. Nutritional items to avoid.

MOTIVATION

"Marathon training made me feel like a whole person—body and mind working together as a team." And other benefits received when you take the 26.2 mile challenge.

You train yourself to be motivated. The left side of our brain tries to hold us back. The creative right brain. Fun, vision and focus. Why I run. The vision exercise. The difference between a dream and a vision. Transforming the vision into a mission. It starts with a date on a calendar. You must believe. Regularity. Your motivation notebook.

Affirming the benefits of exercise. Confidence in the program. Be prepared to back up. The right group will motivate you. It could be low blood sugar. Reduce the anticipated discomfort of the run. How to get out the door after a hard day at work. From the bed to the street.

Forward motion is motivating in itself. Get a mission and write it on the calendar. Don't go too fast. Bring the PowerGel along. Be sure that you're not having a medical problem. On the very tough or fast runs. Mantras for staying motivated. Getting beyond the mid-goal wall.

Rehearse! Benefits of Rehearsal. The mental marathon, step-by-step. The battle: left brain vs right brain. The night before. When the left brain bothers you. Wake up call. The line-up. Don't try to overwhelm the left brain with distracting left brain activity - it doesn't work. The start. Challenges. Gutting it out. On to the finish.

Positive brainwashing. You can use my words, if you wish: relax, power & glide. What happens when you say the magic words. Here's how to make your words magic. Achievement. I'm storing energy. Walking extends resources. No problems will get to me. Muscles—listen to me! I love hills! Short (stride) is better. I'm getting there.

It's time to play tricks on the left brain. Sneak down the road while the left brain is confused. One crazy thought can unlock another. The giant invisible rubber band. Oxygen molecules. Ball bearing atoms. A giant hand. Your inspiration shoes. The PowerBar boost.

The post-race letdown. Select another mission before the big day. The body follows your mental vision. A few seconds of patience. Hydrate and avoid salt and alcohol. At the finish line. Throughout the afternoon. The next day. Two days after. Continue to alternate run days with walk days. Take one week off from racing and speed training for every six miles of the race. Weekend runs can gradually increase in distance. If you've run a marathon and want to run another in the near future. The group will pull you through. The marathon a month club. Before and during, the little things which speed recovery. How soon after a marathon can I realistically think of doing another one?

You can still improve your performance during the last 48 hours. By being positive and staying focused, you assume most of the control over your attitude and your performance. Drink and avoid dehydrating elements. Eat small snacks regularly. Check out the staging area. Rest! Go slowly in the beginning and take your walk breaks. Eat during the second half of the marathon to keep up your blood sugar level—and your attitude. Above all, have fun!

General items. The night before. What to put in your marathon bag. Marathon morning list. Immediately afterward. Recovery routine.

The first three miles. Between three and eight miles. Between 8 and 18 miles. After 18 miles. After 23 miles.

A FASTER MARATHON

The many ways to "win" a marathon. Why run faster in the marathon? Don't attempt a time goal until you've run at least one marathon. So what is a realistic goal? Limit your time goal marathons. From a 2:38 marathon to a 5:10 marathon in one year…and happier! The role of the slow marathon. Framing the marathon. Other marathon missions. The marathon a month club. Questions about slow marathons.

Training prepares the cardiovascular system as you also become mentally tougher. You must have enough recovery time between components. Monitoring overstress. Recovery enhancers. Mileage helps but at great risk. How many running days per week. As we get older. The fatigue-producers. Long runs improve marathon speed—but they must be run slowly. Acceleration-gliders: how to do them.

Hill training rules. Benefits of hill training. Marathon hill training. Hill training form.

When? Warm-up and warm-down. How steep. Hill form. Workouts for: Beginners, Advanced Beginner, Runner, and Competitor. Hill play questions. How a short uphill stride helped me run my fastest marathon at age 35.

The right to have fun. Do things that ensure fun. Where. Speed and endurance simultaneously. Learning how to pace yourself. Recovery. How often. Picking your goal. Predicting your goal. Warm-up. Stretching. Repeat mile intervals. Longer repetitions. Pacing. Adjusting for heat and humidity. Walk between each mile. How many mile repeats. Practice gliding during each mile. Fartlek. Mental Strength. Tempo training. Troubleshooting speed session problems: fading at the end of the workout. Workouts are great, but in the marathon I fade at the end. Isn't jogging between mile repeats better than walking?

Don't be too exuberant. Don't run faster than assigned pace. Start the session slowly and walk between mile repeats. Marathon race form. Form modes. Fun innovations. Setting up the group mile repeat session.

GETTING BETTER AS WE BECOME MORE MATURE

No bone and joint damage after more than 40 years of running. Other studies. Vitality and attitude. Alternative exercise. My favorite running companion, my dad.

PRACTICAL ADVICE

The most common sites of "weak links." How to tell if it's an injury. Inflammation. Loss of function. Pain that doesn't go away. Don't try to "stretch out" a tight muscle! Anti-inflammatory medications: see a doctor first. Treating injuries: get a doctor, don't stretch, stop activity, ice, compression, elevation, massage. Getting back to running.

Coming back from an injury. Sickness. Training interruptions of less than 14 days due to vacation, etc. Bring back the long run. Pacing the long ones. How quickly can you increase the length of the long one and get back into "marathon range."

The top five reasons why you need shoe advice. If you can't find a running specialty store. Bring your worn shoes, socks, foot devices. You're in charge. Spend some time. Tell your shoe expert. Run in each shoe. First, look at function and then go for fit. Which works best on your feet when you run. The DON'Ts of shoe selection. Pronation, Over-pronation, and Supination. Function: are you floppy or rigid? Shape: are you curved or straight? Be sure to lace your shoe securely around the ankle. Don't get locked into specific models or brands. When to buy another shoe.

How to run a marathon efficiently. Posture, Bounce, and Overstride. Correcting forward lean. Correcting overstride. Turnover drill. The battle of Boston 1995. Troubleshooting form problems. Quads: too tired, sore or weak. Discomfort, pain or weakness behind the knee. Shoulder and neck muscles tired and tight. Lower back very tight and over-fatigued. Hamstrings tired or sore. Knee pain. Sore feet and lower legs. Lower back tired and sore. Stretching warning.

How group running helps. Back to our roots. Bonding with others and self. Group fun. Homework assignment: jokes, juicy stories and controversy. The huff & puff rule. Adjusting. Group rules. Don't cut out any walk breaks. You're becoming part of an elite group. Group leaders need your support. Designated sweeper. The victory celebration.

A table which tells you how old your legs feel, based upon fitness level and pounds overweight. This allows big runners to make adjustments before they feel bad.

A table of equivalent performances between 5K, half marathon and marathon. Since this table assumes ideal conditions, add 10 to 20 minutes when moving from a 5K to the marathon. Never try to do a time goal on your first marathon. But you can still use this table. Once you have your marathon equivalent, add at least an hour to the time on your first one.

Once you have a realistic goal, here is your pacing schedule.

WHO IS JEFF GALLOWAY?

*J*eff was an average high school runner who learned, trained hard and made the US Olympic team in 1972. His most satisfying moment, however, was pacing his teammate, Jack Bacheler, through the Olympic Trials Marathon and dropping back at the finish line so that Jack could take the final qualifying spot on the team. Since then, the force of his life has been helping others to enjoy the experience of running and the achievement of finishing a marathon.

Jeff's experience includes being the first winner of the Peachtree Road Race in his hometown of Atlanta GA and finishing over 110 marathons. His book, Galloway's Book on Running has been the best-selling running book over the past decade. Jeff's popular monthly column in Runner's World magazine is circulated to over two million each month.

Jeff's specialty is maximizing the enjoyment and satisfaction of running, while minimizing the time spent, the injuries, and the fatigue. He keeps innovating and articulating techniques which help average people enjoy running more, run faster, and reduce injuries to almost none.

In Jeff's training programs across North America, thousands of beginners finish a marathon six months after taking their first step. More important to Jeff is that most of these folks are hooked on fitness.

Jeff's family includes his wife of nearly 25 years, Barbara, and sons Westin and Brennan, all of whom are runners.

Through his running retreats at Lake Tahoe, Switzerland, and Greece (for the running of the "original" marathon), Jeff works individually with runners of all abilities in a friendly and supportive environment. He conducts over 200 talks and seminars each year, receiving the direct feedback that keeps his articles and books focused on practical, helpful advice.

Jeff still runs over 60 miles a week and hasn't had an overuse running injury in over 15 years.

BEFORE YOU TAKE
THOSE FIRST STEPS...

*T*here are very few people who should not exercise because of cardiovascular, structural, muscular, or other problems. It is very important to ensure that you are not in this risk category.

- Before beginning any exercise, diet or other improvement program, be sure to have yourself and the program evaluated by specialists in the areas you are pursuing.

- The advice in this book is offered as such—advice from one exerciser to another. It is not meant to be a prescription and should be evaluated as noted above and below.

- Specific structures and problems of individuals may require program modifications.

- In each area, find specialists who are also knowledgeable about the positive and other effects of exercise and running.

- Ask several respected leaders in the fitness community for recommendations of specialists.

- Always back off any exercise or program when you feel any risk of injury or health.

- The benefits come from regular exercise and steady adherence to a long-term program.

- Never radically increase the amount of exercise or drastically change diet and other health elements.

- Joining a group helps motivation.

- Have FUN and you'll want to continue.

INTRODUCTION
WHY CHOOSE THE MARATHON?

*O*verwhelming is the best way to describe the floodtide of entrants into marathons. Each year, beginning exercisers by the thousands are targeting a marathon instead of the safer choice of a 5K or 10K. Established marathons are filling their quotas earlier than ever, and the overflow of procrastinators has been absorbed by a mushrooming growth of interesting regional and national 42K events. What started as a once-in-a-lifetime achievement is now being renewed by former couch potatoes every six to 12 months.

At the same time that a majority of the North American population has been labeled "significantly overweight," marathon training has been noted by many experts as the fastest growing activity in the field of exercise. Surely some of the two+ million who train for a marathon each year start with the goal of losing some of the blanket that has been accumulating around their midsections for a decade or so. The overwhelming number of those who continue, however, do so because of the unequaled positive attitude boost, significant stress release, and overall increase in vitality, focus and creativity.

As the average age of the marathoner has increased to 40+, the marathon has become the mid-life mission. It could be worse: when you list the other mid-life diversions,

the marathon is not a bad choice. At this stage of life, a high percentage of these first-time marathoners are accustomed to relying upon key people and leveraging influence through contacts, income and other negotiable items. The marathon stands out as one of the most esteemed of life's achievements, which has to be won by pulling from within oneself the physical, mental and spiritual resources over an extended period of time. The universal respect flows from sedentary observers who wish they could find the fortitude to get out there. Participants discover a mature self-respect, along with the previously dormant strengths and capabilities to meet the challenges on this six-month migration.

Part of the fulfillment must come from getting back to our roots. Our ancient ancestors walked and ran for thousands of miles each year to survive. In the process, they developed and passed on to us a treasury of physical and mental rewards, which we renew on every run. The challenge of a significant physical journey on foot unleashes some primitive connections to our identity as human beings.

Most new marathoners bypass shorter distance events because they know that they need a challenging mission. By writing the marathon date on a calendar, one becomes more motivated to get out the door when the alarm goes off way too early or on days when the weather doesn't cooperate.

If you have read this far, chances are you're ready to go forward with one of most fulfilling experiences of your life. At the very least, you're saying that you want to take responsibility for your health and your attitude. On the long list of benefits from such a program, those two are at the top.

Every marathoner, no matter how experienced, has to dig down and find resources to get through the training program and to finish the marathon. You'll discover strengths that you didn't know were there. Most of those on a marathon mission become more positive and react more directly with life's offerings. As you view the finish banner and realize you're near the end of the journey, even the tough guys let some tears loose.

Over the past four decades, my marathon count has exceeded 110. I've received the same wonderful exhilaration when running them fast (2:16) as I do when running them slowly. To reach the finish line in a marathon is to enter a very elite group: about one tenth of one percent of the population does it. My most treasured marathon was my slowest. I ran with my father in the 1996 Boston Marathon in 5:59:48. He tells folks that if I hadn't been there to slow him down, he'd have run much faster.

To stick with a marathon training program for six months is to become a winner.

To finish a marathon will leave you feeling like a champion!

You can do it!

WHERE DID THE MARATHON COME FROM?

*T*hat's simple. In the first modern Olympics, in 1896, there was a race to commemorate the trek of the ancient messenger from the Plain of Marathon to Athens to report a great Greek victory in 490 BC. But like so many supposedly simple historical facts, this one has many plots and subplots.

Ancient Greek Olympians ran short distance races in stadiums. I have the good fortune to regularly take groups of runners and walkers to visit these sites in Greece. Chillbumps pop up every time I visit and jog down the field. You can put your feet in the grooves of the starting blocks they used and experience a direct connection to the vitality of the ancient Olympic concept. This will keep you motivated to get out the door for weeks or months on your return home!

But there were excellent long distance runners in ancient Greece who never competed but provided fast communication links throughout that civilization. Often logging more than a marathon a day, these endurance specialists could navigate the tricky Greek terrain, covering very long distances faster than horses. They were expected to not only deliver the news but to also interpret it, emphasize key points, and return with a reply, including a description of the facial expression and emotion of the respondent.

Phidippides rose to the challenge in 490 BC. As a messenger for the Athenian army, he and the other soldiers assembled on the hills above the Plain of Marathon, hoping to confront the aggressive and militaristic Persians, who had just invaded Greek soil and set up camp 25 miles from Athens. The enemy had a numerical advantage of about five to one.

This was a crucial period in the development of the democratic experiment in Athens. Contrary to the more autocratic governments of the other great civilizations to that point, the Athenians encouraged individual freedoms and personal growth and achievement. The epitome of this philosophy was the Olympic games, which elevated fitness and sport to a level of respect equal to valued professions. Indeed, the Greeks recorded history according to the four-year Olympiad in which the event occurred. The Persians were determined to snuff out these radical ideas.

The Athenian generals knew that this was a winner-take-all situation. If they lost, the Persians would kill them, burn Athens and enslave their families. The residents of Athens already had a plan to burn the city in order to deprive the Persians of some of their spoils.

The historical record of this period was passed down in oral reports and written down more than two centuries later by Herodotus and others. While the storytelling method of Greek history has been shown to be generally accurate through research and excavation, names and details sometimes became blurred.

Phidippides was mentioned several times in the accounts of the 490 BC campaign. When the committee of three generals who commanded the Athenians looked over the massive beachhead of their opponents, they wisely decided to ask for help, sending a messenger to Sparta. Whereas the Spartans governed by a different philosophy, they certainly would benefit from an Athenian victory; without it, the Persians would be headed their way.

The messenger sent to Sparta (about 130 miles away) was probably Phidippides. A day and a half later he arrived and went before the Spartan rulers to plead for their help. Relatively quickly, they gave him the good news that Sparta would send troops. Unfortunately, they were in the middle of a community ritual and couldn't come for about 10 days.

Another day and a half later, Phidippides had run back to the hills above Marathon and reported to the leadership. Realizing that the Persians wouldn't wait 10 days to attack, they devised an innovative battle plan and attacked with a thin front line. The Persians quickly broke through, thought they had won, and started celebrating. Suddenly the best Greek soldiers hit them from both sides, inflicting massive casualties. Having lost their focus and probably suspecting a supernatural force, the Persians ran for their ships and sailed away. One of the great battles of western civilization had been won.

Historical accounts tell us that a soldier/messenger was then dispatched to Athens to tell of the victory before the Athenians burned their city. Tradition has bestowed the honor of making that "victory lap" upon Phidippides. He covered the long gradual uphill, followed by a gradual downhill into the city and said the unexpected but exhilarating word to the fragile democracy: "Nike" (victory). Athens would live but the wounded and exhausted messenger died.

When the organizers were deciding which events to include in the first modern Olympic games (Athens, 1896), a friend of the prime organizer, De Courbetin, suggested that the run of Phidippides be commemorated in a footrace from the Plain of Marathon to the Olympic stadium. The marathon was born and reporters noted that all of the original competitors walked and ran in that first race. The marathon is one of two events which has been run in every one of the modern Olympic games.

The distance from the tomb at the battlefield to the 1896 stadium is 25 miles, which continued as the official distance until the London Olympics in 1908. The 25-mile course had been measured and marked when the Queen asked if she might be able to watch the start from the palace. The course was extended by 1.2 miles to accommodate the royal request, and the new distance became official. A few years ago, however, as I was walking from the 1896 stadium towards the ancient site of Athens, I realized that Phidippides would have run about 26 miles: the ancient town of Athens is about a mile further down the road from where the 1896 Olympic marathon ended.

A tradition among veteran marathoners when passing the original finish distance at 25 miles is to say "God save the Queen" or something like that. But considering Phidippides' run for reinforcements to Sparta and back, today's marathoners are getting off easy—we could be running 260 miles!

SETTING UP *YOUR* MARATHON PROGRAM

1. The long run gradually increases to 26 miles and gives you the specific endurance needed to complete the marathon.

2. To maintain this endurance, the weekly minimum is 60 minutes of running or walk-running, divided between two to five days.

3. Slower is better on the long ones: the slower you go, the faster you will recover, while receiving all of the endurance.

4. Frequent walk breaks, from the beginning of each long one, add fun and reduce fatigue dramatically.

5. There are almost no injuries among those who adhere to this minimum program.

6. Those who have run a marathon can train for a faster one by doing speed sessions on non-long-run weekends.

THE THREE-DAY-A-WEEK PROGRAM
Goal: To Finish

Mon	Tue	Wed	Thu	Fri	Sat	Sun
walk 30-60 minutes	run-walk 30 minutes	walk 30-60 minutes	run-walk 30 minutes	walk 30-60 minutes	off	long run-walk

ALMOST ANYONE CAN COMPLETE A MARATHON IN SIX MONTHS!

Even if you only have 60 minutes to exercise during the work week, you can train for the marathon. The minimum is actually better for reducing injuries. During the week, you only need to accumulate an hour of running/walking. The long run starts at three miles and gradually increases by one mile each week until it reaches 10 miles. Then, you'll do the long one every other week, with a run-walk of half the distance on the "off" weekend. After you've completed the 18-miler, you'll receive two weekends off for good behavior, shifting to a long one every third week.

LONG RUN ENDURANCE + 60 MINUTES OF MAINTENANCE + REST

Your body is designed to continuously improve its endurance if you gently stress it in a pattern of increases, rest enough for rebuilding, and do regular maintenance so that it won't forget the process. Think of your training program as a sound system. Each exercise session serves as a component designed to produce a specific effect. The long run provides the gentle challenge through mileage extension, which will develop the exact endurance necessary for getting to the finish line of the marathon. The slow and minimal 60 minutes of maintenance run-walks during the week simply maintain the conditioning gained on the weekend. Resting the running muscles on other days is crucial

> **Y**ou can't run too slowly on a long run.

for letting the muscles rebuild, during which they make marvelous adaptations for easier and longer running.

THE LONG RUN BUILDS ENDURANCE

As you extend a mile or three farther on each long one, you push back your endurance limit. It is important to go slowly on each of these (at least two minutes per mile slower than you could run that distance on that day) to make it easy for your muscles to extend their current endurance limit and recover afterward. As you lengthen the long one to 26 miles, you build the exact endurance necessary to complete the marathon. Walk breaks, taken from the beginning (see section below) will also speed your recovery and make the extra distance on each run a gentle challenge.

On the non-long-run weekends, there are several options. Most runners will do a slow run of about half the distance of the current long run (up to 10 miles). On two to four of these "easy" weekends, it is wise to do a 5K road race to predict what you might be able to do in the marathon. (See the Predicting Race Performance page in the Practical Advice section of this book.) Veterans will do speed sessions on some of the non-long weekends. If you're feeling good during these shorter runs, you can run them continuously, but there's no advantage in doing this. In other words, walk breaks are at your discretion on the shorter runs, including the ones during the week.

LONG RUN FACTS:

- Twenty miles with walking breaks equals 20 miles run continuously...at any speed (but you recover faster with walk breaks).

- Forget about speed on long runs. Focus only on the component of endurance.

- You can't run too slowly on the long runs. Run at least two minutes per mile slower than you could run that distance on that day, accounting for heat, humidity, etc.

- You won't usually feel bad when you're running too fast at the beginning of the run so you must force yourself to slow down.

- The day before the long run should be a no-exercise day.

WALK BREAKS ON LONG RUNS

- Must be taken early and often to reduce pounding and fatigue

- Must be taken often to allow the primary running muscles to recover fast—even when increasing long run length

- Will also help most marathoners run faster in the marathon itself

Note: You must still slow down the overall pace to at least two minutes per mile slower than you could run that distance on that day.

The most important walk breaks are the ones taken during the first mile and the second most important set, those taken in the second mile, etc. When taken from the beginning of all long ones, walk breaks erase fatigue, speed recovery, reduce injury, and yet bestow all of the endurance of the distance covered. In other words, a slow long run with walk breaks gives you the same distance conditioning as a fast one, when both cover the same distance.

Everyone should take a one to two-minute walk break every two to eight minutes on every long run. If you're just beginning to run, you'll walk more than you'll run. Experienced marathoners will recover much faster from their long ones when they take one-minute walk breaks at least every eight

> **The "Two-Minute Rule":** On long runs, you must run at least two minutes per mile slower than you could run that distance on that day (accounting for heat, humidity, hills, etc.).

minutes. The walk breaks can be done at a fast or an easy pace. See the chapter on walk breaks for more information.

DOING "THE MINIMUM" WILL DECREASE YOUR CHANCE OF INJURY AND FATIGUE

The bad news: When you extend your endurance limits on each long one, you'll stress and break down the muscle and energy systems. The good news comes after rest days. When you give the running muscles a chance to recover, they make dozens of adaptations, gearing you up for an even greater challenge one to three weeks later. If you're not getting enough rest, your muscles will accumulate pockets of micro-tears, which will continue to accumulate until you experience extreme fatigue or injury.

Tens of thousands of average people have gone through our program, with almost no injuries among those who follow the minimum. There are always some, however, who have to push the envelope. The few who get injured in our training groups are almost always those who add distance, speed or exercise days to our recommended schedule.

Because this is a bare-bones program, it's very important to do every one of the 60 minutes of exercise during the week to maintain long run endurance and speed recovery by increased blood flow to the muscles. You can run/walk these in as short as 10-minute segments, accumulating the magic hour of exercise over a four to five-day period. As is true with "cramming" before exams, it's not effective to get in all 60 minutes during the two days before the next long run. The day before the long one should be devoid of exercise—or at least no exercise for the calf muscles in the lower leg.

REST AND CROSS TRAINING

Significant rest is as important as the stress components of the program. It's actually during the rest days from running that your muscles rebuild stronger and make adaptations for greater efficiency. Only if you back off enough from the stress will the muscles recover enough to prevent injury or lingering tiredness.

To maximize the chance of having resilient legs, it's very important to rest the muscles on the day before the long run. Cross training can be done on other non-running days, as long as the lower leg muscles can recover and you don't seem to be accumulating overall fatigue. Avoid exercises such as stair machines, leg strength exercise, cycling that involves standing up, and step aerobics classes. The most common cross training exercises are walking, swimming, cycling, and upper body strength exercise.

Cross training won't improve your marathon time, and it's not necessary for finishing the marathon. It will provide attitude-boosting endorphins, stress release, and fat-burning on the days when you need to let your running muscles recover. For more on cross training, consult the chapter in this book.

SPEED

Only those who have run a marathon before should even consider a time goal. The primary benefit in this program comes from covering the gradually increasing distance of the long run. After having run over 60 marathons for time and over 50 just to finish, I believe that time improvement is for the ego, but there's nothing wrong with that. The speed game can be interesting, but most of the satisfaction in running in a marathon comes from crossing the finish

5

Y*es, it's possible to train for the marathon and have a life.*

line. The first marathon should be done at a slow enough pace so that you reach the finish line knowing that you could run faster and that you want to run another.

Veterans who have run a marathon or few and want to improve their times can add a speed component on some of the non-long-run weekends. You'll find my recommended schedule of hill play and then mile repeats listed in the training schedules and in the Speedplay chapter in this book. Please be careful because the addition of speed will increase your chance of injury. As long as your goal is realistic, you're taking suffi-cient rest, and you adapt the speedwork pace to weather conditions, you'll give the body the creative stress it needs to help you improve in a series of steps. Don't add to the program, and monitor your "weak links" to minimize the chance of overstress and injury.

Veterans will increase their chance of time goal fulfillment by increasing the length of the long one to 28 to 29 miles. This builds extra endurance, which gives your legs the capacity to keep pushing during the latter stages of the marathon itself. On these extra long ones, the recommended pace reduction from the beginning is at least two and a half minutes per mile slower than you could run that distance on that day.

BEWARE OF MIXING COMPONENTS

Running too fast on the long one will leave you much more tired, with multiples of damaged muscle cells, than you've experi-enced by following the Two-Minute Rule. Not only does this increase the chance of injury, but veterans who try to put speed into the endurance run will sacrifice the quantity or quality of their speedplay later in the week. Often this fatigue is so subtle that you don't feel it for two or three long

ones, due to the release of stress hormones, which mask the sensations of tiredness.

Running too long or too fast during speedplay sessions will reduce the prospec-tive benefit. Speed in endurance events is developed, like endurance, in a series of many speed sessions, each pushing only a little further than the one before. Going further or faster than you have been in the recent past will increase recovery time and complicate the rebuilding process. When too many of the muscle cells are damaged, the muscle doesn't rebuild stronger for a long time.

Maintenance runs that are too fast will slow down recovery and increase the buildup of fatigue. It is important that your 60 minutes of maintenance exercise during the week is done slowly enough so the muscles will recover from the previous weekend. When in doubt, go slower.

IT HELPS TO HAVE A GROUP

One of the most delightful things I do is help set up training groups around North America. Each group member finds a significant motivation boost to do the long ones and to get in the 60 minutes during the week. You'll be inspired by your "team-mates" some days, and you'll inspire them on others. Choose a team that has the same fitness condition as you. The goal is to go slowly enough on long runs that even the least conditioned members of the group can keep up. In each of the cities where we have groups, we have several sub-groups, based upon fitness level.

WHERE IS *THE WALL?*

Most marathoners who start their long runs too fast or exceed the length of their current long run by more than three miles or both

Yes, it's possible to complete every long one, even a 26-miler, without hitting the couch or bed all afternoon and evening.

will experience a fatigue "wall" at the end of the run. If you're running within your capabilities from the beginning, you'll be tired as you reach the mileage of your longest run in the past two to three weeks. Most runners can go one to two miles beyond that point, accumulating more fatigue quickly but able to move ahead as before. The wall hits you quickly as you reach your limits. Within a few yards, you go from feeling tired but capable of continuing forward to feeling like you can't go more than a few steps. The muscles have gone too far beyond their limit and can't handle any more running. Because of the physical stress, your left brain is sending you streams of negative messages which tell you to quit, question your sanity, and ask you philosophical questions such as: "Why are you doing this?"

So your wall is normally the length of your longest run within the last two to three weeks, provided you are running the pace you could run that distance on that day. Even a little too fast in the beginning will introduce you to the wall sooner. On a hot, humid day, you'll bump into that wall before you should—if you don't slow your pace down even more than normal from the beginning. Even those who have missed a long run in the marathon schedule have been able to do the next long one by slowing down to at least three minutes per mile slower than they could run and by taking walk breaks much more frequently. The more conservative you are, in pace and in walking, from the beginning of the run, the more you can push your wall back farther and farther with little risk of fatigue or injury.

WHY DO I NEED TO RUN A 26-MILE TRAINING RUN BEFORE THE MARATHON?

I get a lot of feedback on this one. My name is used in vain, they tell me, during the 26-mile training run. But within 24 hours, the wonderful realization and confidence takes hold: "I'm a marathoner!"

On each long run, including the 26-miler, most who are training for their first marathon are running farther than they have ever gone in their lives, by two to three miles. After running the 26-mile training run, the training is complete. You won't have to push your wall back during the marathon itself. You have arrived.

The confidence bestowed by that 26-mile achievement will take away many of the nervous anxieties leading up to the marathon itself. You're going to have some negative messages from that left side of the brain anytime you attempt a challenge like this. You'll reduce them down to a manageable level after the completion of this, the ultimate long training run.

I'VE HEARD THAT GOING BEYOND 20 MILES BREAKS YOU DOWN

Only if you run too fast. Impatient runners and "type A" running personalities have spread the breakdown rumors after running too fast on a long one. They are so tired after an 18 to 20-mile run that they can't imagine how anyone could run longer than that without dire consequences. When long runs become races, the body accumulates fatigue, which may not be erased by marathon day.

7

> *Y*es, it's possible to finish a marathon and celebrate with friends and family that evening.

It's an entirely different story when you run at least two minutes per mile slower than you could run on that day and take the walk breaks which you need. On each long one you gently push your endurance barrier back another two to three miles. Gentle fatigue, yes; breakdown, no. Tens of thousands of marathoners have pushed their walls back gently without breaking down. You can too!

How do I know if I'm running two minutes per mile slower than I could run on that day?

You don't. Even veteran athletes have to guess when invoking the Two-Minute Rule. When you guess on the conservative side, you win. You'll recover faster, feel good that evening, and reduce the chance of aches, pains and injuries, while receiving all of the endurance bestowed by the distance of that run.

The **"huff and puff"** rule may help: If you're huffing and puffing so much during the last two to three miles of a long run that you can't carry on a conversation, you went too fast from the beginning of that run. On the next run, significantly slow down, take walk breaks more frequently, or both. Remember to write a note to yourself, which you'll read just before starting your next long one.

But I have a time goal, even if it's my first one...

A time goal puts stress on you before and during the first marathon, which will reduce your enjoyment of the big moment. By backing off by two minutes per mile slower than you could run that distance on that day, you'll be able to enjoy the course,

talk to your fellow runners and share the experience. You'll cross that finish line knowing that you could run faster, and this will motivate you to do just that...if you want to.

I ran my first 60 marathons hard. Now I've run more than 50 running within myself. I have received the same satisfaction, sense of achievement, and internal glow from all of the slow ones as I did from the fast ones. The main difference is that I could appreciate the satisfaction and celebrate the achievement on the slow ones. I wasn't very social for very long after the fast ones.

Doesn't slow running produce a slow runner?

Actually, running a fast long training run will produce an even slower runner—one with dead legs that don't recover between long ones. There is only one purpose of the long run: to build endurance. The most effective way to do this is to slowly cover two to three miles further than you went on your previous long one. The slower you run, the more quickly you'll recover so that you can do the speed you need to get faster. See the section on speedplay, which will produce a faster runner.

What type of medical clearance do I need?

Before you start a strenuous training program, be sure to get clearance from a doctor who knows the benefits of exercise. The chance is tiny that you'll have a problem that will prevent you from continuing, but let's make sure.

8

THE LONG RUN *IS* YOUR MARATHON TRAINING PROGRAM!

"Since I've been running 26-milers in training, I don't hit the wall any more."

Whatever your goal, the long run will help you more than any component of your running program. By going slowly, you can burn more fat, push back your endurance barriers, and run faster at shorter distance races.

WHAT IS A LONG RUN?

The long run starts with the longest distance you've covered within the last two weeks and increases by one mile on a weekly long one up to 10 miles. At that point, you'll shift to running long every other weekend, increasing by two miles each time. Once you reach 18 miles, increase by three miles every third week.

THE MENTAL BENEFITS

While there are significant and continuing physical benefits from running long runs regularly, the mental ones are greater. Each week, I hear from beginning marathoners after they have just run the longest run of their lives. This produces mental momentum, self-confidence and a positive attitude. By slowing the pace and taking walk breaks, you can also experience a series of victories over fatigue with almost no risk of injury.

PUSHING BACK YOUR LIMITS

As you push a mile or three farther on each long one, you push back your endurance limit. It's important to go slowly on each of these (at least two minutes per mile slower than you could run that distance on that day) to make it easy for your muscles to extend their current endurance limit. When it's really hot and humid, for example, you'll need to run two and a half or three minutes per mile slower.

THE MOST DIRECT WAY TO PREPARE FOR THE MARATHON

As you extend the long one to 26 miles, you build the exact endurance necessary to complete the marathon (14 to 15 for the half marathon, eight to 10 for the 10K). Those who have marathon time goals can extend their capacity by running as far as 30 miles three to four weeks before the marathon. You're actually pushing back your "endurance wall" with each long run.

WALK BREAKS SPEED RECOVERY

Walk breaks, taken from the beginning, will also speed your recovery and make the extra distance on each run nothing more than a gentle challenge. By walking one to

> **I**t hurts no one to slow down on the long run, but it hurts those who are having a bad day if they try to run faster.

two minutes, after two to eight minutes of running, you shift the use of the muscle and reduce the intensity. Because you're not using the muscle the same way continuously, you significantly increase the distance you can cover before fatigue sets in.

AS THE LONG RUNS GET LONGER...

- Slow down the pace, from the beginning, by running at least two minutes per mile slower than you could run that distance on that day.

- Increase the frequency of walk breaks.

Signs that you went too fast on a long one:

- You must hit the couch or bed and rest for an hour or more

- Muscle soreness or leg fatigue which lasts for more than two days, making it uncomfortable to run

- Aches and/or pains that last for more than four days after a long one

- Huffing and puffing so much during the last two to three miles that you can't carry on a conversation

- Struggling during the last two to three miles to maintain pace or slowing down

- An increase in nausea and irritation at the end of the run

Example: If you started running five minutes and walking one minute,

- at 18 miles, run four minutes and walk one minute

- at 20 to 23 miles, run three minutes and walk one minute for the first 15 miles, then go to four and one if you're feeling good

- on the 26-miler, run three minutes and walk one for the whole run

PACING OF LONG RUNS: THE TWO-MINUTE RULE

Run all of the long ones at least two minutes per mile slower than you could run that distance on that day. The walk breaks will help you to slow the pace, but you must run slower as well. You get the same endurance from the long one if you run slowly as you would if you ran fast. However, you'll recover much faster from a slow long run.

ADJUST FOR HEAT, HUMIDITY, HILLS, ETC.

The warmer and more humid it is, the slower you must go (two and a half to three minutes/mile slower than you could run that distance on that day). Be sure to stay hydrated and avoid too much salt intake during the 36 hours before the long run, during the long one and through the run. The slower you go, from the beginning of the run, the less damage you'll incur from the heat, humidity and distance covered. More frequent (or longer) walk breaks will also lower the damage without detracting from the endurance of that long run.

You get more of your money's worth on a long run—you get to experience it longer.

NON-LONG-RUN WEEKENDS

On the non-long-run weekends, you have several options. Most runners will do a slow run of about half the distance of the current long run. On two to four of these "easy" weekends, it's wise to do a 5K road race to predict what you might be able to do in the marathon. Veterans will do speed sessions on some of the non-long weekends. If you're feeling good on these shorter runs, you can run them continuously, but there's no advantage in doing this. In other words, walk breaks are at your discretion on the shorter runs, including the ones during the week.

ALMOST EVERYONE HAS AT LEAST ONE "BAD" LONG RUN

You may never be able to discover why, but if you know, learn! The tough ones teach you that you have hidden inner strengths, which you can draw upon on future challenges, both in running and in life itself. This will particularly help your confidence and your ability to withstand adversity in the marathon itself.

Long run facts:

- Twenty miles with walking breaks equals 20 miles run continuously...at any speed (but you recover faster with walk breaks).

- Forget about speed on long runs. Focus only on the component of endurance.

- You can't run too slowly on the long runs. Run at least two minutes per mile slower than you could run that distance on that day, accounting for heat, humidity, etc.

- You won't usually feel bad when you're running too fast at the beginning of the run; you must force yourself to slow down.

- The day before the long run should be a no-exercise day.

11

BEGINNER PROGRAM

Week #	Mon	Tue	Wed	Thu	Fri	Sat	Sun
1.	walk 30 min	run/walk 30min	walk 30 min	run/walk 30 min	walk 30 min	off	3-4 run/walk
2.	walk 30 min	run/walk 30min	walk 30 min	run/walk 30 min	walk 30 min	off	4-5 run/walk
3.	walk 30 min	run/walk 30min	walk 30 min	run/walk 30 min	walk 30 min	off	5-6 run/walk
4.	walk 30 min	run/walk 30min	walk 30 min	run/walk 30 min	walk 30 min	off	6-7 run/walk
5.	walk 30 min	run/walk 30min	walk 30 min	run/walk 30 min	walk 30 min	off	7-8 run/walk
6.	walk 30 min	run/walk 30min	walk 30 min	run/walk 30 min	walk 30 min	off	8-9 mi
7.	walk 30 min	run/walk 30min	walk 30 min	run/walk 30 min	walk 30 min	off	9-10 mi
8.	walk 30 min	run/walk 30min	walk 30 min	run/walk 30 min	walk 30 min	off	10-11 mi
9.	walk 30 min	run/walk 30min	walk 30 min	run/walk 30 min	walk 30 min	off	11-12 mi
10.	walk 30 min	run/walk 30min	walk 30 min	run/walk 30 min	walk 30 min	off	6 mi
11.	walk 30 min	run/walk 30min	walk 30 min	run/walk 30 min	walk 30 min	off	13-14 mi
12.	walk 30 min	run/walk 30min	walk 30 min	run/walk 30 min	walk 30 min	off	7 mi
13.	walk 30 min	run/walk 30min	walk 30 min	run/walk 30 min	walk 30 min	off	15-16 mi
14.	walk 30 min	run/walk 30min	walk 30 min	run/walk 30 min	walk 30 min	off	7 mi
15.	walk 30 min	run/walk 30min	walk 30 min	run/walk 30 min	walk 30 min	off	17-18 mi
16.	walk 30 min	run/walk 30min	walk 30 min	run/walk 30 min	walk 30 min	off	8 mi
17	walk 30 min	run/walk 30min	walk 30 min	run/walk 30 min	walk 30 min	off	19-20 mi
18.	walk 30 min	run/walk 30min	walk 30 min	run/walk 30 min	walk 30 min	off	8-9 mi
19.	walk 30 min	run/walk 30min	walk 30 min	run/walk 30 min	walk 30 min	off	8-9 mi
20.	walk 30 min	run/walk 30min	walk 30 min	run/walk 30 min	walk 30 min	off	22-23 mi
21.	walk 30 min	run/walk 30min	walk 30 min	run/walk 30 min	walk 30 min	off	8-10 mi
22.	walk 30 min	run/walk 30min	walk 30 min	run/walk 30 min	walk 30 min	off	8-10 mi
23.	walk 30 min	run/walk 30min	walk 30 min	run/walk 30 min	walk 30 min	off	24-26 mi
24.	walk 30 min	run/walk 30min	walk 30 min	run/walk 30 min	walk 30 min	off	8-10 mi
25.	walk 30 min	run/walk 30min	walk 30 min	run/walk 30 min	walk 30 min	off	8-10 mi
26.	walk 30 min	off	walk 30 min	off	walk 30 min	off	The Marathon*
27.	walk 45 min	run/walk 45 min	walk 30-60 min	run/walk 40 min	walk 30-60 min	off	7-10 mi run/walk
28.	walk 45 min	run/walk 45 min	walk 30-60 min	run/walk 45 min	walk 30-60 min	off	9-15 mi run/walk
29.	walk 45 min	run/walk 45 min	walk 30-60 min	run/walk 45 min	walk 30-60 min	off	12-20 mi run/walk

12

- Stay conversational on all of your exercise sessions. This means that you should be exerting yourself at a low enough level that you could talk. It's okay to take deep breaths between sentences, but you don't want to "huff and puff" between every word.

- For the first few weeks, you will be doing more walking than running. On every "run/walk" day, walk for 2-3 minutes and jog 1-2 minutes. Every 3-4 weeks you may evaluate how you're feeling. If you want to increase the running, start by taking a 3-minute walk with a 2-minute run. Many of our beginners don't get further than this. However, advanced beginners progress to a maximum of running for 2 minutes and walking for 2 minutes.

- Be sure to do the running portion slow enough at the beginning of every run (especially the long one) so that you'll feel tired but strong at the end. This conservatism will allow you to recover faster.

- Don't wait to take walk breaks! By alternating walking and running from the beginning, you speed recovery without losing any of the endurance effect of the long one.

- Best results will be achieved when you increase the long one to 26 miles. If your last one is only 24 miles, you must run slowly and take a few more walking breaks during the first 5 and 10 miles of the marathon itself.

- As the runs get longer, be sure to keep your blood sugar boosted by eating a PowerBar (or equivalent) about an hour before exercise and pieces of a PowerBar (or equivalent) during the second half of the long run or marathon. Drink water continuously before and during exercise and with all food. Gradually introduce your system to the nutrients on your long runs.

- Above all, HAVE FUN!

13

"TO FINISH" PROGRAM

Week #	Mon	Tue	Wed	Thu	Fri	Sat	Sun
1.	walk/XT 40 min	run 30-45 min	walk or XT	run 30-45 min	walk or XT	off	3 mi easy
2.	walk/XT 40 min	run 30-45 min	walk or XT	run 30-45 min	walk or XT	off	4 mi
3.	walk/XT 40 min	run 30-45 min	walk or XT	run 30-45 min	walk or XT	off	5 mi
4.	walk/XT 40 min	run 30-45 min	walk or XT	run 30-45 min	walk or XT	off	6 mi
5.	walk/XT 40 min	run 30-45 min	walk or XT	run 30-45 min	walk or XT	off	7 mi
6.	walk/XT 40 min	run 30-45 min	walk or XT	run 30-45 min	walk or XT	off	8 mi
7.	walk/XT 40 min	run 30-45 min	walk or XT	run 30-45 min	walk or XT	off	9 mi
8.	walk/XT 40 min	run 30-45 min	walk or XT	run 30-45 min	walk or XT	off	10 mi
9.	walk/XT 40 min	run 30-45 min	walk or XT	run 30-45 min	walk or XT	off	11-12 mi
10.	walk/XT 40 min	run 30-45 min	walk or XT	run 30-45 min	walk or XT	off	6 mi
11.	walk/XT 40 min	run 30-45 min	walk or XT	run 30-45 min	walk or XT	off	13-14 mi
12.	walk/XT 40 min	run 30-45 min	walk or XT	run 30-45 min	walk or XT	off	7 mi
13.	walk/XT 40 min	run 30-45 min	walk or XT	run 30-45 min	walk or XT	off	15-16
14.	walk/XT 40 min	run 30-45 min	walk or XT	run 30-45 min	walk or XT	off	8 mi
15.	walk/XT 40 min	run 30-45 min	walk or XT	run 30-45 min	walk or XT	off	17-18
16.	walk/XT 40 min	run 30-45 min	walk or XT	run 30-45 min	walk or XT	off	8-10 mi
17	walk/XT 40 min	run 30-45 min	walk or XT	run 30-45 min	walk or XT	off	19-20
18.	walk/XT 40 min	run 30-45 min	walk or XT	run 30-45 min	walk or XT	off	5K race or 8-10
19.	walk/XT 40 min	run 30-45 min	walk or XT	run 30-45 min	walk or XT	off	8-9 mi
20.	walk/XT 40 min	run 30-45 min	walk or XT	run 30-45 min	walk or XT	off	22-23
21.	walk/XT 40 min	run 30-45 min	walk or XT	run 30-45 min	walk or XT	off	5K race or 8-10
22.	walk/XT 40 min	run 30-45 min	walk or XT	run 30-45 min	walk or XT	off	8-10 mi
23.	walk/XT 40 min	run 30-45 min	walk or XT	run 30-45 min	walk or XT	off	24-26 mi
24.	walk/XT 40 min	run 30-45 min	walk or XT	run 30-45 min	walk or XT	off	5K race or 8-10
25.	walk/XT 40 min	run 30-45 min	walk or XT	run 30-45 min	walk or XT	off	8-10 mi
26.	run 40 min	off	run 30 min	off	run/walk 30 min	off	**The Marathon**
27.	walk 45 min	run/walk 30 min	walk 30-60 min	run/walk 45 min	walk 30-60 min	off	7-10 mi run/walk
28.	walk 45 min	run/walk 45 min	walk 30-60 min	run/walk 45 min	walk 30-60 min	off	9-15 mi run/walk
29.	walk 45 min	run/walk 45 min	walk 30-60 min	run/walk 45 min	walk 30-60 min	off	12-20 mi run/walk

14

- Every other day you can cross-train (XT) or walk. It's your choice: cross-country ski machines, water running, cycling and any other mode which you find fun and interesting (but non-pounding). You don't have to do the cross training to finish the marathon, but these activities will improve overall fitness.

- Stay conversational on all of your exercise sessions. This means that you should be exerting yourself at a low enough level that allows you to talk. It's okay to take deep breaths between sentences, but you don't want to "huff and puff" between every word.

- Be sure to do the running portion slow enough at the beginning of every run (especially the long one) so that you'll feel tired but strong at the end. This conservatism will allow you to recover faster.

- When in doubt, slow down the pace and take more walk breaks-from the beginning.

- Don't wait to take walk breaks! By alternating walking and running from the beginning, you speed recovery without losing any of the endurance effect of the long one.

- As the runs get longer, be sure to keep your blood sugar boosted by eating a PowerBar or whatever you like for a pre-run breakfast about an hour before the start. During the second half of the long run or marathon take PowerGel (etc.) with water. Gradually introduce your system to the nutrients on your long runs and follow the feeding schedule that works for you during the marathon.

- Best results will be achieved when you increase the long run to 26 miles. If your last one is only 24 miles, you must run slowly and take a few more walk breaks during the first 5-10 miles of the marathon itself.

Above all, HAVE FUN!

15

TIME GOAL MARATHON: 4:40

Week #	Mon	Tue	Wed	Thu	Fri	Sat	Sun
1.	XT	40-50 min	20-30 min	XT	40-50 min	off	4-6 hills (5-7 mi)
2.	XT	40-50 min	20-30 min	XT	40-50 min	off	5K race (6-7 mi)
3.	XT	40-50 min	20-30 min	XT	40-50 min	off	7-8 hills (7-8 mi)
4.	XT	40-50 min	20-30 min	XT	40-50 min	off	9-10 hills (8-9 mi)
5.	XT	45-50 min	25-35 min	XT	45-50 min	off	5K race (9-10 mi)
6.	XT	45-50 min	25-35 min	XT	45-50 min	off	3-4 x 1 mi (11 mi)
7.	XT	45-50 min	25-35 min	XT	45-50 min	off	4-5 x 1 mi (8 mi)
8.	XT	45-50 min	25-35 min	XT	45-50 min	off	5-6 x 1 mi (13 mi)
9.	XT	45-50 min	25-35 min	XT	45-50 min	off	5K race (6 mi)
10.	XT	45-55 min	25-40 min	XT	45-55 min	off	15-16 mi easy
11.	XT	45-55 min	25-40 min	XT	45-55 min	off	5K race (6 mi)
12.	XT	45-55 min	25-40 min	XT	45-55 min	off	17-18 mi easy
13.	XT	45-55 min	25-40 min	XT	45-55 min	off	5-6 x1 mi
14.	XT	45-55 min	25-40 min	XT	45-55 min	off	19-20 mi easy
15.	XT	45-55 min	25-40 min	XT	45-55 min	off	5K race (10 mi)
16.	XT	45-55 min	25-40 min	XT	45-55 min	off	5 x1 mi
17.	XT	45-55 min	25-40 min	XT	45-55 min	off	22-23 mi easy
18.	XT	45-55 min	25-40 min	XT	45-55 min	off	5K race
19.	XT	45-55 min	25-40 min	XT	45-55 min	off	4 x 1 mi
20.	XT	45-55 min	25-40 min	XT	45-55 min	off	24-26 mi easy
21.	XT	45-55 min	25-40 min	XT	45-55 min	off	5K race
22.	XT	45-55 min	25-40 min	XT	45-55 min	off	3-4 x 1 mi
23.	XT	45-55 min	25-40 min	XT	45-55 min	off	27-28 mi easy
24.	XT	45-55 min	25-40 min	XT	45-55 min	off	5K or 3 x 1 mi
25.	XT	40-45 min	20-25 min	XT	40-45 min	off	3 x 1 mi
26.	run 40 min	off	run 30 min	off	run 30 min	off	**The Marathon**
27.	walk 45 min	run/walk 30 min	walk 30-60 min	run/walk 40 min	walk 30-60 min	off	7-10 mi run/walk
28.	walk 45 min	run/walk 45 min	walk 30-60 min	run/walk 45 min	walk 30-60 min	off	9-15 mi run/walk
29.	walk 45 min	run/walk 45 min	walk 30-60 min	run/walk 45 min	walk 30-60 min	off	12-20 mirun/walk

16

FROM JEFF GALLOWAY'S MARATHON!   1-800-200-2771   WWW.JEFFGALLOWAY.COM

- After hill and speed sessions and 5K races you'll see the total mileage recommendation for the day in parentheses. This can be accumulated by adding up the warm-up, the warm-down, hill distance, and any other running during the session.

- On the XT (cross-training) days you can swim, run in the water, use exercise machines such as rowing, cross-country ski, and cycle. Don't use the stair machines. If you miss one of these XT days, don't worry.

- Run the long ones at least 2 minutes per mile slower than you could run that same distance on that day (adjust for heat, humidity, hills, etc.). By running slower, you'll speed recovery and reduce the chance of injury.

- Take a one-minute walk break every 3-5 minutes from the beginning of every long run. On the first few long ones, you may run 5 minutes between breaks. But when the long one reaches 18-20 miles, shift to a one-minute break every 4 minutes. For runs 23-26 miles, take a walk break every 3 minutes. These breaks shift the use of the muscles before they get over-fatigued. You'll have better muscle response late in the run and will recover faster. There is NO reduction of endurance when you take walk breaks.

- Early in the schedule, hill play is recommended on the weekend. Do not sprint. After a relaxed warm-up, do 4-8 accelerations. Then run each hill at about 10K race pace. Keep feet low to the ground and avoid tension in the leg muscles (especially the hamstring). Run up and over the top of the hill, and walk down. Walk more before the next hill if you need more recovery.

- Follow the same warm-up procedure for mile repeats. For a time goal of 4:40, run each mile repeat in 10:15. This

- prepares you for the pace you'll be running between walk breaks in the marathon. If you're unrealistically optimistic in predicting your marathon goal pace, you'll run the mile repeats too fast and risk overtraining and injury. So if this pace causes you to breathe heavily, shift to a slower pace and adjust your marathon goal accordingly. Be sure to walk (don't jog) between mile repeats for at least 4 minutes.

- 5K races help you predict a realistic goal in the marathon. Take your performance times on accurately measured courses, and use the "Predicting Race Performance" chart in Galloway's Book On Running. The more races you have, the more accurate your prediction will be. Adjust your mile repeat sessions accordingly.

- Marathon pace running can be done on two other days during the week (Wednesday and Friday). After a slow warm-up, followed by 4-8 acceleration GLIDERS, run 1-3 miles at the marathon pace your 5K races are predicting. This tells you what it's like to run at marathon goal pace. Make sure that you've recovered from the weekend run, and break up the paced miles with slow jogging between.

- The pace of the Tuesday run should be at least one minute per mile slower than marathon goal pace and slower if you're still tired from the weekend session. You may also do a few acceleration-GLIDERS on this day, but be careful. Never hesitate to slow down on the Tuesday, Wednesday and Friday runs.

- You have some flexibility on the number of minutes to be run during the week. Never increase the amount more than 10 percent above what you have been doing the week before. Don't hesitate to cut back on some of these days if you're feeling tired from the (hopefully) playful but tiring weekend.

TIME GOAL MARATHON: 4:20

Week #	Mon	Tue	Wed	Thu	Fri	Sat	Sun
1.	XT	40-50 min	20-30 min	XT	40-50 min	off	4-6 hills (5-7 mi)
2.	XT	40-50 min	20-30 min	XT	40-50 min	off	5K race (6-7 mi)
3.	XT	40-50 min	20-30 min	XT	40-50 min	off	7-8 hills (7-8 mi)
4.	XT	40-50 min	20-30 min	XT	40-50 min	off	9-10 hills (8-9 mi)
5.	XT	45-50 min	25-35 min	XT	45-50 min	off	5K race (9-10 mi)
6.	XT	45-50 min	25-35 min	XT	45-50 min	off	3-4 x 1 mi (11 mi)
7.	XT	45-50 min	25-35 min	XT	45-50 min	off	4-5 x 1 mi (8 mi)
8.	XT	45-50 min	25-35 min	XT	45-50 min	off	5-6 x 1 mi (13mi)
9.	XT	45-50 min	25-35 min	XT	45-50 min	off	5K race (6 mi)
10.	XT	45-55 min	25-40 min	XT	45-55 min	off	15-16 mi easy
11.	XT	45-55 min	25-40 min	XT	45-55 min	off	5K race (9 mi)
12.	XT	45-55 min	25-40 min	XT	45-55 min	off	17-18 mi easy
13.	XT	45-55 min	25-40 min	XT	45-55 min	off	6-7 x 1 mi
14.	XT	45-55 min	25-40 min	XT	45-55 min	off	19-20 mi easy
15.	XT	45-55 min	25-40 min	XT	45-55 min	off	5K race (10 mi)
16.	XT	45-55 min	25-40 min	XT	45-55 min	off	6 x1 mi
17.	XT	45-55 min	25-40 min	XT	45-55 min	off	22-23 mi easy
18.	XT	45-55 min	25-40 min	XT	45-55 min	off	5K race
19.	XT	45-55 min	25-40 min	XT	45-55 min	off	5 x 1 mi
20.	XT	45-55 min	25-40 min	XT	45-55 min	off	24-26 mi easy
21.	XT	45-55 min	25-40 min	XT	45-55 min	off	5K race
22.	XT	45-55 min	25-40 min	XT	45-55 min	off	3-5 x 1 mi
23.	XT	45-55 min	25-40 min	XT	45-55 min	off	27-28 mi easy
24.	XT	45-55 min	25-40 min	XT	45-55 min	off	5K or 3 x 1 mi
25.	XT	40-45 min	20-25 min	XT	40-45 min	off	3 x 1 mi
							The Marathon
26.	run 40 min	off	run 30 min	off	run 30 min	off	off
27.	walk 45 min	run/walk 30 min	walk 30-60 min	run/walk 45 min	walk 30-60 min	off	7-10 mi run/walk
28.	walk 45 min	run/walk 45 min	walk 30-60 min	run/walk 45 min	walk 30-60 min	off	9-15 mi run/walk
29.	walk 45 min	run/walk 45 min	walk 30-60 min	run/walk 45 min	walk 30-60 min	off	12-20 mi run/walk

- After hill and speed sessions and 5K races you'll see the total mileage recommendation for the day in parentheses. This can be accumulated by adding up the warm-up, the warm-down, hill distance, and any other running during the session.

- On the XT (cross-training) days you can swim, run in the water, use exercise machines such as rowing, cross-country ski, and cycle. Don't use the stair machines. If you miss one of these XT days, don't worry.

- Run the long ones at least 2 minutes per mile slower than you could run that same distance on that day (adjust for heat, humidity, hills, etc.). By running slower, you'll speed recovery and reduce the chance of injury.

- Take a one-minute walkbreak every 4-6 minutes from the beginning of every long run. On the first few long ones, you may run 6 minutes between breaks. But when the long one reaches 18-20 miles, shift to a one-minute break every 5 minutes. For runs 23-26 miles, take a walk break every 4 minutes. These breaks shift the use of the muscles before they get over-fatigued. You'll have better muscle response late in the run and will recover faster. There is NO reduction of endurance when you take walk breaks.

- Early in the schedule, hill play is recommended on the weekend. Do not sprint. After a relaxed warm-up, do 4-8 accelerations. Then run each hill at about 10K race pace. Keep feet low to the ground and avoid tension in the leg muscles (especially the hamstring). Run up and over the top of the hill, and walk down. Walk more before the next hill if you need more recovery.

- Follow the same warm-up procedure for mile repeats. For a time goal of 4:20, run each mile repeat in 9:30. This pre- pares you for the pace you'll be running between walk breaks in the marathon. If you're unrealistically optimistic in predicting your marathon goal pace, you'll run the mile repeats too fast and risk overtraining and injury. So if this pace causes you to breathe heavily, shift to a slower pace and adjust your marathon goal accordingly. Be sure to walk (don't jog) between mile repeats for at least 4 minutes.

- 5K races help you predict a realistic goal in the marathon. Take your performance times on accurately measured courses, and use the "Predicting Race Performance" chart in Galloway's Book On Running. The more races you have, the more accurate your prediction will be. Adjust your mile repeat sessions accordingly.

- Marathon pace running can be done on two other days during the week (Wednesday and Friday). After a slow warm-up followed by 4-8 acceleration GLIDERS, run 1-3 miles at the marathon pace your 5K races are predicting. This tells you what it's like to run at marathon goal pace. Make sure that you've recovered from the weekend run, and break up the paced miles with slow jogging between.

- The pace of the Tuesday run should be at least one minute per mile slower than marathon goal pace and slower if you're still tired from the weekend session. You may also do a few acceleration-GLIDERS on this day, but be careful. Never hesitate to slow down on the Tuesday, Wednesday and Friday runs.

- You have some flexibility on the number of minutes to be run during the week. Never increase the amount more than 10 percent above what you have been doing the week before. Don't hesitate to cut back on some of these days if you're feeling tired from the (hopefully) playful but tiring weekend.

TIME GOAL MARATHON: 4 HOURS

20

Week #	Mon	Tue	Wed	Thu	Fri	Sat	Sun
1.	XT	40-50 min	20-30 min	XT	40-50 min	off	4-6 hills (5-7 mi)
2.	XT	40-50 min	20-30 min	XT	40-50 min	off	5K race (6-7 mi)
3.	XT	40-50 min	20-30 min	XT	40-50 min	off	7-8 hills (7-8 mi)
4.	XT	40-50 min	20-30 min	XT	40-50 min	off	9-10 hills (8-9 mi)
5.	XT	45-50 min	25-35 min	XT	45-50 min	off	5K race (9-10 mi)
6.	XT	45-50 min	25-35 min	XT	45-50 min	off	3-5 x 1mi (11 mi)
7.	XT	45-50 min	25-35 min	XT	45-50 min	off	5K race (8 mi)
8.	XT	45-50 min	25-35 min	XT	45-50 min	off	5-7 x 1mi(14mi)
9.	XT	45-50 min	25-35 min	XT	45-50 min	off	5K race (7 mi)
10.	XT	45-55 min	25-40 min	XT	45-55 min	off	15-16 mi easy
11.	XT	45-55 min	25-40 min	XT	45-55 min	off	5K race (9 mi)
12.	XT	45-55 min	25-40 min	XT	45-55 min	off	17-18 mi easy
13.	XT	45-55 min	25-40 min	XT	45-55 min	off	6-8 x 1mi
14.	XT	45-55 min	25-40 min	XT	45-55 min	off	19-20 mi easy
15.	XT	45-55 min	25-40 min	XT	45-55 min	off	5K race (10 mi)
16.	XT	45-55 min	25-40 min	XT	45-55 min	off	6-8 x 1mi
17.	XT	45-55 min	25-40 min	XT	45-55 min	off	22-23 mi easy
18.	XT	45-55 min	25-40 min	XT	45-55 min	off	5K race
19.	XT	45-55 min	25-40 min	XT	45-55 min	off	4-6 x 1 mi
20.	XT	45-55 min	25-40 min	XT	45-55 min	off	25-26 mi easy
21.	XT	45-55 min	25-40 min	XT	45-55 min	off	5K race
22.	XT	45-55 min	25-40 min	XT	45-55 min	off	3-5 x 1 mi
23.	XT	45-55 min	25-40 min	XT	45-55 min	off	27-28 mi easy
24.	XT	45-55 min	25-40 min	XT	45-55 min	off	5K or 4 x 1 mi
25.	XT	40-45 min	20-25 min	XT	40-45 min	off	4 x 1 mi
26.	run 40 min	off	run 30 min	off	run 30 min	off	**The Marathon**
27.	walk 45 min	run/walk 30 min	walk 30-60 min	run/walk 40 min	walk 30-60 min		7-10 run/walk
28.	walk 45 min	run/walk 45 min	walk 30-60 min	run/walk 45 min	walk 30-60 min		9-15 mi run/walk
29.	walk 45 min	run/walk 45 min	walk 30-60 min	run/walk 45 min	walk 30-60 min		12-20 mi run/walk

prepares you for the pace you'll be running between walk breaks in the marathon. If you're unrealistically optimistic in predicting your marathon goal pace, you'll run the mile repeats too fast and risk overtraining and injury. So if this pace causes you to breathe heavily, shift to a slower pace and adjust your marathon goal accordingly. Be sure to walk (don't jog) between mile repeats for at least 4 minutes.

- 5K races help you predict a realistic goal in the marathon. Take your performance times on accurately measured courses, and use the "Predicting Race Performance" chart in Galloway's Book On Running. The more races you have, the more accurate your prediction will be. Adjust your mile repeat sessions accordingly.

- Marathon pace running can be done on two other days during the week (Wednesday and Friday). After a slow warm-up followed by 4-8 acceleration GLIDERS, run 1-3 miles at the marathon pace your 5K races are predicting. This tells you what it's like to run at marathon goal pace. Make sure that you've recovered from the weekend run, and break up the paced miles with slow jogging between.

- The pace of the Tuesday run should be at least one minute per mile slower than marathon goal pace and slower if you're still tired from the weekend session. You may also do a few acceleration-GLIDERS on this day, but be careful. Never hesitate to slow down on the Tuesday, Wednesday and Friday runs.

- You have some flexibility on the number of minutes to be run during the week. Never increase the amount more than 10 percent above what you have been doing the week before. Don't hesitate to cut back on some of these days if you're feeling tired from the (hopefully) playful but tiring weekend.

21

After hill and speed sessions and 5K races you'll see the total mileage recommendation for the day in parentheses. This can be accumulated by adding up the warm-up, the warm-down, hill distance, and any other running during the session.

- On the XT (cross-training) days you can swim, run in the water, use exercise machines such as rowing, cross-country ski, and cycle. Don't use the stair machines. If you miss one of these XT days, don't worry.

- Run the long ones at least 2 minutes per mile slower than you could run that same distance on that day (adjust for heat, humidity, hills, etc.). By running slower, you'll speed recovery and reduce the chance of injury.

- Take a one-minute walk-break every 4-6 minutes from the beginning of every long run. On the first few long ones, you may run 6 minutes between breaks. But when the long one reaches 18-20 miles, shift to a one-minute break every 5 minutes. For runs 23-26 miles, take a walk break every 4 minutes. These breaks shift the use of the muscles before they get over-fatigued. You'll have better muscle response late in the run and will recover faster. There is NO reduction of endurance when you take walk breaks.

- Early in the schedule, hill play is recommended on the weekend. Do not sprint. After a relaxed warm-up, do 4-8 accelerations. Then run each hill at about 10K race pace. Keep feet low to the ground, avoid tension in the leg muscles (especially the hamstring). Run up and over the top of the hill, and walk down. Walk more before the next hill if you need more recovery.

- Follow the same warm-up procedure for mile repeats. For a time goal of 4 hours, run each mile repeat in 8:40. This

TIME GOAL MARATHON: 3:45

Week #	Mon	Tue	Wed	Thu	Fri	Sat	Sun
1.	XT	40-50 min	20-30 min	XT	40-50 min	off	4-6 hills (5-7 mi)
2.	XT	40-50 min	20-30 min	XT	40-50 min	off	5K race (6-7 mi)
3.	XT	40-50 min	20-30 min	XT	40-50 min	off	7-8 hills (7-8 mi)
4.	XT	40-50 min	20-30 min	XT	40-50 min	off	9-10 hills (8-9 mi)
5.	XT	45-50 min	25-35 min	XT	45-50 min	off	5K race (9-10 mi)
6.	XT	45-50 min	25-35 min	XT	45-50 min	off	3-5 x 1mi (12 mi)
7.	XT	45-50 min	25-35 min	XT	45-50 min	off	4-6 x 1mi (8 mi)
8.	XT	45-50 min	25-35 min	XT	45-50 min	off	5-7x 1mi (14 mi)
9.	XT	45-50 min	25-35 min	XT	45-50 min	off	5K race (7 mi)
10.	XT	45-55 min	25-40 min	XT	45-55 min	off	15-16 mi easy
11.	XT	45-55 min	25-40 min	XT	45-55 min	off	5K race (9 mi)
12.	XT	45-55 min	25-40 min	XT	45-55 min	off	17-18 mi easy
13.	XT	45-55 min	25-40 min	XT	45-55 min	off	6-8 x 1 mi
14.	XT	45-55 min	25-40 min	XT	45-55 min	off	19-20 mi easy
15.	XT	45-55 min	25-40 min	XT	45-55 min	off	5K race (10 mi)
16.	XT	45-55 min	25-40 min	XT	45-55 min	off	7-9 x 1 mi
17.	XT	45-55 min	25-40 min	XT	45-55 min	off	22-23 mi easy
18.	XT	45-55 min	25-40 min	XT	45-55 min	off	5K race
19.	XT	45-55 min	25-40 min	XT	45-55 min	off	5-7 x 1 mi
20.	XT	45-55 min	25-40 min	XT	45-55 min	off	25-26 mi easy
21.	XT	45-55 min	25-40 min	XT	45-55 min	off	5K race
22.	XT	45-55 min	25-40 min	XT	45-55 min	off	4-6 x 1 mi
23.	XT	45-55 min	25-40 min	XT	45-55 min	off	28-29 mi easy
24.	XT	45-55 min	25-40 min	XT	45-55 min	off	5K or 4 x 1 mi
25.	XT	40-45 min	20-25 min	XT	40-45 min	off	4-5 x 1 mi
							The Marathon
26.	run 40 min	off	run 30 min	off	run 30 min	off	off
27.	walk 45 min	run/walk 30 min	walk 30-60 min	run/walk 40 min	walk 30-60 min		7-10 mi run/walk
28.	walk 45 min	run/walk 45 min	walk 30-60 min	run/walk 45 min	walk 30-60 min		9-15mi run/walk
29.	walk 45 min	run/walk 45 min	walk 30-60 min	run/walk 45 min	walk 30-60 min		12-20 mi run/walk

22

- After hill and speed sessions and 5K races you'll see the total mileage recommendation for the day in parentheses. This can be accumulated by adding up the warm-up, the warm-down, hill distance, and any other running during the session.

- On the XT (cross-training) days you can swim, run in the water, use exercise machines such as rowing, cross-country ski, and cycle. Don't use the stair machines. If you miss one of these XT days, don't worry.

- Run the long ones at least 2 minutes per mile slower than you could run that same distance on that day (adjust for heat, humidity, hills, etc.). By running slower, you'll speed recovery and reduce the chance of injury.

- Take a one-minute walk-break every 4-6 minutes from the beginning of every long run. On the first few long ones, you may run 6 minutes between breaks. But when the long one reaches 18-20 miles, shift to a one-minute break every 5 minutes. For runs 23-26 miles, take a walk break every 4 minutes. These breaks shift the use of the muscles before they get over-fatigued. You'll have better muscle response late in the run and will recover faster. There is NO reduction of endurance when you take walk breaks.

- Early in the schedule, hill play is recommended on the weekend. Do not sprint. After a relaxed warm-up, do 4-8 accelerations. Then run each hill at about 10K race pace. Keep feet low to the ground and avoid tension in the leg muscles (especially the hamstring). Run up and over the top of the hill and walk down. Walk more before the next hill if you need more recovery.

- Follow the same warm-up procedure for mile repeats. For a time goal of 3:45, run each mile repeat in 8:05. This pre-pares you for the pace you'll be running between walk breaks in the marathon. If you're unrealistically optimistic in predicting your marathon goal pace, you'll run the mile repeats too fast and risk overtraining and injury. So if this pace causes you to breathe heavily, shift to a slower pace, and adjust your marathon goal accordingly. Be sure to walk (don't jog) between mile repeats for at least 4 minutes.

- 5K races help you predict a realistic goal in the marathon. Take your performance times on accurately measured courses, and use the "Predicting Race Performance" chart in Galloway's Book On Running. The more races you have, the more accurate your prediction will be. Adjust your mile repeat sessions accordingly.

- Marathon pace running can be done on two other days during the week (Wednesday and Friday). After a slow warm-up, followed by 4-8 acceleration GLIDERS, run 1-3 miles at the marathon pace your 5K races are predicting. This tells you what it's like to run at marathon goal pace. Make sure that you've recovered from the weekend run and break up the paced miles with slow jogging between.

- The pace of the Tuesday run should be at least one minute per mile slower than marathon goal pace and slower if you're still tired from the weekend session. You may also do a few acceleration-GLIDERS on this day, but be careful. Never hesitate to slow down on the Tuesday, Wednesday and Friday runs.

- You have some flexibility on the number of minutes to be run during the week. Never increase the amount more than 10 percent above what you have been doing the week before. Don't hesitate to cut back on some of these days if you're feeling tired from the (hopefully) playful but tiring weekend.

TIME GOAL MARATHON: 3:30

Week #	Mon	Tue	Wed	Thu	Fri	Sat	Sun
1.	XT	40-60 min	20-30 min	XT	40-60 min	off	4-6 hills (5-7 mi)
2.	XT	40-60 min	20-30 min	XT	40-60 min	off	5K race (6-7 mi)
3.	XT	40-60 min	20-30 min	XT	40-60 min	off	7-8 hills (7-8 mi)
4.	XT	40-60 min	20-30 min	XT	40-60 min	off	9-10 hills (8-9 mi)
5.	XT	45-60 min	25-35 min	XT	45-60 min	off	5K race (9-10 mi)
6.	XT	45-60 min	25-35 min	XT	45-60 min	off	3-5 x 1mi (12 mi)
7.	XT	45-60 min	25-35 min	XT	45-60 min	off	5K race (8 mi)
8.	XT	45-60 min	25-35 min	XT	45-60 min	off	6-8 x 1mi (14 mi)
9.	XT	45-60 min	25-35 min	XT	45-60 min	off	5K race (8 mi)
10.	XT	45-65 min	25-40 min	XT	45-65 min	off	15-16 mi easy
11.	XT	45-65 min	25-40 min	XT	45-65 min	off	5K race (9 mi)
12.	XT	45-65 min	25-40 min	XT	45-65 min	off	17-18 mi easy
13.	XT	45-65 min	25-40 min	XT	45-65 min	off	7-9 x1 mi
14.	XT	45-65 min	25-40 min	XT	45-65 min	off	19-20 mi easy
15.	XT	45-65 min	25-40 min	XT	45-65 min	off	5K race (10 mi)
16.	XT	45-65 min	25-40 min	XT	45-65 min	off	8-10 x 1 mi
17.	XT	45-65 min	25-40 min	XT	45-65 min	off	22-23 mi easy
18.	XT	45-65 min	25-40 min	XT	45-65 min	off	5K race
19.	XT	45-65 min	25-40 min	XT	45-65 min	off	5-7 x 1 mi
20.	XT	45-65 min	25-40 min	XT	45-65 min	off	25-26 mi easy
21.	XT	45-65 min	25-40 min	XT	45-65 min	off	5K race
22.	XT	45-65 min	25-40 min	XT	45-65 min	off	4-6 x 1 mi
23.	XT	45-65 min	25-40 min	XT	45-65 min	off	28-29 mi easy
24.	XT	45-55 min	25-40 min	XT	45-55 min	off	5K or 4 x 1 mi
25.	XT	40-45 min	20-25 min	XT	40-45 min	off	4-5 x 1 mi
26.	run 40 min	off	run 30 min	off	run 30 min	off	**The Marathon**
27.	walk 45 min	run/walk 30 min	walk 30-60 min	run/walk 45 min	walk 30-60 min	off	7-10 mi run/walk
28.	walk 45 min	run/walk 45 min	walk 30-60 min	run/walk 45 min	walk 30-60 min	off	9-15 mi run/walk
29.	walk 45 min	run/walk 45 min	walk 30-60 min	run/walk 45 min	walk 30-60 min	off	12-20 mi run/walk

- After hill and speed sessions and 5K races you'll see the total mileage recommendation for the day in parentheses. This can be accumulated by adding up the warm-up, the warm-down, hill distance, and any other running during the session.

- On the XT (cross-training) days you can swim, run in the water, use exercise machines such as rowing, cross-country ski, and cycle. Don't use the stair machines. If you miss one of these XT days, don't worry.

- Run the long ones at least 2 minutes per mile slower than you could run that same distance on that day (adjust for heat, humidity, hills, etc.). By running slower, you'll speed recovery and reduce the chance of injury.

- Take a one-minute walk break every 4-6 minutes from the beginning of every long run. On the first few long ones, you may run 6 minutes between breaks. But when the long one reaches 18-20 miles, shift to a one-minute break every 5 minutes. For runs 23-26 miles, take a walk break every 4 minutes. These breaks shift the use of the muscles before they get over-fatigued. You'll have better muscle response late in the run and will recover faster. There is NO reduction of endurance when you take walk breaks.

- Early in the schedule, hill play is recommended on the weekend. Do not sprint. After a relaxed warm-up, do 4-8 accelerations. Then run each hill at about 10K race pace. Keep feet low to the ground and avoid tension in the leg muscles (especially the hamstring). Run up and over the top of the hill, and walk down. Walk more before the next hill if you need more recovery.

- Follow the same warm-up procedure for mile repeats. For a time goal of 3:30, run each mile repeat in 7:40. This pre-pares you for the pace you'll be running between walk breaks in the marathon. If you're unrealistically optimistic in predicting your marathon goal pace, you'll run the mile repeats too fast and risk overtraining and injury. So if this pace causes you to breathe heavily, shift to a slower pace and adjust your marathon goal accordingly. Be sure to walk (don't jog) between mile repeats for at least 4 minutes.

- 5K races help you predict a realistic goal in the marathon. Take your performance times on accurately measured courses, and use the "Predicting Race Performance" chart in Galloway's Book On Running. The more races you have, the more accurate your prediction will be. Adjust your mile repeat sessions accordingly.

- Marathon pace running can be done on two other days during the week (Wednesday and Friday). After a slow warm-up followed by 4-8 acceleration GLIDERS, run 1-3 miles at the marathon pace your 5K races are predicting. This tells you what it's like to run at marathon goal pace. Make sure that you've recovered from the weekend run and break up the paced miles with slow jogging between.

- The pace of the Tuesday run should be at least one minute per mile slower than marathon goal pace and slower if you're still tired from the weekend session. You may also do a few acceleration-GLIDERS on this day, but be careful. Never hesitate to slow down on the Tuesday, Wednesday and Friday runs.

- You have some flexibility on the number of minutes to be run during the week. Never increase the amount more than 10 percent above what you have been doing the week before. Don't hesitate to cut back on some of these days if you're feeling tired from the (hopefully) playful but tiring weekend.

25

TIME GOAL MARATHON: 3:15

Week #	Mon	Tue	Wed	Thu	Fri	Sat	Sun
1.	XT or 3 easy	40-55 min	20-50 min	XT	40-55 min	off	4-6 hills (5-7 mi)
2.	XT or 3 easy	40-55 min	20-50 min	XT	40-55 min	off	5K race (6-7 mi)
3.	XT or 3 easy	40-55 min	20-50 min	XT	40-55 min	off	7-8 hills (7-8 mi)
4.	XT or 3 easy	40-65 min	20-50 min	XT	40-55 min	off	9-10 hills (8-9 mi)
5.	XT or 3 easy	45-70 min	25-55 min	XT	45-50 min	off	5K race (9-10 mi)
6.	XT or 3 easy	45-70 min	25-55 min	XT	45-70 min	off	3-5 x 1mi (12 mi)
7.	XT or 3 easy	45-70 min	25-55 min	XT	45-70 min	off	5K race (8 mi)
8.	XT or 4 easy	45-70 min	25-55 min	XT	45-70 min	off	6-8 x 1mi (14 mi)
9.	XT or 4 easy	45-70 min	25-55 min	XT	45-70 min	off	5Krace (8mi)
10.	XT or 4 easy	45-75 min	25-60 min	XT	45-75 min	off	15-16 mi easy
11.	XT or 4 easy	45-75 min	25-60 min	XT	45-75 min	off	5K race (9 mi)
12.	XT or 4 easy	45-75 min	25-60 min	XT	45-75 min	off	17-18 mi easy
13.	XT or 4 easy	45-75 min	25-60 min	XT	45-75 min	off	7-9 x1mi
14.	XT or 4 easy	45-75 min	25-60 min	XT	45-75 min	off	19-20 mi easy
15.	XT or 4 easy	45-75 min	25-60 min	XT	45-75 min	off	5K race (10 mi)
16.	XT or 4 easy	45-75 min	25-60 min	XT	45-75 min	off	9-11x1mi
17.	XT or 4 easy	45-75 min	25-60 min	XT	45-75 min	off	22-23 mi easy
18.	XT or 4 easy	45-75 min	25-60 min	XT	45-75 min	off	5K race
19.	XT or 4 easy	45-75 min	25-60 min	XT	45-75 min	off	5-8 x 1mi
20.	XT or 4 easy	45-75 min	25-60 min	XT	45-75 min	off	25-26 mi easy
21.	XT or 4 easy	45-75 min	25-60 min	XT	45-75 min	off	5K race
22.	XT or 4 easy	45-75 min	25-60 min	XT	45-75 min	off	5-8 x 1 mi
23.	XT or 4 easy	45-75 min	25-60 min	XT	45-75 min	off	28-29 mi easy
24.	XT	45-55 min	25-50 min	XT	45-55 min	off	5K or 4 x 1mi
25.	XT	40 min	20-35 min	XT	40 min	off	4-6 x 1 mi
26.	run 40 min	off	run 30 min	off	run 30 min	off	**The Marathon**
27.	XT 45 min	run/walk 30 min	XT 30-60 min	run/walk 40 min	XT 30-60 min	off	7-10 mi run/walk
28.	XT 45 min	run/walk 45 min	XT 30-60 min	run/walk 45 min	XT 30-60 min	off	9-15 mi run/walk
29.	XT 45 min	run/walk 45 min	XT 30-60 min	run/walk 45 min	XT 30-60 min		12-20 mi run/walk

- After hill and speed sessions and 5K races you'll see the total mileage recommendation for the day in parentheses. This can be accumulated by adding up the warm-up, the warm-down, hill distance, and any other running during the session.

- On the XT (cross-training) days you can swim, run in the water, use exercise machines such as rowing, cross-country ski, and cycle. Don't use the stair machines. If you miss one of these XT days, don't worry.

- Run the long ones at least 2 minutes per mile slower than you could run that same distance on that day (adjust for heat, humidity, hills, etc.). By running slower, you'll speed recovery and reduce the chance of injury.

- Take a one-minute walk-break every 5-7 minutes from the beginning of of every long run. On the first few long ones, you may run 7 minutes between breaks. But when the long one reaches 18-20 miles, shift to a one-minute break every 6 minutes. For runs 23-26 miles, take a walk break every 5 minutes. These breaks shift the use of the muscles before they get over-fatigued. You'll have better muscle response late in the run and will recover faster. There is NO reduction of endurance when you take walk breaks.

- Early in the schedule, hill play is recommended on the weekend. Do not sprint. After a relaxed warm-up, dq 4-8 accelerations. Then run each hill at about 10K race pace. Keep feet low to the ground, avoid tension in the leg muscles (especially the hamstring). Run up and over the top of the hill, and walk down. Walk more before the next hill if you need more recovery.

- Follow the same warm-up procedure for mile repeats. For a time goal of 3:15, run each mile repeat in 7:05 This pre-

- pares you for the pace you'll be running between walk breaks in the marathon. If you're unrealistically optimistic in predicting your marathon goal pace, you'll run the mile repeats too fast and risk overtraining and injury. So if this pace causes you to breathe heavily, shift to a slower pace and adjust your marathon goal accordingly. Be sure to walk (don't jog) between mile repeats for at least 4 minutes.

- 5K races help you predict a realistic goal in the marathon. Take your performance times on accurately measured courses, and use the "Predicting Race Performance" chart in Galloway's Book On Running. The more races you have, the more accurate your prediction will be. Adjust your mile repeat sessions accordingly.

- Marathon pace running can be done on two other days during the week (Wednesday and Friday). After a slow warm-up followed by 4-8 acceleration GLIDERS, run 1-3 miles at the marathon pace your 5K races are predicting. This tells you what it's like to run at marathon goal pace. Make sure that you've recovered from the weekend run and break up the paced miles with slow jogging between.

- The pace of the Tuesday run should be at least one minute per mile slower than marathon goal pace and slower if you're still tired from the weekend session. You may also do a few acceleration-GLIDERS on this day, but be careful. Never hesitate to slow down on the Tuesday, Wednesday and Friday runs.

- You have some flexibility on the number of minutes to be run during the week. Never increase the amount more than 10 percent above what you have been doing the week before. Don't hesitate to cut back on some of these days if you're feeling tired from the (hopefully) playful but tiring weekend.

TIME GOAL MARATHON: 2:59

Week #	Mon	Tue	Wed	Thu	Fri	Sat	Sun
1.	XT or 3 easy	40-55 min	20-50 min	XT	40-55 min	off	4-6 hills (5-7 mi)
2.	XT or 3 easy	40-60 min	20-50 min	XT	40-60 min	off	5K race (6-7 mi)
3.	XT or 3 easy	40-65 min	20-50 min	XT	40-60 min	off	7-8 hills (7-8 mi)
4.	XT or 3 easy	40-65 min	20-50 min	XT	40-60 min	off	9-10 hills (8-9 mi)
5.	XT or 3 easy	45-75 min	25-55 min	XT	45-65 min	off	5K race (9-10 mi)
6.	XT or 3 easy	45-80 min	25-55 min	XT	45-65 min	off	5-7 x 1mi (12 mi)
7.	XT or 3 easy	45-80 min	25-55 min	XT	45-70 min	off	5K race (8 mi)
8.	XT or 4 easy	45-80 min	25-55 min	XT	45-75 min	off	6-8 x 1mi (14 mi)
9.	XT or 4 easy	45-80 min	25-55 min	XT	45-80 min	off	7-9 x 1mi (10 mi)
10.	XT or 4 easy	45-85 min	25-60 min	XT	45-80 min	off	15-16 mi easy
11.	XT or 4 easy	45-85 min	25-60 min	XT	45-85 min	off	5K race (9 mi)
12.	XT or 4 easy	45-85 min	25-60 min	XT	45-85 min	off	17-18 mi easy
13.	XT or 4 easy	45-85 min	25-60 min	XT	45-85 min	off	9-11 x1 mi
14.	XT or 4 easy	45-85 min	25-60 min	XT	45-85 min	off	19-20 mi easy
15.	XT or 4 easy	45-85 min	25-60 min	XT	45-85 min	off	5K race (10 mi)
16.	XT or 4 easy	45-85 min	25-60 min	XT	45-85 min	off	10-12 x1 mi
17.	XT or 4 easy	45-85 min	25-60 min	XT	45-85 min	off	22-23 mi easy
18.	XT or 4 easy	45-85 min	25-60 min	XT	45-85 min	off	5K race
19.	XT or easy	45-85 min	25-60 min	XT	45-85 min	off	5-8 x 1 mi
20.	XT or 4 easy	45-85 min	25-60 min	XT	45-85 min	off	25-26 mi easy
21.	XT or 4 easy	45-85 min	25-60 min	XT	45-85 min	off	5K race
22.	XT or easy	45-85 min	25-60 min	XT	45-85 min	off	5-8 x 1 mi
23.	XT or 4 easy	45-75 min	25-60 min	XT	45-75 min	off	28-30 mi easy
24.	XT	45-55 min	25-50 min	XT	45-55 min	off	5K or 4 x 1mi
25.	XT	40 min	20-35 min	XT	40 min	off	4-6 x 1 mi
26.	run 40 min	off	run 30 min	off	run 30 min	off	**The Marathon**
27.	XT 45 min	run/walk 30 min	XT 30-60 min	run/walk 40 min	XT 30-60 min	off	7-10 mi run/walk
28.	XT 45 min	run/walk 45 min	XT 30-60 min	run/walk 45 min	XT 30-60 min	off	9-15 mi run/walk
29.	XT 45 min	run/walk 45 min	XT 30-60 min	run/walk 45 min	XT 30-60 min	off	12-20 mi run/walk

■ After hill and speed sessions and 5K races you'll see the total mileage recommendation for the day in parentheses. This can be accumulated by adding up the warm-up, the warm-down, hill distance, and any other running during the session.

■ On the XT (cross-training) days you can swim, run in the water, use exercise machines such as rowing, cross-country ski, and cycle. Don't use the stair machines. If you miss one of these XT days, don't worry.

■ Run the long ones at least 2 minutes per mile slower than you could run that same distance on that day (adjust for heat, humidity, hills, etc.). By running slower, you'll speed recovery and reduce the chance of injury.

■ Take a one-minute walk-break every 8-10 minutes from the beginning of every long run. On the first few long ones, you may run 10 minutes between breaks. But when the long one reaches 18 miles (and further), shift to a one-minute break about every mile. Be sure to adjust to more frequent breaks if needed. These breaks shift the use of the muscles before they get over-fatigued. You'll have better muscle response late in the run and will recover faster. There is NO reduction of endurance when you take walk breaks.

■ Early in the schedule, hill play is recommended on the weekend. Do not sprint. After a relaxed warm-up, do 4-8 accelerations. Then run each hill at about 10K race pace. Keep feet low to the ground and avoid tension in the leg muscles (especially the hamstring). Run up and over the top of the hill, and walk down. Walk more before the next hill if you need more recovery.

■ Follow the same warm-up procedure for mile repeats. For a time goal of 2:59, run each mile repeat in 6:32. This prepares you for the pace you'll be running between walk breaks in the marathon. If you're unrealistically optimistic in predicting your marathon goal pace, you'll run the mile repeats too fast and risk overtraining and injury. So if this pace causes you to breathe heavily, shift to a slower pace and adjust your marathon goal accordingly. Be sure to walk (don't jog) between mile repeats for at least 4 minutes.

■ 5K races help you predict a realistic goal in the marathon. Take your performance times on accurately measured courses, and use the "Predicting Race Performance" chart in Galloway's Book On Running. The more races you have, the more accurate your prediction will be. Adjust your mile repeat sessions accordingly.

■ Marathon pace running can be done on two other days during the week (Wednesday and Friday). After a slow warm-up followed by 4-8 acceleration GLIDERS, run 1-3 miles at the marathon pace your 5K races are predicting. This tells you what it's like to run at marathon goal pace. Make sure that you've recovered from the weekend run and break up the paced miles with slow jogging between. Hopefully your legs will feel good enough to do 1-2 of these marathon pace miles on the Wednesday and Friday before your marathon (unless the marathon is on Saturday and then shift to Tuesday and Thursday).

■ The pace of the Tuesday run should be at least one minute per mile slower than marathon goal pace and slower if you're still tired from the weekend session. You may also do a few acceleration-GLIDERS on this day, but be careful. Never hesitate to slow down on the Tuesday, Wednesday and Friday runs.

■ You have some flexibility on the number of minutes to be run during the week. Never increase the amount more than 10 percent above what you have been doing the week before. Don't hesitate to cut back on some of these days if you're feeling tired from the (hopefully) playful but tiring weekend.

29

Time Goal Marathon: 2:39

Week #	Mon	Tue	Wed	Thu	Fri	Sat	Sun
1.	XT or 3 easy	40-55 min	20-50min	XT	40-55 min	off	4-6 hills (5-7 mi)
2.	XT or 3 easy	40-60 min	20-50min	XT	40-60 min	off	5K race (6-7 mi)
3.	XT or 3 easy	40-65 min	20-50min	XT	40-60 min	off	7-8 hills (7-8 mi)
4.	XT or 3 easy	40-65 min	20-50min	XT	40-60 min	off	9-10 hills (8-9 mi)
5.	XT or 3 easy	45-75 min	25-55min	XT	45-65 min	off	5K race (9-10 mi)
6.	XT or 3 easy	45-80 min	25-55min	XT	45-65 min	off	5-7 x 1mi (11 mi)
7.	XT or 3 easy	45-80 min	25-55min	XT	45-70 min	off	5K race (8 mi)
8.	XT or 4 easy	45-80 min	25-55min	XT	45-75 min	off	6-8 x 1mi (13 mi)
9.	XT or 4 easy	45-80 min	25-55min	XT	45-80 min	off	8-10x 1mi (12 mi)
10.	XT or 4 easy	45-85 min	25-60min	XT	45-80 min	off	15-16 mi easy
11.	XT or 4 easy	45-85 min	25-60min	XT	45-85 min	off	5K race (9 mi)
12.	XT or 4 easy	45-85 min	25-60min	XT	45-85 min	off	17-18 mi easy
13.	XT or 4 easy	45-85 min	25-60min	XT	45-85 min	off	10-11 x1 mi
14.	XT or 4 easy	45-85 min	25-60min	XT	45-85 min	off	19-20 mi easy
15.	XT or 4 easy	45-85 min	25-60min	XT	45-85 min	off	5K race (10 mi)
16.	XT or 4 easy	45-85 min	25-60min	XT	45-85 min	off	11-13 x1 mi
17.	XT or 4 easy	45-85 min	25-60min	XT	45-85 min	off	22-23 mi easy
18.	XT or 4 easy	45-85 min	25-60min	XT	45-85 min	off	5K race
19.	XT or 4 easy	45-85 min	25-60min	XT	45-85 min	off	5-8 x 1 mi
20.	XT or 4 easy	45-85 min	25-60min	XT	45-85 min	off	25-26 mi easy
21.	XT or 4 easy	45-85 min	25-60min	XT	45-85 min	off	5K race
22.	XT or 4 easy	45-85 min	25-60min	XT	45-85 min	off	5-8 x 1 mi
23.	XT or 4 easy	45-75 min	25-60min	XT	45-75 min	off	28-30 mi easy
24.	XT	45-55 min	25-50min	XT	45-55 min	off	5K or 4 x 1 mi
25.	XT	40 min	20-35min	XT	40 min	off	4-6 x 1 mi
26.	run 40 min	off	run 30 min	off	run 30 min	off	**The Marathon**
27.	XT 45 min	run/walk 40 min	XT 30-60 min	run/walk 40 min	XT 30-60 min	off	7-10 mi run/walk
28.	XT 45 min	run/walk 45 min	XT 30-60 min	run/walk 45 min	XT 30-60 min	off	9-15 mi run/walk
29.	XT 45 min	run/walk 45 min	XT 30-60 min	run/walk 45 min	XT 30-60 min	off	12-20 mi run/walk

- After hill and speed sessions and 5K races you'll see the total mileage recommendation for the day in parentheses. This can be accumulated by adding up the warm-up, the warm-down, hill distance, and any other running during the session.

- On the XT (cross-training) days you can swim, run in the water, use exercise machines such as rowing, cross-country ski, and cycle. Don't use the stair machines. If you miss one of these XT days, don't worry.

- Run the long ones at least 2 minutes per mile slower than you could run that same distance on that day (adjust for heat, humidity, hills, etc.). By running slower, you'll speed recovery and reduce the chance of injury.

- Take a one-minute walk break every 8-10 minutes from the beginning of every long run. On the first few long ones, you may run 10 minutes between breaks. But when the long one reaches 18 miles (and further) shift to a one-minute break about every mile. Be sure to adjust to more frequent breaks if needed. These breaks shift the use of the muscles before they get over-fatigued. You'll have better muscle response late in the run and will recover faster. There is NO reduction of endurance when you take walk breaks.

- Early in the schedule, hill play is recommended on the weekend. Do not sprint. After a relaxed warm-up, do 4-8 accelerations. Then run each hill at about 10K race pace. Keep feet low to the ground and avoid tension in the leg muscles (especially the hamstring). Run up and over the top of the hill, and walk down. Walk more before the next hill if you need more recovery.

- Follow the same warm-up procedure for mile repeats. For a time goal of 2:39, run each mile repeat in 5:40. This prepares you for the pace you'll be running between walk breaks in the marathon. If you're unrealistically optimistic in predicting your marathon goal pace, you'll run the mile repeats too fast and risk overtraining and injury. So if this pace causes you to

- breathe heavily, shift to a slower pace and adjust your marathon goal accordingly. Be sure to walk (don't jog) between mile repeats for at least 4 minutes.

- 5K races help you predict a realistic goal in the marathon. Take your performance times on accurately measured courses, and use the "Predicting Race Performance" chart in Galloway's Book On Running. The more races you have, the more accurate your prediction will be. Adjust your mile repeat sessions accordingly.

- Marathon pace running can be done on two other days during the week (Wednesday and Friday). After a slow warm-up, followed by 4-8 acceleration GLIDERS, run 1-3 miles at the marathon pace your 5K races are predicting. This tells you what it's like to run at marathon goal pace. Make sure that you've recovered from the weekend run and break up the paced miles with slow jogging between. Hopefully, your legs will feel good enough to do 1-2 of these marathon pace miles on the Wednesday and Friday before your marathon (unless the marathon is on Saturday and then shift to Tuesday and Thursday).

- The pace of the Tuesday run should be at least one minute per mile slower than marathon goal pace and slower if you're still tired from the weekend session. You may also do a few acceleration-GLIDERS on this day, but be careful. Never hesitate to slow down on the Tuesday, Wednesday and Friday runs.

- You have some flexibility on the number of minutes to be run during the week. Never increase the amount more than 10 percent above what you have been doing the week before. Don't hesitate to cut back on some of these days if you're feeling tired from the (hopefully) playful but tiring weekend.

FAT-BURNING TRAINING

Week #	Mon	Tue	Wed	Thu	Fri	Sat	Sun
1	30 min walk/jog	xt	30 min walk	xt	30 min walk/jog	walk	3 mi easy
2	30 min walk/jog	xt	35 min walk/jog	xt	35 min walk/jog	walk	4 mi
3	30 min walk/jog	xt	40 min walk/jog	xt	40 min walk/jog	walk	5 mi
4	30 min walk/jog	xt	45 min walk/jog	xt	45 min walk/jog	walk	6 mi
5	30 min walk/jog	xt	45-50 min walk/jog	xt	45-50 min walk/jog	walk	7 mi
6	30 min walk/jog	xt	45-50 min walk/jog	xt	45-50 min walk/jog	walk	8 mi
7	30 min walk/jog	xt	50-55 min walk/jog	xt	50-55 min walk/jog	walk	9 mi
8	30 min walk/jog	xt	50-55 min walk/jog	xt	50-55 min walk/jog	walk	10 mi
9	30 min walk/jog	xt	55-60 min walk/jog	xt	55-60 min walk/jog	walk	11-12 mi
10	30 min walk/jog	xt	55-60 min walk/jog	xt	55-60 min walk/jog	walk	6 mi
11	30 min walk/jog	xt	60-65 min walk/jog	xt	60-65 min walk/jog	walk	13-14 mi
12	30 min walk/jog	xt	60-65 min walk/jog	xt	60-65 min walk/jog	walk	7 mi
13	30 min walk/jog	xt	60-70 min walk/jog	xt	60-70 min walk/jog	walk	15-16 mi
14	30 min walk/jog	xt	60-70 min walk/jog	xt	60-70 min walk/jog	walk	8 mi
15	30 min walk/jog	xt	60-75 min walk/jog	xt	60-75 min walk/jog	walk	17-18 mi
16	30 min walk/jog	xt	60-75 min walk/jog	xt	60-75 min walk/jog	walk	8-10 mi
17	30 min walk/jog	xt	60-80 min walk/jog	xt	60-80 min walk/jog	walk	19-20 mi
18	30 min walk/jog	xt	60-80 min walk/jog	xt	60-80 min walk/jog	walk	5K race or 8-10 mi
19	30 min walk/jog	xt	60-85 min walk/jog	xt	60-85 min walk/jog	walk	8-9 mi
20	30 min walk/jog	xt	60-85 min walk/jog	xt	60-85 min walk/jog	walk	22-23 mi
21	30 min walk/jog	xt	60-90 min walk/jog	xt	60-90 min walk/jog	walk	5K race or 8-10 mi
22	30 min walk/jog	xt	60-90 min walk/jog	xt	60-90 min walk/jog	walk	8-10 mi
23	30 min walk/jog	xt	45-60 min walk/jog	xt	45-60 min walk/jog	walk	24-26 mi
24	30 min walk/jog	xt	45-60 min walk/jog	xt	45-60 min walk/jog	walk	5K race or 8-10 mi
25	30 min walk/jog	xt	45-60 min walk/jog	xt	45-60 min walk/jog	walk	8-10 mi
26	30 min walk/jog	xt	45-60 min walk/jog	xt	45-60 min walk/jog	walk	The Marathon
27	30 min walk/jog	xt	45 min walk/jog	xt	45 min walk/jog	walk	7-10 mi run/walk
28	30 min walk/jog	xt	60 min walk/jog	xt	60 min walk/jog	walk	9-15 mi run/walk
29	30 min walk/jog	xt	60 min walk/jog	xt	60 min walk/jog	walk	12-20 run/walk

- As the runs get longer, be sure to keep your blood sugar boosted by eating a PowerBar or whatever you like for a pre-run breakfast about an hour before the start. During the second half of the long run or marathon take PowerGel (etc.) with water. Gradually introduce your system to the nutrients on your long runs and follow the feeding schedule that works for you during the marathon.

- Best results will be achieved when you increase the long run to 26 miles. If your last one is only 24 miles, you must run slowly and take a few more walk breaks during the first 5-10 miles of the marathon itself.

- Every other day you can cross-train (XT) or walk. It's your choice: cross-country ski machines, cycling and any other mode which you find fun and interesting (but non-pounding). You don't have to do the cross training to finish the marathon, but these activities will improve overall fitness and fat burning. It's better to do exercises that build up body heat to a level that you can stand for at least 45 minutes. If this means taking it very easy in the beginning, do so. It's also fine to alternate segments of 10-15 minutes of different exercises but move quickly between segments.

- Stay conversational on all of your exercise sessions. This means that you should be exerting yourself at a low enough level that allows you to talk. It's okay to take deep breaths between sentences, but you don't want to "huff and puff" between every word. This is the test for staying aerobic and therefore inside the fat-burning zone.

- Beginners with no exercise background may need to take sit-down breaks of 1-2 minutes, every 4-10 minutes of walking, run-walking or cross training. If taking these breaks allows you to do more exercise and recover faster, take them.

- Be sure to do the running portion slow enough at the beginning of every run (especially the long one) so that you'll be able to continue past the 45-minute mark inside the fat-burning zone (the "no puffing" zone). This conservatism will also speed recovery.

- When in doubt, slow down the pace and take more walk breaks from the beginning. It is the distance covered, not the speed, that determines how much fat you've burned. Slow down, burn more and feel better during your exercise tomorrow as well as today.

- Don't wait to take walk breaks! By alternating walking and running from the beginning, you speed recovery without losing any of the endurance effect of the long one.

WALK BREAKS

Walking
Breakthrough

"Without walk breaks, I could only run three miles, with difficulty. Using walk breaks, I've finished three marathons feeling strong."

Walk breaks will...

...allow those who can only run two miles to go three or four and feel fine

...help beginners or heavy runners to increase their endurance to 5K, 10K or even the marathon in as soon as six months

...bestow the endurance for runners of all abilities to go beyond "the wall"

...allow runners over the age of 40 to not only do their first marathon but to improve times in most cases

...help runners of all ages to improve times because legs are strong at the end

...reduce the chance of injury and overtraining to almost nothing

As one who has pridefully run for more than four decades, it's sometimes hard to admit something, but here goes. Our bodies weren't designed to run continuously for long distances, especially distances as far as the marathon. Sure we can adapt, but there is a better way to increase endurance than by running continuously. By alternating walking and running, from the start, there's virtually no limit to the distance you can cover. Thousands of people in their 40s and 50s with no exercise background have used the walk-run method to complete a marathon in six months. Once we find the ideal ratio for a given distance, walk breaks allow us to feel strong to the end and recover fast, while bestowing the same stamina and conditioning we would have received if we had run continuously.

Most runners will record significantly faster times when they take walk breaks because they don't slow down at the end of a long run. Thousands of time-goal-oriented veterans have improved by 10, 20, 30 minutes and more in marathons by taking walk breaks early and often in their goal race. You can easily spot these folks in races. They're the ones who are picking up speed during the last two to six miles when everyone else is slowing down.

Walk-running is what we were designed to do

Our ancient ancestors had to walk and run thousands of miles every year to survive. Because they moved on to greener pastures and away from predators, we're here to philosophize about walk breaks. So it's a fact that each of us inherited an organism that was designed to move forward for long distances. As often happens with behaviors which enhance survival, a series of very complex and internally satisfying rewards have developed, which relax the muscles, stimulate the creative and intuitive side of our brain, and energize our spirit. By

> *"When I moved my weekend long run up to 10 miles, I started to feel, after each long one, some primitive feelings—like I was the first one blazing a trail for others to follow."*

getting out the door and moving forward three or more times a week, even the most out-of-shape couch potato will discover this enhanced sense of self worth and improved attitude.

While walking is our most efficient exercise pattern, we can adapt to running and do well. Indeed, most walkers who add running to their exercise say they get a better boost in their after-exercise attitude. But running continuously can quickly push anyone beyond the capacity of leg muscles. When we alternate between walking and running, early and often, we are going back to the type of exertion that brought our forebears across continents, over deserts and mountain ranges.

36 EVEN A SHORT WALK BREAK WHEN TAKEN EARLY AND REGULARLY WILL:

- Extend the capacity of the running muscles at the end of the run because you're shifting the workload between the walking and the running muscles

- Virtually erase fatigue with each early walk break by keeping your pace and effort level conservative in the early stages

- Allow those with some types of previous injuries to knees, ankles, hips, feet, etc. to train for marathons without further injury

- Restore resiliency to the main running muscles before they fatigue—like getting a muscle strength booster shot each break

- Allow runners to improve 10 to 40 minutes in their marathon compared with running continuously

- Speed up recovery from each long run—even from 23 and 26-mile training runs

- Leave you feeling good enough to carry on social and family activities—even after the very long long runs

WALK BREAKS WERE PART OF THE MARATHON——FROM THE BEGINNING

Ancient Greek messengers such as the original marathoner Phidippides (see his story in the first section of this book) regularly covered distances of more than 100 kilometers a day by walking and running. The accounts of the original marathon race, in the 1896 Olympics, described significant periods of walking for *all* competitors, including the winner Spiros Louis.

Elite marathoners continue to use walk breaks. The great American marathoner, Bill Rodgers, has said many times that he had to walk at water stations during his Boston and NYC marathon victories in order to get the water into his stomach (instead of wearing it on his shirt). Fabian Roncero took several walk breaks during his victory in the '98 Rotterdam Marathon to gather his resources. If anyone tells you that by taking walk breaks you are not a marathoner, he or she should be the one to tell this 2:07:26 champion that he is not a marathoner.

The label of "marathoner" has, from the beginning, been awarded to those who went the distance under their own power, whether they ran, walked, crawled or tiptoed. When you cross that finish line, you've entered an elite group. About one tenth of one percent of the population has done it. Don't let anyone take that great achievement away from you.

> **"I** *tried to train for three marathons without walk breaks and became injured each time. Walk breaks allowed me to get to the starting line and then to the marathon finish line...injury free!"*

I've now done well over 100 marathons, about half of them without walk breaks. On every one of the walk-break marathons, I received the same sense of accomplishment, all of the internal rewards, and the indescribable exhilaration of finishing as on the non-walk marathons. But when I inserted walk breaks throughout, I was able to enjoy the accomplishment afterward.

WHY DO WALK BREAKS WORK?

BY USING MUSCLES IN DIFFERENT WAYS—FROM THE BEGINNING—YOUR LEGS KEEP THEIR BOUNCE AS THEY CONSERVE RESOURCES.

Walk breaks keep you from using up your resources early. By alternating the exertion level and the way you're using your running muscles, these prime movers have a chance to recover before they accumulate fatigue. On each successive walk, most or all of the fatigue is erased, bestowing strength at the end. This reduces the damage to the muscle dramatically, allowing you to carry on your life activities even after a marathon.

Walk breaks force you to slow down early in the run so that you don't start too fast. This reduction of the intensity of muscle use from the beginning conserves your energy, fluids and muscle capacity. On each walk break, the running muscles make internal adaptations, which give you the option to finish under control, increase the pace, or go even further.

When a muscle group, such as your calf, is used continuously step by step, it fatigues relatively soon. The weak areas get overused and force you to slow down later or scream at you in pain afterward. By shifting back and forth between walking and running muscles, you distribute the workload among a variety of muscles, increasing your overall performance capacity. For veteran marathoners, this is often the difference between achieving a time goal...or not.

Walk breaks will significantly speed up recovery because there is less damage to repair. The early walk breaks erase fatigue, and the later walk breaks will reduce or eliminate overuse muscle breakdown.

WALK BREAKS CAN ELIMINATE INJURY

Many runners who were injured during previous training programs (because they ran continuously) have stayed injury-free when they add walk breaks to long runs. Without walking from the beginning, the leg muscles fatigue more quickly and can't keep these lower extremities moving efficiently in their proper range of motion. The resulting "wobble" allows the leg to extend too far forward in an overstride. This abuses the tendons and injures the small muscle groups which try to keep the body on its proper mechanical track but don't have the horsepower to completely control the body weight moving forward.

Walk breaks taken early in the run keep the muscles strong and resilient enough so that the legs can move with strength and efficiency throughout. This will significantly reduce or eliminate the excess stress around the knees, ankles, feet, etc., which produces injury. The little "back-up" muscle groups can stay in reserve and fine-tune the running motion after fatigue sets in.

HOW TO SET UP WALK BREAKS

Walk breaks can change a bad run into a regular one and sometimes a great one.

ON LONG TRAINING RUNS: THE MORE OFTEN YOU TAKE WALK BREAKS, THE BETTER YOUR LEGS FEEL AT THE END

- Beginners take jogging breaks in their walks (one minute jogs, every five minutes or so of walking).

- As beginners get in better shape, they may reduce the walking segments gradually (1-4, then 1-3, 1-2, 1-1).

- Fitness runners will take a two-minute walk break after two to three minutes of jogging.

- Average runners take one to two-minute walk breaks after three to eight minutes of running.

- Advanced runners take one-minute walk breaks or "shuffle breaks" every mile (after about eight to 10 minutes of running).

WHEN TO TAKE WALK BREAKS

Walk breaks can change a bad run into a regular one—and sometimes a great one. We don't usually know the reason we don't feel good as we start a run. Instead of quitting or suffering through (and not wanting to run the next time), try a one to two-minute walk break every three to eight minutes. By breaking up your run early and often, you can cover the distance you'd like to cover on that day, burn the calories you'd like to burn, and increase the chance that you'll enjoy the experience of running itself.

You don't need to take walk breaks on runs that are short enough and easy for you to run continuously. For example, if your current long run is 10 miles and you feel good as you start your Tuesday five-miler, you don't need to put in walk breaks. If the walk breaks can make the experience better, however, take them!

THE EARLIER YOU TAKE THE WALK BREAKS, THE MORE THEY HELP YOU!

To receive maximum benefit, you must start the walk breaks before you feel any fatigue, in the first mile. If you wait until you feel the need for a walk break, you've already reduced your potential performance. Even waiting until the two-mile mark to take the first one will reduce the resiliency you could regain from walking in the first mile.

Would you like a discount? To put it in shopping terms, walk breaks give a discount from the pounding on legs and feet.

"I waited until the 10-mile mark to take walk breaks in my first two marathons—and was wiped out for two weeks. When I took them every mile, from the beginning, I improved my time by 20 minutes, recovered fast, and danced afterwards."

If you walk often enough, start early enough, and keep the pace slow enough, a 10-mile run only leaves five to seven miles of fatigue, and a 20-miler produces only 12 to 15 miles of tiredness.

Hint: If you feel self-conscious about walking early, carry an empty water bottle and pretend to drink as you walk. You can also blame me: Tell those who pass you that Jeff Galloway made you do it!

WHEN IN DOUBT, WALK MORE AND WALK EARLIER

It's much better to take a one-minute walk break every five minutes than to take a five-minute walk every 25 minutes. By breaking up your run early—even with a short break—you allow for quicker and more effective recovery. If you're used to walking one minute every four minutes but are not feeling good at the beginning of a run, go to 4-2 or 2-1.

There's very little difference in benefit between a 4-2 and a 2-1. The more frequent break (2-1) will keep the legs fresher. The longer you run continuously, the more fatigued the legs become. Remember that you only lose about 17 seconds when you walk for a minute. The small amount of distance you lose on extra walking earlier will almost always be recovered at the end—because you kept your legs fresh. Those who put this concept to the test almost always find that taking more frequent walk breaks doesn't slow the overall time of long runs—when the long runs are done at the correct slow pace.

HOW FAST SHOULD YOU WALK ON THE WALK BREAK?

A slow walk is fine. When you walk fast for a minute, most runners will lose about 15 seconds over running at their regular pace. But if you walk slowly, you'll lose only about 20 seconds. If you have a "type A" running personality and want to walk fast, make sure that you don't lengthen your walking stride too much. Monitor the tightness of your hamstring and the tendons behind the knee. If you feel tension there, walk slowly with bent knees to keep that area relaxed. Again, a slow walk is just as good as a fast one and may keep the leg muscles from getting tight.

Racewalk technique is also okay. As long as you receive qualified instruction and practice this regularly, racewalking will allow many runners to go faster during the walk breaks. Because a racewalk uses different muscle groups than those used in running, this is an appropriate shifting of muscle use and allows the prime running muscles to recover and rebuild.

HOW FAST SHOULD MY RUNNING PACE BE?

The overall pace of all long runs should be at least two minutes per mile slower than

39

"This marathon season I ran two minutes and walked two minutes. Last season I ran three minutes and walked one minute. When I checked my training journals for this and last year, I was amazed to find that my running times for the same distances with 2/2 were about the same as 3/1. I recovered so much faster when I went to 2 and 2."

you could race the distance. If you don't have a clue how fast this is, use the "talk test": If you're huffing so much at the end of a long run that you can't carry on a coherent conversation, you went too fast earlier in the run. On each successive long one, slow down until the puffing is minimal.

Since a one-minute walk break only slows you down by 15-20 seconds, you'll need to purposely run slower than you usually run, as well as taking the walk breaks. This will allow you to comply with the two-minute rule which says that long runs should be run at least two minutes slower than you could race that distance on that day. You can't run too slowly. You'll receive the same endurance from a long run as you do from a fast one. Slow down and enjoy the scenery.

40 As the long runs get longer, take the walk breaks more often.

A runner that is comfortable running six minutes and walking one minute will move to 5-1 at 15 to 18 miles, then to 4-1 at 20 miles, and 3-1 when the long runs reach 23 miles.

DON'T GET TOO RIGIDLY LOCKED INTO A SPECIFIC RATIO OF WALK BREAKS—ADJUST AS NEEDED

Even if you run the same distance every day, you'll find that you'll need to vary the walk break frequency to adjust for speed, hills, heat, humidity, time off from training, etc. If you anticipate that your run will be more difficult or will produce a longer recovery, take more frequent walk breaks (or longer walks) and you may be surprised at how quickly you recover. On cold days, you may not need to take the walks as often (although it's not wise to reduce walk breaks in any run longer than 17 miles).

HOW WALK BREAKS CAN SPEED YOU UP IN THE MARATHON

A survey of veteran marathoners showed an average improvement of 13 minutes when they put walk breaks into their marathon, compared with running continuously under the same conditions. By saving the strength and efficiency of the running muscles through early walk breaks, you'll avoid the slowdown in the last six miles, where most continuous runners lose their momentum. You'll be passing people and picking up speed if you paced yourself conservatively and walked enough from the first mile.

WHY DO YOU SPEED UP WITH WALK BREAKS?

When you pace yourself correctly and take the walk breaks you need in the first mile of a race, you'll virtually erase the fatigue of mile one. By continuing to walk before you get tired, you conserve resources and can run with strength to the finish line. Most runners who don't take walk breaks slow down significantly during the last six to eight miles. Walk-break-takers at least avoid the seven to 15-minute slowdown at the end. With proper speed training, pacing and the right walk-run ratio, you'll run faster during the last six to eight miles only because you walked early.

A GAME OF "CHASE"

After a few miles into your marathon, you'll settle into a pace and notice some of the folks around you. As you take your walk break, track one or two of them so that you catch up with them by the time you start your next walk break. You'll have to pick new "markers" around the halfway point. Because they're running continuously, they'll probably start slowing down about then.

THE MENTAL BENEFIT: BREAKING 26 MILES INTO SEGMENTS WHICH YOU KNOW YOU CAN DO

Even sub-three-hour runners continue to take their walk breaks to the end. One of them explained it this way: "Instead of thinking at 20 miles that I had six more gut-wrenching miles to go, I was saying to myself 'one more mile until my break.' Even when it was tough, I always felt that I could go one more mile." A three-minute run/one-minute walk person told me that she got over the tough parts by saying "three more minutes."

> **O**ver four dozen runners have broken three hours in the marathon for the first time after inserting a walk break every mile.

WALK BREAKS IN THE MARATHON: HOW LONG AND HOW OFTEN?

The following is recommended until 18 miles in the marathon. After that point, walk breaks can be reduced or eliminated as desired.

Beginning runners should follow the program you've used in training as long as you aren't slowing down at the end. If you struggled during the last few miles, take walk breaks more often from the beginning. A minimum beginners program would be two to three minutes of walking for every one to two minutes of jogging.

First-time marathoners who don't enter races should follow the program you've used in training as long as you haven't been slowing down at the end of the long ones. If you struggled during the last few miles, take walk breaks more often from the beginning. A minimum suggestion for first-time marathoners would be one minute of walking for every three to four minutes of running.

If you haven't run more than 20 miles in training, there's still hope. Let's say that you just picked up this book less than three weeks before your marathon and your longest run is only 18 miles. If you had no trouble with your last long run and have been taking walk breaks, add one minute to each walk (a five-minute run, one-minute walk becomes five running minutes and two walking minutes). If you haven't been taking walk breaks at all or haven't been taking them as often as the schedule below, add one minute to each walk break on this schedule.

All others should monitor walk breaks by goal pace (first-time marathoners should run their first one at least an hour slower than they could run on that day).

Time Goal of more than 6 hours:
1-2 minutes of walking every 1-2 minutes of running

Time Goal of 5:30-6:00 hours and slower:
1 minute of walking after every 4-5 minutes of running

Time Goal of 5:00-5:29:
1 minute of walking after every 5-6 minutes of running

Time Goal of 4:30-4:59:
1-2 minutes of walking after every 6-7 minutes of running

Time Goal of 4:00-4:29:
1 minute of walking after every 7-8 minutes of running

Time Goal of 3:30-3:59:
1 minute of walking after every mile

Time Goal of 3:22-3:29:
30 seconds after every mile

Time Goal of 3:16-3:21:
20 seconds of walking after every mile

Time Goal of 3:08-3:15:
15 seconds of walking after every mile

Time Goal of 2:50-3:07:
10 seconds of walking after every mile

42

Jeff Galloway's Experience

His Choice: A 3:40 marathon *without* walking breaks...

or a 3:25 marathon *with* walking breaks

Most of you who have time goals will record a faster time, as this gentleman did, if you take the walk breaks early and often.

A friend of mine in his late 40s had been trying for years to run a 3:30 marathon and should have done it, but 3:40 was as fast as he could run. His 5K and 10K performances predicted about 3:25, and he had done plenty of intense training in three different marathon campaigns, including high mileage, lots of speedwork, two runs a day, etc.

Finally, he sent in his entry form for my program, only after I told him that if he didn't run below 3:30 in his goal marathon, I'd return his check. Never did I mention the walk breaks because I knew he would say something about 'sissy stuff' and not sign up.

I knew that in the past he had been physically trained (probably overtrained) for his goal and mainly needed to run with a group to slow down his pace on the long one. The group support during speed sessions also helped him enjoy doing mile repeats for the first time in his life.

After the first session he came up to me, irate, and demanded his money back. 'I can't do these walk breaks: they're sissy stuff!' I refused to return his check, reminding him that *a deal was a deal.*

He went through the program, complaining during just about every walk break. Secretly, he told friends in his pace group that he wasn't going to walk during the marathon itself.

On marathon morning, his group leader lined up with him and physically restrained him for one minute each mile...walking. At 18 miles, he looked at my friend and said 'Well, you seem to have just enough life in your legs so run along now!' And he did.

His time was 3:25. He had run 15 minutes faster than he had ever run!

At first, he couldn't believe that he could improve that much while walking every mile. But when he analyzed where he had slowed down in past marathons, it was always in the last six to eight miles. In his recent marathon he kept picking up the pace after 18 and knocked five minutes off his pace in that final segment. He finally admitted that the early and regular 'muscle shifts' left his legs feeling strong and responsive all the way to the finish line.

43

WALK BREAK QUESTIONS

"SHOULD I CHANGE MY RUN/ WALK RATIO DURING THE MARATHON?"

If you're feeling good at 13 to 15 miles, you could stretch the run segments to one additional minute (i.e., from running four minutes and walking one minute, you could extend to running five minutes and walking one minute). After 18 miles, you could stay the same, stretch another minute, or take out the walk breaks entirely. While it's your choice, most marathoners who are feeling good keep at least a 30-second break every mile. If you're having a bad day, however, the sooner you can increase the frequency of walk breaks or walk more during each break, the less you will tend to slow down at the end of the marathon.

"IF I'VE NEVER TRIED THE WALK BREAKS IN TRAINING RUNS, WOULD YOU ADVISE TAKING THEM IN THE MARATHON?"

They will only help you. I've received hundreds of letters, faxes, emails and calls from those who heard about the walk break concept the evening before the marathon and tried it the next day. Their response is very similar to this one:

"When I heard you recommend walk breaks at the seminar before the marathon, I didn't want to think about it. I don't know why but it just seemed demeaning for a real runner like me to walk like that. You see, I've run 10 marathons with a personal best of 3:57 and have been proud of the fact that I've never walked.

"But after thinking about it overnight, I decided to prove you wrong by doing exactly what you suggested. To tell you the honest truth, I'd been sick for the last couple of weeks or so and calculated that I probably couldn't run a personal best anyway.

"I walked for a minute every mile and ran my original goal pace for a 3:55 finish during the running portions.

"By the first half of the marathon I was behind my goal pace by three minutes. Aha, I said to myself, Galloway is going to be wrong. If I'm already three minutes behind at the half, I'll be way behind at the finish.

"At 20 miles, I was beginning to feel stronger than I had ever felt at that stage of the marathon. I cut out the walk breaks and ran to the finish, except for short breaks at water stops. While tired during the last six miles, I felt good and passed a lot of people, not really aware of my pace.

"I couldn't believe my time at the finish: 3:52—five minutes faster than I had ever run in my life…and after a bad cold! How did that happen?"

"ARE YOU SAYING THAT I CAN BENEFIT FROM A WALK BREAK—EVEN THOUGH I'M TRAINING FOR A SUB-THREE-HOUR MARATHON?"

Yes, dozens of runners have reported breaking three hours by taking walk breaks when they couldn't do so by running continuously. A growing number of runners have run below 2:50 by taking walk breaks at least during the first 18 miles. Everyone benefits from walk breaks. They reduce the pounding, allow for water consumption, and speed up recovery from long runs. Competitive runners can erase enough fatigue during the first half so that they can race the second half. The demands of a time goal program require quick recovery, which walk breaks allow. In two to four days, you can be recovered enough from a 26 to 28 mile run to do speed training—by running at least two minutes per mile slower than you could run that same distance on that day and taking liberal walk breaks from the beginning.

"DO I HAVE TO TAKE WALK BREAKS AT THE END OF MY RUNS IF MY LEGS ARE TIGHTENING UP?"

Take them as long as you can because they will speed your recovery. If your legs cramp up later during walk breaks then just shuffle through the breaks (by keeping your feet low to the ground with a short stride). At the end, you want to stay as fluid as you can while still alternating the use of the muscle groups. Cramping at the end tells you to start slower in the next long run and to avoid dehydration the day before the run, the morning of the run and during the run itself.

"DO I NEED TO TAKE WALK BREAKS ON THE SHORT RUNS DURING THE WEEK?"

If you can run continuously now on shorter midweek runs, you don't have to take the walk breaks. If you want to take them, do so. Walk breaks on midweek runs will insure that you recover from the long ones at the fastest pace.

45

FOOD AND FAT-BURNING

FAT-BURNING AS A WAY OF LIFE

"After seven marathons in five years, I've lost 35 pounds and kept it off. I must say, however, that I was disappointed that I didn't lose a single pound while training for my first one."

If running is one of the very best ways to burn fat, then why do so few marathoners lose weight—at least in their first campaign? Among the many good answers to this one is that a novice marathoner should reduce mileage and other running stresses to arrive at the starting line and the finish line injury-free. The low mileage associated with this insurance policy will not burn much fat off the body.

Significant dietary changes usually disrupt your metabolism, cause an inconsistent mental focus, and lead to energy surges and withdrawals. Other problems encountered by those who change diet and train for a marathon at the same time are the following: stress fractures, nutritional

deficiencies and blood sugar level reductions. All can leave you unmotivated to exercise. It's no wonder that we see a lot of program dropouts among those who radically change their diets.

After crossing that marathon finish line for the first time, you're free to set up a five-year plan for making nutritional changes. Check the Schedules section for a "Fat-Burning Schedule" with an expanded program of exercise and cross training.

But first, let's look into the, unfortunately, expanding world of fat. To better understand how to take it off, we'll look first at how it goes on and the powerful biological instincts that try to keep it in storage. After a good look at the income side, we'll focus on the long-term ways of burning it off as a lifestyle. Once you transform yourself into a fat-burning organism, you'll feel better all day long as you burn more fat.

FAT AS FUEL

Our "set point" determines how much we store

*T*he human organism is lazy. With a primary mission of survival, each of us is programmed to slowly build up extra fat storage. For millions of years, this has been a proven "insurance policy," which allowed our ancient ancestors to survive through periods of starvation and sickness. The mechanisms of fat storage, described below, support a well-established principle called "set point." This powerful regulatory mechanism increases your appetite for weeks or months, after periods of fat loss due to reduced calorie intake, illness, and even psychological deprivation. Unfortunately, it does its job too well, leaving you fatter than you were before the fat loss. Understanding how the set point works as your hedge against starvation is the most important step in learning how to adjust it downward, or at least manage it, for the rest of your life.

WHAT IS FAT?

When you eat a pat of butter, you might as well inject it onto your thigh or stomach. While dietary fat is directly deposited, protein and carbohydrates (even sugar) will be converted into fat only when you've consumed too many calories from those sources throughout the day. If you're trying to reduce the fat blanket, it helps to eat complex carbohydrates (baked potatoes, rice, whole grains, vegetables) and lean protein sources (legumes, turkey breast, nonfat dairy products, etc.).

AN UNLIMITED SUPPLY OF THE BEST FUEL FOR RUNNING

Only body fat is used as fuel, not the fat in your diet. It is an excellent energy source, leaving a small amount of waste product, which is easily removed through the increased blood flow of exercise. While stored sugar is limited, you can't run far enough to use up your fat storage. Even a 140-pound person with the unusually low level of two percent body fat has hundreds of miles of fuel on board.

ANOTHER DIFFERENCE BETWEEN MEN AND WOMEN

Men tend to store fat on the surface of the body, often on the outside of the stomach area. Most females store fat internally at first. Thousands of areas between muscle cells are filled up first. Many young women feel that some dramatic change has occurred around the age of 30 when they suddenly start showing fat accumulation on the outside of their bodies, while maintaining the same diet and level of exercise. They've actually been storing fat inside for many years. Once the inner areas are filled, women notice a dramatic change

47

on the outside of their thighs or stomachs, often in less than a year.

THE SET POINT IS PROGRAMMED TO INCREASE YOUR FAT ACCUMULATION, SLIGHTLY, EACH YEAR

By the time humans enter their mid-20s, most have settled into an accustomed level of calorie-burning and calorie consumption. Your set point is adjusted for the amount of fat you've collected to that point. Very slowly, your basal metabolism rate (the calories which are burned each day to keep you alive, doing routine activities) is reduced. Since your appetite doesn't adjust downward very quickly, most humans consume a few more calories than they need, each week, producing a slow increase in fat accumulation. The internal set point quickly adjusts to the higher level of fat, as the new "set point." Increased fat levels are biologically reinforced with each additional year of age as fat helps one survive a prolonged illness or other major interruption of health or food intake.

DIETS DON'T WORK BECAUSE THEY READJUST THE METABOLISM "THERMOSTAT" IN THE WRONG DIRECTION

By depriving yourself of food, you can reduce your body fat temporarily as you reduce your metabolism rate and your motivation to exercise. As soon as the diet is over, however, your set point mechanism unleashes a starvation reflex that keeps you eating until the fat levels are slightly higher than they were before the diet. At the same time, your metabolism rate stays low to help you store fat more quickly. No matter how mentally focused you are, you'll find yourself with more fat on your frame when you mess with that very powerful survival mechanism.

48

THE STARVATION REFLEX

By now you know that diets are read by your intuitive set point mechanism as a form of starvation, planting a future seed for increased fat storage. Over millions of years, our ancient ancestors withstood regular famines, establishing very complex and quick reactions to prepare for even the possibility of food reduction. If you're getting food in adequate quantity and frequency, your system doesn't feel the need to store fat. But the reflex starts into action when you've waited too long between snacks or meals on any day. The longer you wait to eat your next food, the more you stimulate the fat-depositing enzymes. When you eat your next food, more of it will be processed into fat. But that's not all of the bad news. A longer wait between meals increases your appetite, which leads to overeating—during the next meal or over the next few hours. Even if you've eaten three to five times a day but have eaten too few calories for that day's activities, you'll experience an increased appetite during the next 12 to 36 hours.

PSYCHOLOGICAL STARVATION

The negative power of the subconscious mind will crush your attempts to restrict your food intake. Almost everyone feels guilty about eating certain delicious items that tend to put fat on our bodies due to fat, sugar content or quantity. If you tell yourself that next week (or next month) you're going to go on a diet that will really get the fat off your body, you give yourself a license to overeat calories and decadent foods, quickly, before the diet begins. Not only does this make your fat reduction task more difficult, but it often results in a steady delay in the start date of the perceived austere diet.

Depriving yourself of one or more foods that you dearly love will start a psychological time bomb ticking away. Yes, you can tell yourself that you'll never eat another doughnut, hamburger, french fry, etc. You may even be able to abstain for an extended period of time. But at some point in the future, when the food is around and no one else is, your starvation reflex will grab hold of you in a binge. Over time, the binges will lead you to consume more of that decadent food than you deprived yourself of during the period of prohibition.

True Confessions: An Ice Cream Addiction Is Broken

I've always enjoyed ice cream, but until about 1970 my cravings for it were under control. Then, I discovered Breyer's Chocolate Chip Mint ice cream. At first it was a special treat eaten about once a week, say after a long run or a very hard workout. Gradually, I increased the reward frequency, as I was increasing my daily mileage from 10 miles to as much as 30 miles. I justified the speed it took to empty a half gallon box of my daily reward by the number of extra calories burned on the track, road and trail. It seemed to me then that the supermarkets had installed a super magnet in the frozen food section and my shopping cart was pulled there almost under its own power.

In the mid-1980s, as my wife, Barb, and I celebrated our tenth anniversary, we were determined to improve our diets. Knowing that our almost daily dose of the smooth, light-tasting ice cream couldn't be good for our arteries, we made an austere New Year's resolution: no more Breyer's ice cream.

For two years we survived the "cold turkey" diet. Then, one fateful day, we held a birthday party at our house, and some well-meaning friend brought over a box of the banned substance. Both Barb and I did well during the party, but during the cleanup the box was melting on the counter with only a little left. We jointly decided that one spoonful wouldn't kill us. The taste brought back the submerged cravings, which had been there all along. I'm sure we ate more Breyer's Chocolate Chip Mint in the next six months than we had deprived ourselves of over the two-year prohibition.

At that point, I decided to try a five-year moderation plan. I visualized myself five years in the future, eating a bowl of that ice cream every fifth night and being completely satisfied. Somewhat understanding the psychological starvation with which I had shocked my system, I kept telling myself that the ice cream would always be available if I wanted it more often. When things got tough and I felt deprived, I gave into a bowl, while visualizing that in five to six years, even with it in the freezer, I only wanted to eat it every fifth or sixth night.

Continuing to bring the visualization to the present, I saw myself four years hence, eating a bowl of it every three to four nights. Three years from that date, I would enjoy a bowl every two to three nights, and by two years from that time, a bowl every night would satisfy me. You must know that at the starting point, I was consuming about a quart every night.

Each time I got out the ice cream, for the next year, I went through my visualizations for the next five years. I filled in my eating rehearsal with changes in eating frequency—to avoid being so hungry in the evening. Over the years, I filled in these visualizations with an ever-expanding variety of foods that I learned to like but which were much lower in fat.

It worked! Before 60 months had elapsed, I was eating a bowl of full-fat ice cream every sixth night—at the most. Normally, the amount that has been consumed is much less than that. While I have made some integrated changes to my diet, I'm not gloating. I keep telling myself that the Breyer's is in the freezer.

49

BURNING IT OFF
BIG AND LITTLE THINGS THAT CAN BURN FAT AND KEEP IT OFF

...REGULAR EXERCISE IMPROVES DISEASE RESISTANCE

In the last chapter we talked about the "set point" which regulates your appetite to maintain fat accumulation at a certain level, which gradually increases each five to 10 years. One of the very best and proven ways of readjusting the set point is by doing regular endurance exercise. We're not just talking about increased fat-burning during exercise. The increased health benefits of regular exercise (enhanced resistance to disease, stronger heart, more efficient cardiovascular system, etc.) give intuitive signals to the body that there is lowered risk of long-term health problems, thus reducing the need for increased fat levels. A fit 70-year-old, for example, can often fight off a disease better and quicker than an average (and not very fit) 30-year-old. Your set point mechanism seems to have a sensor that intuitively monitors long-term trends in your body. In most cases, the set point is adjusted higher in those who suffer a series of health set-backs. In combination with regular exercise, however, it's possible to lower the monitored fat level. Let's look at some of the many reasons why exercise controls fat buildup.

...BY BURNING OFF THAT PIECE OF PIE

Regular running and walking keeps fat off the body, burning off excess calories. Most beginning runners experience some fat burn-off, even when their weight stays the same, particularly when diet is not dramatically increased. If you've consumed more calories than you've burned during a given day, you can literally burn them off with an after-dinner walk or jog. This is particularly helpful if you've consumed excess calories from carbohydrates on a given day.

...BY BURNING MORE FAT WHEN WE'RE ASLEEP

Running regularly for more than 45 minutes (even with walk breaks) trains our exercising muscle cells to be fat-burners at all times of the night and day. After months of regular distance running, you will have transformed a vast number of running muscle cells into fat-burners which prefer fat as a fuel, even when sitting around all day or when asleep at night. Long runs which exceed 90 minutes, when done every two to three weeks, speed up the transformation of the muscle cells from sugar-burners to fat-burners.

SUGAR-BURNING PRODUCES WASTE BUILDUP—SO SLOW DOWN!

Glycogen is the form of sugar that is stored in the muscles for quick energy. Not only is this the fuel that gets us started, but it sustains us for the first half hour of exercise. Unfortunately, when this form of sugar is used for exercise, it leaves behind a lot of waste product. Running even a little too fast at the beginning depletes valuable glycogen quicker as it fills up the muscles and slows them down. This is why many runners don't feel great during the first few miles of a run. The faster the starting pace, the more uncomfortable we'll feel. Most of this discomfort can be eliminated with a slow start and more frequent or longer early walk breaks - in short, a better warm-up. But there will be still more waste produced from glycogen than that experienced when burning fat.

The supply of glycogen is very limited, and it is necessary for brain function. A small amount of this "muscle sugar" is burned every mile, even after you've shifted primarily into fat-burning. So it's very important on long runs to conserve this resource by keeping the pace very slow from the beginning. When supplies run low, your "energy control" will hold back enough for your most crucial organ and force a breakdown of fat and protein—a very uncomfortable process. You'll avoid this negative effect by gradually increasing your distance, by putting in more walk breaks from the beginning, and by running at least three days a week (regularity of exercise).

FROM 15-45 MINUTES, YOUR MUSCLES GRADUALLY SHIFT INTO FAT-BURNING

Your body must not believe that you're really going out on a distance run until you keep moving forward for more than a quarter hour. At this point, you begin to break down body fat for fuel (dietary fat is converted directly into body fat and is not burned for energy). It takes some work to break down the "excess baggage" on your body into free fatty acids and triglycerides that can keep you running mile after mile. If you continue exercising longer than about 15 minutes at a pace that is within your capacity, you start shifting into fat-burning. As your exercise continues past the quarter-hour mark, you start a transition into fat-burning as long as you continue to exercise at a level of exertion that is within your capacity.

51

IF YOU'RE STILL EXERCISING COMFORTABLY AFTER 45 MINUTES, YOU'LL BE BURNING ALMOST EXCLUSIVELY FAT AS FUEL

By starting at a slow pace and taking walk breaks as needed, you can lower your exertion level enough to stay in the fat-burning zone for an extended time. This conserves glycogen for later use as you burn off the extra blanket around your stomach or thighs.

UNTRAINED MUSCLES MUST LEARN HOW TO BURN FAT

Those who are not in shape for endurance activity must train the muscles to burn fat. Beginning exercisers may have to walk only until they get up to an hour or more of continuous activity. Instead of walk breaks, some totally out-of-shape beginners need to take one to two minute "sit down" breaks every five to eight minutes to stay in the fat-burning zone. After a few weeks, however, most of these novices can improve to continuous 45 to 60-minute walks at a steady pace. At that point, they may increase the walking or hold the distance steady and add jogging breaks. See the "Walking Breakthrough" chapter for specific guidance in this area. Some people take longer to progress. Everyone needs to exercise patience.

SLOW AEROBIC EXERCISE BURNS FAT; FAST ANAEROBIC EXERCISE BURNS SUGAR

Fat can only be burned in the muscle cell when there's an adequate supply of oxygen. This is "aerobic exercise": exertions that are done at an easy enough pace so that the blood can provide all of the oxygen needed by the muscles. As soon as you increase the pace beyond your current capacity or go farther than your muscles are trained to go, the running muscles can't get enough oxygen to burn fat and shift back to the readily available but inefficient energy source, glycogen. You're now "anaerobic," meaning that the muscles aren't getting enough oxygen. The longer and faster you run anaerobically, the worse you'll feel and the sooner you'll quit because of waste product accumulation. (For a more detailed explanation of this process, see <u>Galloway's Book On Running</u>.)

WALK BREAKS AND A SLOW START PACE KEEP YOU IN THE FAT-BURNING ZONE LONGER

Not only does an easy pace from the start reduce the waste product buildup in the first quarter hour, it pushes back your wall. If you're used to running five miles (at a 12-minute/mile pace) with no walk breaks, running a 14 to 16-minute pace will reduce

the exertion so that you can run six to eight miles while feeling the same way you felt after five. When you add a one-minute walk break every five minutes, you can push the wall back to seven to 10 miles, while feeling as though you covered only about half that distance. I'm not recommending that you make this type of an increase in one or two runs for it's always better to gradually increase your mileage. However, it is a fact that slower running with walk breaks will allow you to do this with little or no risk of injury or overfatigue. The extra mileage means that you are burning more calories and fat.

LONG RUNS TRAIN YOUR MUSCLE CELLS TO BE FAT-BURNING FURNACES

The continuous movement of the body during long, slow runs and walks mobilizes an incredible number of muscle cells in the legs, back, butt and related areas. By slowly covering several miles, three times a week, this network of muscles specializes in the work that can keep moving the body in the most efficient way. Since fat is the most efficient and abundant fuel, the muscles will adapt to become fat-burners if this over 45-minute run-walk is done regularly enough.

The adaptation to fat-burning is more difficult for those who've done little or no exercise before. If you're in this category, do more walking and stick with it. The same fat-burning process works for you as it does for world class athletes. You may not notice it for a while because the changes are going on inside the muscle cells. Keep telling yourself "I'm becoming a fat-burning furnace" because you are!

BURNING MORE FAT WHILE ASLEEP

As more of the muscle cells adapt to fat metabolism through training, you'll be burning more fat throughout the day. Once they've run enough long runs, regularly, sedentary office workers will burn it while sitting in their office or while on the couch at night. Endurance-trained fat-burning cells will choose more fat as their fuel even while asleep. When you're engaged in a "battle of the bulge," you'll be able to enlist thousands of cells as your soldiers, gobbling fat all day and all night.

THE MORE 45+-MINUTE EXERCISE SESSIONS, THE MORE EFFECTIVE THE FAT METABOLISM CHANGE

By slowing down enough to be able to break the 45-minute barrier, you show your body that you're serious about endurance. It responds by adapting the former sugar-burning cells into fat-burners. The minimum necessary is one 45+-minute session per week (but the process is put into "fast forward" by going 90 minutes+ every two weeks. As the long run distance increases significantly in a marathon (or half marathon) program, you force more and more cells into the more efficient mode of fat metabolism and keep them there.

REGULARITY IS VERY IMPORTANT

To maintain the capacity of your expanding fat furnace, you'll need at least two other 30-minute sessions a week. If these can be increased to at least 45 minutes, you'll improve the adaptation. It's better to slow down from the beginning of exercise so that you'll feel better, be more motivated to continue, and go further.

RAISING YOUR CORE BODY TEMPERATURE INCREASE TRIGGERS FAT BURN-OFF

Running and walking elevates your core body temperature. Many experts believe that this produces a healthy "fever" which often kills off infections before they cause colds or worse. But the greater your blanket of body fat, the more heat you'll retain, which can lead to excessive fluid loss through sweating. Your body's temperature control mechanism will try to reduce this source of stress if you run regularly. After months of regular long runs, you'll slowly burn off the blanket, reducing your set point and therefore your body fat.

IT'S COUNTER-PRODUCTIVE TO DRAMATICALLY INCREASE YOUR DISTANCE QUICKLY

North Americans often want changes to occur too rapidly. If a little exercise burns x amount of fat, it's tempting to log twice as many miles to double your fat-burning. This doesn't work. By adding too much distance, too soon, you'll get tired or injured, forcing you to stop exercising or cut back dramatically. Even worse is the possibility that you'll get mentally burned out. If you continue to run slowly and increase total weekly mileage by no more than 10 percent, you'll reduce your chance of injury and burn-out to almost nothing.

THE START IS CRUCIAL

The biggest mistake runners make is starting a run too hard, too fast. This is so easy to do because it usually doesn't *feel* too hard, but six to 10 minutes later you're wishing that you were finished. By forcing yourself to start much more slowly than you want, you'll receive a stream of benefits, speeding your entry into the fat zone and setting yourself up for more enjoyment

53

later. The slower you go at the start, the easier it will be at the end to increase distance. Slow starts also speed up your recovery, which will improve your motivation to get out there for the next one.

ESTIMATED EFFECT OF WALK BREAKS ON CALORIE-BURNING

Recreational Walking————————
@ 50 calories per mile

1 min. jog, after 4-5 min. of walking———-
@ 55 calories per mile

1 min. jog, after 3-4 min. of walking———
@ 60 calories per mile

1 min. jog, after 2 min. of walking———
@ 65 calories per mile

1 min. jog, after 1 min. of walking———
@ 70 calories per mile

racewalking————————————
@ 75 calories per mile

2 min jog, 2 min. walk————————
@ 75 calories per mile

2 min. jog, 1 min. walk————————
@ 80 calories per mile

3 min. jog, 1 min. walk————————
@ 85 calories per mile

4-5 min. jog, 1 min. walk——————
@ 90 calories per mile

6-7 min. jog, 1 min. walk——————
@ 95 calories per mile

8-9 min. jog, 1 min. walk——————
@ 98 calories per mile

Running continuously————————
@ 100 calories per mile

HOW TO BURN MORE FAT BY TAKING WALK BREAKS

To show you why it's better to go slowly, let's look at the math in the table above. Continuous running (whether slow or fast) burns about 100 calories per mile. If you're walking normally, you're burning about 50 calories per mile. Even if you're running two minutes and walking one minute, you're closer to the running side of the graph, burning about 80 calories per mile.

So...lets suppose you're running five miles on four days a week. If you slowed down and inserted a one-minute walk break every three minutes of running, you'd feel about the same after covering eight miles—as you would have if you'd run five continuously. Here's the math:

8 miles x 85 calories per mile = 680 calories per run

5 miles x 100 calories per mile = 500 calories per run

_____

that's an increase of   180 calories per run

In one year, this burns off an extra 10 pounds of fat!

WHY DIDN'T I LOSE WEIGHT DURING MY MARATHON PROGRAMS?

Don't use the scales as your gauge of fat loss. You've probably lost fat, even though your weight stays the same. While fat is burned during your runs, there are other physiological changes which will increase your body weight in a healthy way, helping you to improve exercise performance. More water and glycogen is stored in the muscle cells so that you can stay cooler and maintain energy during exercise. Blood volume also increases when you do regular endurance running and walking to more easily supply the exercising muscles with oxygen and nutrients. All three of these changes increase body weight in a good way, preparing you for easier and better running.

IT'S NOT A GOOD IDEA TO TRY TO LOSE A LOT OF WEIGHT WHILE TRAINING FOR A MARATHON

A four to six-month endurance program produces enough lifestyle challenges without adding the stress of a diet change. To accomplish your goal, you need a steady flow of energy. When you're strenuously training while on a diet, the energy supply is often interrupted, resulting in low motivation and negative feelings during and after runs.

When gearing up the body to go 26 miles, I want you to focus on three items:

1. Incorporating regular endurance exercise into your lifestyle,

2. Building the endurance necessary to go the distance, and

3. Learning how to enjoy the process so you'll want to do it again.

If you try to change diet during this mission, you're very likely to suffer from confused priorities. It's so easy to think you're eating healthier foods while you omit certain nutrients needed for performance. Unfortunately, the loss of these nutritional building blocks isn't noticed until weeks or months later when you're dragging around—unmotivated to exercise.

Unless you had nutritional problems before the program started, stick with the diet that you've been using. Certainly it's okay to divide up your food into more small meals a day (see next chapter) and to reduce fat intake a little, but don't make any radical changes. If you feel that you have some nutritional problems at any time, see a sports nutritionist, especially one that has had success in working with long distance runners.

During a marathon program it's okay to say "I'm starting my diet later"...after the marathon.

55

HOW YOU EAT DETERMINES HOW GOOD YOU FEEL... AND HOW MUCH FAT YOU STORE

THE INCOME SIDE OF THE LEDGER

"I love being able to eat all day long, while losing five pounds in four months."

A successful eating plan is one which provides all essential nutrients, allows you to maintain a good energy level for exercise and for daily activities, while maintaining the body fat level with which you feel comfortable. For fat level management, you must stay in touch with the principles of your set point and be honest with yourself. This means balancing what you want to look like with the type of eating plan you're willing to follow, not for a month or so, but as a lifestyle. Most successful dietary changes are small ones, which allow you to feel good all day long so that you can exercise and burn off the pounds of fat you want to lose.

The primary purpose of this chapter is to help you set up an eating plan that will give you sufficient energy for your daily activities as well as marathon training. Fat-burning should be a longer term activity and integrated into lifestyle, taking a back seat to the establishment of exercise as the prime mover in your personal wellness program.

So exercise burns the fat, is the furnace that keeps it off, and gives you the good attitude and the reason to continue working toward your goal. Just knowing that you're burning it off gives purpose to your dietary changes. But it works both ways. Your eating plan can give you the energy you need to be motivated to exercise as it delivers the nutrients for muscle exertion and repair. Most runners find that only a few changes in eating frequency and food choices make the difference in keeping off the baggage that they worked so hard to get rid of.

The primary mission of eating is to give you the essential nutrients with a steady metabolism boost so that you can maintain a motivational level of blood sugar to do all of life's activities. Your energy level is somewhat determined by what you eat and significantly influenced by how much and how often you eat.

56

Lose a little here...a little there

Fat loss in a year	Method
Up to 10 lbs.	Eating the same foods in the same quantity but eating eight to 10 times a day instead of three or less
1-3 lbs.	Getting out of your chair at work or couch at home several times a day (metabolism increase)
1-3 lbs.	Doing more of your runs because of a motivational level of blood sugar
1-3 lbs.	Parking 100 meters further away from each supermarket trip
2-5 lbs.	Going farther on numerous runs because your blood sugar level is at a higher level
2-5 lbs.	Substituting a baked potato for a large fries once a week
2-5 lbs.	Walking around the block (sometimes twice) after supper

EATING ALL DAY LONG!

Yes, it's better for fat control and your energy level if you eat every 90 minutes or so. Our human digestion system was designed for grazing: taking in modest amounts of food all day long. Each time we eat, even small amounts, our digestive system gears up to process the nutrients and dispose of the bulk. This means that you're burning calories for an extended period beyond the eating of the snack—in order to digest the food.

On the other hand, the starvation reflex kicks into fat-depositing when your metabolism slows down. Even if you wait three hours to eat, you'll increase the fat-depositing enzymes so that more of the next meal becomes fat. To prevent starvation, you have an intuitive mechanism that conserves resources and adds fat to the body if you're not grazing regularly.

The longer you go without food, the more your metabolism will shut down into a fasting or low level of energy. If you're not eating enough food, "metabolism control" will cut your flow of energy so that you don't burn up your reserve. The longer you fast, the more likely you will want to be

sedentary and resist moving around. So if you're trying to exercise in the afternoon, five hours after your last meal or snack, your metabolism controller will probably be steering you toward the couch instead of the track or trail.

SMALL MEALS ENERGIZE; BIG MEALS PUT YOU TO SLEEP

Your digestive system gears up whenever there is any food consumed. A small to moderate snack will give you a significant metabolism increase and can be processed efficiently. A big meal will take a while to process. Your metabolism gears up to process it, but so many resources are needed (especially blood supply) that your body organism wants to shut down other activities to process the bulk in your extended gastrointestinal complex. This is why you feel sleepy and unmotivated about half an hour after a big meal.

WHAT YOU EAT MAKES A DIFFERENCE

A good balance of fresh, complex carbohydrates along with some protein and a little fat will leave you satisfied for an extended

57

period after eating. Too much food, too much sugar and starch, and too much fat in a meal will lead to fat accumulation.

Carbohydrates give you the energy you need in a form the body can easily use. Complex carbohydrates (such as vegetables, fruits, whole grain products, legumes, etc.) have fiber and various other nutrients neatly packaged with the energy. The more fiber, the longer you'll feel satisfied afterward because it takes the body a longer time to process the food. Simple carbohydrates (sugar, starch, etc.) are broken down so fast that you can consume a great quantity of calories without feeling satisfied. Excess calories that accumulate during a day are processed into fat when they haven't been needed for energy for several hours.

Fat is directly deposited on your body—you might as well inject it on your stomach or thigh. A little fat in each snack or meal will keep you from being hungry for a longer period. But once the fat content exceeds about 25 percent of the calories, particularly in a meal, you'll be storing significant quantities. Since fat slows down digestion, you'll be more uncomfortable if you want to run too soon after eating. The more fat you eat, the more lethargic you will feel.

Eating fat after exercise also slows down your restocking of glycogen. Studies have shown that a high carbohydrate meal within 30 to 120 minutes after a run will help you re-stock the vital energy supply you need for the first 15 to 30 minutes of exercise. When too much fat is consumed, the glycogen is not replenished and you don't feel very good as you start each successive run.

Sugar and starch are simple carbohydrates which are processed so quickly that you usually get hungry before you've even had a chance to burn them off. Since we tend to

follow our hunger, eating meals with sugar and starch almost always leads to more calories consumed in a 24-hour period than we are burning off. Excess calories are transformed into body fat. A small amount of simple carbohydrates is okay—especially if it's a food that you dearly love. So don't prevent yourself from eating that piece of pizza; just enforce the one-slice rule.

Protein is the building block of our muscles. We need some each day to replace the normal wear and tear of our muscles and other tissue. By eating some protein with each of your snacks, you'll prolong your feeling of satisfaction—extending the time before you feel hungry. You can certainly eat too much protein. If your total consumption of calories during a day is more than you've burned up, the excess will be converted into fat—whether the surplus comes from carbs, protein, fat or all of the above. Too much protein in the diet can cause other health problems. Most nutritionists I've interviewed have told me that even a steady diet of 30 percent or more of protein can lead to kidney damage.

Fiber will also keep you from getting hungry for a while. Many types of soluble fiber, such as oat bran, coat the lining of the stomach, slowing down the release of sugars into the bloodstream. I've found that PowerBar, which has a very effective form of soluble fiber, keeps me from getting hungry for about twice the time as other energy bars with the same number of calories. Practically any fiber that is in a food will increase the feeling of satisfaction. A baked potato, for example, leaves me satisfied about three times as long as an apple, when each has the same number of calories. The baked potato fiber is much more complex than that found in apples, and the latter has much more sugar. When you substitute an apple for a piece of pie or a bowl of ice cream, you reduce calories and fat.

*E*ven a PowerBar, eaten an hour before exercise with a glass of water, will raise my blood sugar level to workout motivation levels. It's still better, however, to eat snacks all day long, instead of waiting until you feel extremely hungry.

Putting it all on the table

Here's an exercise which will help you lose up to 10 pounds a year without cutting any of your food intake or increasing exercise. Now I know that this sounds like one of those TV ads for "thigh cream" or something like that, but trust me and read on.

1. On a piece of paper, write down all the food you eat in a week. You can actually collect this info by taking a journal with you and recording everything you eat, day by day. Write the food and the amount (you may need to bring with you a tiny gram scale). When possible, get the recipe and/or the nutrient breakdown (calories from fat, protein and carbohydrate).

2. Once you have your weekly totals, imagine that you're putting all of this food on a table. It may take a big table. You'll probably be surprised at your findings. Actually, you will be working your mind and your pencil.

3. List each food and total the number of grams or ounces you've consumed of each. There are a number of great resource books in libraries and bookstores which will help you analyze each food.

4. Now for the fun! Arrange the total into about 60 to 70 small meals so that you've used up all of the amounts of each food. Try to combine so that you have some fat (10 to 20 percent of the calories), some protein (10 to 25 percent of the calories), and the rest carbohydrates in every small meal. Also, try to have some fiber in every meal. You'll have some larger meals every day and lots of small ones.

5. Once you get into food-combining, you'll discover the proportions of fat, protein and fiber which keep you satisfied and the amount of carbohydrates which give you energy. Don't use someone else's combinations because each of us responds differently to specific foods.

6. For individual help with your diet, consult a sports nutritionist. A great reference book is <u>Sports</u> <u>Nutrition</u> <u>Handbook</u> by Nancy Clark, MS, RD.

59

BLOOD SUGAR LEVEL (BSL)

Your motivation (to exercise, to work, to play with the kids, etc.) will also vary with the level of sugar in your blood. If you have too little, you'll tend to be lazy and sleepy and will find it difficult to concentrate on anything. But if there's too much sugar in the food you eat, your blood sugar level will rise quickly and make you feel very good for a short while...and then crash. An elevated BSL will trigger a release of insulin, which does two negative things. It sends the BSL lower than it was before you ate your snack or meal. But insulin is also the chemical that promotes fat storage so it starts to process that excess energy into your storage areas. Eating all day long helps to maintain a moderately elevated BSL (but not too high) and maximizes the chance that you'll feel motivated and energized to be more active in everything you do.

COMPLEX CARBOHYDRATES GIVE YOU A DISCOUNT RATE

The more complex the fiber in a food, the more calories are burned in the processing of that food. Take a baked potato, for example. If you eat the skin and all, you'll be burning up to 25 percent of the calories to process it. Contrast this with the fact that virtually 100 percent of the fat calories in french fries, for example, are directly deposited on your body.

A GRACE PERIOD

Even if you eat too many calories in carbohydrates and protein, you can still go out for a walk or jog and burn them off. Here's another way to gain control over your weight and fat level.

SET POINT REGULATES HUNGER

Over a month's time, research has shown that we tend to eat the number of calories that we burn up, controlled by our intuitive "set point mechanism" (SPM). When it (SPM) senses that we're engaging the starvation reflex, it will trigger more hunger and we'll eat more calories than we're burning, producing a weight gain. By eating small meals every few hours,

60

Galloway's picks:

LOWFAT FOODS THAT INCREASE SATISFACTION*

Protein:

Nonfat or lowfat chicken breasts (frozen)

Nonfat or lowfat deli turkey

Egg whites

Soy burgers

Some white fish (many fish have a high fat content)

Vegetables

Most cooked vegetables

Salads

Cole slaw with nonfat mayonnaise

Soup—in cans or dry mix in a cup

Filler foods

Baked potatoes

Brown rice (feel satisfied longer)

White rice

Cereal

Grape Nuts can be added to many snacks to prolong satisfaction

Oatmeal with fruit or in a smoothie

Oat bran can be added to drinks, soup, pancakes, muffins and bread

Fruits

Smoothies with oat bran

Baked goods

Whole grain or crusty and fibrous bread

Small meals

Oat bran pancakes or waffles with smoothie topping (bananas, strawberries and orange juice)

Grape Nuts, banana, grapes or sliced apples

Whole grain or oat bran bagel with lowfat or fatfree cream cheese

Baked potato (skin and all), fatfree cream cheese, low or nonfat cole slaw

Turkey breast or ground turkey burgers with vegetable of choice

Chicken breast with rice, vegetables, whole grain breads

Smoothie: any fruit (1-3 varieties) and fruit juice

Example: banana, frozen strawberries, OJ concentrate, yogurt, oat bran (if desired)

PowerBars

* remember to drink water with every snack

exercising regularly, eating complex carbs, etc., we'll tend to stay the same or burn off more calories than we've consumed. This results in fat reduction. Simple sugars and starches just slide through with no discount, producing surplus calories that are converted into body fat.

THE RELOADING ZONE

The best window for reloading after exercise is within 30 minutes of finishing your run. But you can still get increased reloading benefits for the next two hours. Be sure to drink water or other fluids (except for those with caffeine and alcohol) during the reloading process. By drinking fluid and eating some quality carbohydrate snack (enhanced by adding about 20 percent protein by calorie count), you can maximize glycogen reloading and therefore feel better and stronger during your next run.

VITAMINS AND MINERALS

I'm not a proponent of filling up your shelves with pills. A variety of fresh fruits and vegetables with lean protein will usually give you more of the nutrients than you need. If you suspect that your diet is not delivering, take a "one a day" type vitamin. Some good research points to the possibility of cancer reduction if you take Vitamin C (500mg) and Vitamin E (400iu) every day. Vitamin C definitely speeds up the healing process. Women who exercise regularly tend to be low in iron and sometimes calcium.

ALCOHOL

This central nervous system depressant is almost certain to lower your performance if consumed within about 12 hours of exercise. The more you drink, the longer the depressing effect lasts. Alcohol dehy-drates you also. It's not a good idea to drink the night before a significant run (long, fast, or a race).

CAFFEINE

Caffeine is a central nervous system stimulant that can enhance exercise performance and enjoyment. But there are a few individuals who shouldn't partake. Those who have irregular heartbeat problems, for example, shouldn't be drinking coffee. If you suspect that you are one of these few people, check with your doctor or a sports nutritionist.

You will lose about half the water in a cup of coffee or diet cola. This means that half of the fluid is available for absorption. It is still wise to moderate your use of caffeine products. A cup of coffee before a race is fine if you're accustomed to doing this before running. It's not a great idea, however, to drink three or more cups or diet drinks before going to the starting line.

I dearly enjoy my cup of coffee before my run. It not only raises my awareness, concentration and motivation, but it seems to get the right brain working its intuitive magic and cranking out creative thoughts.

Research shows that caffeine stimulates an early breakdown of your body fat into substances that can be burned as fuel, free fatty acids and triglycerides. There's also good evidence that drinking a cup of coffee about an hour before exercise improves your endurance.

I just feel better on a run after a cup of coffee...or two.

LONG TERM NUTRITIONAL HEALTH

I recommend that you do additional reading in sports nutrition and gradually modify your diet. After reading through five or 10 good resource books on nutrition, you'll see that the principles in agreement are the following:

- It's important to reduce dietary fat over time.

- It's best to get your nutrients mostly in food.

- A variety of foods, including fresh fruit and vegetables, will deliver nutrients well.

- It's better to eat seven to nine meals a day rather than two to three bigger ones.

- In each meal, try to balance mostly complex carbohydrates with some protein and a little fat.

- Most women and some men tend to be low in iron and should supplement.

- Supplementing vitamins E and C can help in preventing certain types of cancer.

- In changing your diet, do it over three to five years, five being better than three.

The percentages vary as do the programs to deliver nutrients. You will find the combinations that work best for you.

BOOSTING BLOOD SUGAR— AND MOTIVATION

"Eating during my marathon allowed me to mentally feel great after the marathon and celebrate with my friends all evening."

*D*uring my first 70 marathons or so, I didn't eat anything. On each of these, my blood sugar level was so low at the end that I hardly enjoyed the exhilaration of even the better ones. I thought that low blood sugar was a given, that it would crash regardless of what I did on all runs beyond 20 miles. Even on my best marathons, I finished feeling exhausted, unmotivated, unable to concentrate very well, and very hungry but often nauseous. A good nap usually turned into a long evening hibernation. Without eating, the vitality wasn't in the legs or spirit the next morning—even after some 12-hour slumbers.

I've now run my last 40+ marathons using PowerBar as my blood sugar booster and have enjoyed the afterglow of each—even the tough ones. By attacking the blood sugar condition before it got too low, I learned that you can not only feel good during the latter stages of a marathon but you can also have a good attitude all evening.

Each runner needs to try out various blood sugar boosters during training runs and then stick with the plan that works best: how much to take and when to eat. Before going into the specifics, let's look at the reasons why we need to eat and some of the problems to avoid.

THE BLOOD SUGAR CHALLENGE

When you run farther than about 12 miles, your blood sugar is going to go downhill. If you do nothing about it, you'll be feeling very low, mentally, at the end of the marathon. It only takes a small amount of carbohydrate, taken regularly, to maintain blood sugar at a stable level. So what is this blood sugar thing anyway?

The level of sugar in your blood will determine your current feeling of well-being. If the blood sugar level (BSL) is in a good, normal range, you will concentrate well, feel more motivated and will reduce the number of negative messages from your left brain. When you let the BSL go too low, you'll get hungry, feel drowsy, lose your focus, and be susceptible to quitting early or reducing a legitimate goal for that day.

Most folks wake up in the morning with a BSL that is stable, while slightly slow. Eating snacks or meals, throughout the day, that include complex carbohydrates, protein, and a little fat will elevate the level slightly and keep it stable. But foods that are too high in sugar (or other simple carbohydrates) will boost the sugar level too high, too quickly.

When the BSL gets too high, your monitoring system automatically secretes insulin

63

which results in a BSL that is lower than it was before you ate the snack. As a further insult, insulin processes the extra sugar into body fat.

Low BSL is a major stress to your system and activates a negative stream of messages from the left side of your brain. Expect to hear a series of logical but motivation-reducing line of thoughts designed to get you to quit or to even stop thinking about exercise: "Why are you doing this?" "Slow down and you'll feel better," "Stop this exercise and you'll feel great." Within half an hour or less, you can often stop these messages completely. Just eat a PowerBar or another energy-boosting snack. Here are some other guidelines which will reduce the rise of the BSL:

64

- Choose complex carbohydrates instead of sugar foods (simple carbs): baked potatoes, rice (especially brown rice), lowfat whole-grain breads, or whole-grain pasta with lowfat sauces.

- Soluble fiber in snacks like PowerBar will coat the lining of the stomach. This can keep the BSL from rising to the level that will trigger an insulin release, and it will slow down the release of sugars in the food over an extended period of time.

- Combine complex carbohydrates with a modest amount of protein to stabilize the BSL.

- Example: Two thick pieces of whole-grain bread or bagel coated with mustard or nonfat cream cheese, with a slice or two of lowfat turkey breast.

MANY OF THE "MIDDLE-AGE CROWD" NOTICE BLOOD SUGAR LETDOWNS

Some look on it as another betrayal of the 35+ body, when they experience hypoglycemia or low blood sugar symptoms for the first time in their lives. Relax, this is a common occurrence. More reassurance is the realization that you can do something about it. Older runners who have this low blood sugar condition will need to ensure that they're eating often enough.

EATING CONSTANTLY, ALL DAY LONG

Your BSL is best maintained by eating a modest breakfast and then a series of small snacks all day long. By eating a small or modest amount, before you get hungry, you'll avoid the "starvation reflex" which leads to overeating.

Breakfast gives you a sustained feeling of well-being throughout the morning and reduces the chance of a significant drop in BSL. By eating lowfat snacks (such as pretzels, bagels, PowerBars) at the first sign of a slight hunger or BSL drop, you'll maintain energy, mental concentration and attitude. Without some breakfast, you'll probably get behind in the blood sugar war, staying hungry all day and overeating at some point.

You don't have to eat a big breakfast. By having a modest amount of fuel in the stomach (healthy snacks throughout the day and night), you've got a better chance to maintain a steady BSL, avoid hunger which leads to overeating, and maintain a good energy level.

Sample Breakfasts:

- 1-2 bagel(s), fatfree cream cheese, fruit

- 1-2 bowl(s) of cereal, skim milk, two pieces of toast with light jam

- 1 bowl of oatmeal or other hot cereal, two pieces of toast, juice

- 2 egg-substitute eggs (or 4 egg whites), toast or bagel, juice

- 4-8 ounces of fatfree yogurt, Grape Nuts, fruit cocktail, juice

THE STARVATION REFLEX

If you want to burn fat and/or maintain a good energy level, it's counterproductive to extend the time between snacks or meals. A blood sugar "debt" is often produced by waiting, causing you to go on an eating frenzy, which further increases fat accumulation:

- The longer you wait, the more you'll stimulate the fat-depositing enzymes

- So...more of your next meal will be deposited as fat on your body.

- The waiting period increases appetite, causing you to overeat later.

WAITING TOO LONG BETWEEN SNACKS WILL LOWER YOUR MOTIVATION

You may not feel like exercising in the afternoon because it's been too long since you've had a snack. As the time increases between significant snacks of food, your BSL drops and so does your motivation, concentration and attitude.

INCREASING THE LONG RUN WILL HELP YOU MANAGE THE BLOOD SUGAR LEVEL (BSL)

By gradually increasing the length of your long run (with walking breaks), you'll push

back the threshold of this blood sugar crash. As the muscles become better fat-burners, they make many adaptations which increase the efficiency of each use of glycogen. This reduces the quantity of glycogen needed for any use: long run, daily activity, etc. This means that there is more glycogen available to you later to maintain BSL at a higher level for a greater time and distance. It is most important that you run the long ones at least two minutes slower than you could run that same distance on that day.

As you extend your endurance barriers, you'll go further before experiencing the discomfort of low blood sugar. Your energy system becomes increasingly "stingy" with the glycogen you have and delivers a better quality of fuel at the same time.

Long runs also stimulate the exercising muscles to store more glycogen. By the time you have increased your long one to 20 miles and more, you not only use less glycogen per mile, you'll have a greater deposit in your bank.

65

The significant improvement in the storage, shifting of supplies, and consumption of glycogen is a prime example of how the human organism is designed to improve when faced with a series of challenges. On each long run as you push further than you've gone before, you stress the limits of glycogen resources. This stimulates the systems to improve in every way to deliver better quality and quantity on your next long one. Further efficiencies in the use of glycogen are realized as you repeat this challenge in a series of long runs.

COUNTERATTACKING LOW BLOOD SUGAR LEVEL ON LONG RUNS

Even if your BSL is ideal at the beginning of a run, it is certain to be dramatically reduced as you push your limits beyond 15 miles (and many runners experience the "crash" before this). Almost everyone will suffer low blood sugar at the end of these runs if he or she does not eat quality carbohydrate snacks before the start and during the second half of the long one.

BLOOD SUGAR BOOSTERS

Even the most conditioned marathoner will suffer a blood sugar crisis when he or she goes more than about 15 miles. The only way to win this battle and boost the BSL is to counterattack. Whether you use PowerBars or other foods, here are the principles which have led to blood sugar success:

1. Choose a food that is low in fat (less than 10 percent of the total calories of the food in fat) but which contains significant soluble fiber.

2. Most runners need 200 to 250 calories about an hour before the long run to keep the blood sugar level sustained until the halfway point (of a run beyond 15 miles).

3. If the food is a solid, like PowerBar, be sure to drink at least four ounces of water for every 100 calories of the food.

4. Cut the solid food up into small pieces for easier consumption during the second half of the long run.

5. Drink water with each piece.

6. Test your eating routine during long runs to find the right time sequence, quantity, etc. for you.

CHOOSING AND TESTING ENERGY FOOD

There are many foods advertised as sports energizers. As is found in all commercial products, some brands make inflated claims. First, determine what you need from the snack. Next, evaluate the possible products, with the help of knowledgeable running friends, sports nutritionists, or trustworthy running store staff.

Next, try several of these in long and short runs and choose one or two to fine-tune for the marathon itself. Use your chosen foods on as many runs as possible before using them in the marathon.

You and your digestive tract can learn to like just about anything. Don't give up on a food because it doesn't taste good at first or doesn't seem to work for you the first time. Take small amounts of the food with water at first. Over time, you can increase the amount of the food as your systems learn to digest and use it.

ENERGY-BOOSTING CHOICES

◆ High carbohydrate foods with soluble fiber (PowerBar and related products)

Supplying a moderate boost of energy, these products usually deliver a good BSL for an extended period. Be sure to check the label of the product you choose to ensure that it is low in fat (fat calories are less than 10 percent total calories). Eat a portion about one hour before the run and pieces of the product throughout the second half of the run— always with water.

◆ High carbohydrate "goos"

These thick-but-sweet products have the consistency of paste. They usually deliver a stronger BSL boost at first, which wears off after several minutes. Read and follow the directions on the package, and try them out in training runs extensively. Because they are somewhat liquid, they get into the blood stream quicker than the "bar" products, but it is still wise to take water with each packet, if available. Once you start taking these, you must continue consuming them until the end of the run to avoid blood sugar letdown.

♦ Fluids with sugar (mostly electrolyte beverages)

While these can be an excellent fluid replacement before and after training runs, the electrolyte beverages tend to send the BSL into a rollercoaster ride when taken in the marathon itself. Without a substance such as soluble fiber to slow down the absorption of the sugar (and maintain the level), you can easily encourage an insulin reaction by drinking them regularly. If you are desperate and feel the need to drink some of these products, dilute them with water.

♦ Concentrated carbohydrate fuels

There are several fluids on the market which offer a great amount of carbohydrate in a small bottle. Similar to syrup, these fluids take a while to digest and require fluid from your body to do so. As they will tend to dehydrate you, they are not recommended for drinking either the day before, the morning before, or during the marathon itself (or during comparable times in training runs). Their concentration will often cause fat accumulation.

The fluid goes so quickly through your digestive system that you're hungry before you've had a chance to burn off the significant number of calories.

♦ Hard candies, etc.

One of the most reliable "boosters" is the inexpensive, little hard candies. Each one of these supplies so few total calories that insulin response is unlikely. If you start eating one about every mile during the second half of the marathon, you will gain some BSL boost.

It's always better to drink water at every stop when taking these candies. In addition, a pre-marathon snack of quality carbohydrate is recommended to maintain BSL until the halfway, hard candy boosters. As they have no soluble fiber, keep taking them. Unlike the "bar" products, sugar candies don't provide a long-lasting boost.

Look at the fat content of any exercise snack—and energy bars specifically. It is recommended that you choose bars in which the fat calories comprise less than 10 percent of the total calories. The more fat, the longer it takes for them to be digested, and the more likely it will be that the food will give you a lethargic reaction instead of an energetic one.

67

THE MARATHON DIET

"At first I had stomach trouble on most of my runs. Then I wrote down what I ate the day before and eliminated the problems. I almost never have stomach problems now."

24 HOURS BEFORE THE MARATHON AND 24 HOURS AFTER

If you want to know which pill or snack you can eat to send you zooming to top performance, then get another book. Over my four decades of running, I've heard just about every claim made by a nutritional product, and almost none of them seem to deliver what they promise. While you'll find below a listing of foods that will give you energy and reduce gastrointestinal problems, I believe that steady training with rest produces successful marathon success. Food will give you energy to train and the raw material to rebuild muscle.

Even though North Americans tend to eat a lot of junk food, they generally get enough nutrients during a six-month period to train for and complete a marathon without incident. But even if you are deficient in some nutritional way as you walk to the starting line, it's too late to do anything about it. Except for the issue of maintaining blood sugar level, noted in this chapter, by that time your nutritional homework has either been done or not.

TRAIN YOUR STOMACH FOR THE MARATHON

Just as you must train your legs to go the distance, your digestive system must be fine-tuned to deliver the nutrients under the stress of long runs. In this process, you'll steadily eliminate (or adjust the intake of) foods that produce negative effects. You want to get into a routine, knowing exactly what to eat, when to eat it, how much to drink with it, etc. If you adjust this during your series of long runs, you'll reduce the chance of problems in the marathon to almost nothing. Your stomach and GI tract can adapt to delivering nutrients with little or no negative reactions throughout a strenuous endurance event.

ELIMINATING PROBLEM FOODS

While a variety of foods is great for overall nutrition, your pre-marathon diet will be more focused. Analyze your eating the day before and the morning of long runs. Over the months, eliminate foods that cause problems. If you had a problem on a run, eliminate the food or foods that could have caused it. Realize that it may have been the quantity of food. It's better to err on the side of eating too little than eating too much. But, please, don't starve yourself. Continue to eat small meals or snacks (which you know will digest quickly) all day long into the evening.

CONTROL YOUR FOOD DESTINY THE DAY BEFORE WITH A SCHEDULE

Start with the foods that have digested quickly for you leading up to long runs and didn't cause stomach or other GI problems. Write down the schedule in a journal or notebook where you can review it before your next long run. After each snack, note the amount, the time, and any fluid you consumed with it. As you work on the right quantity and timetable, you'll gain control over how you feel the day before and the morning of the long run or marathon.

Jeff Galloway's Eating Countdown

The following is the most I would ever eat before a marathon. Usually, I leave out some of the items. This is not meant to be a suggestion for what you should eat—set the schedule which works best for you. When you drink, remember to adhere to the sloshing rule.

The day before the long run or marathon

9:00 a.m.	Cereal or bagel with lowfat cream cheese, coffee (or tea with orange juice)
	Drink 8 ounces OJ or Sports drink
10:30 a.m.	PowerBar or whole-grain bagel or baked potato with nonfat cole slaw
	Drink 8 ounces of water or sports drink
12:00 noon	Grilled chicken sandwich or sliced turkey breast on whole-grain bread, steamed broccoli or spinach salad
	Drink 8 ounces of water or sports drink
1:30-2:00 p.m.	PowerBar or cereal or baked potato with nonfat sour cream
	Drink 8 ounces of water or sports drink
3:30-4:00 p.m.	Grilled chicken sandwich or turkey breast burrito with pinto beans and sliced tomatoes, PowerBar
	Drink 8 ounces of water or sports drink
5:30-6:00 p.m.	Baked potato with nonfat sour cream or brown rice with steamed broccoli, PowerBar, if hungry
	Drink 8 ounces of water
7:00-7:30 p.m.	PowerBar
	Drink 8 ounces of water
9:00 p.m.	PowerBar, if hungry
	8 ounces of water

Marathon morning

5 a.m.	Wake up
	Drink 8 ounces of water
6 a.m.	PowerBar, cup of coffee
	Drink 8 ounces of water
6:30 a.m.	Drink 4-8 ounces of water, if there's no sloshing in the stomach
7:00 a.m.	Start Race

69

DRINK UNTIL YOU HEAR SLOSHING

On the day before and on the morning of the marathon, drink some non-dehydrating fluid regularly. But don't overdo it. When I hear sloshing in my stomach or feel that my stomach is loaded with water, I don't drink for a while. When the sloshing sound goes away, I resume drinking.

There is a potentially serious health problem if your sodium levels are low and you continue to drink beyond the point of being well hydrated. This is called water intoxication, a life-threatening disruption of the necessary flow of fluids during exercise. The chance of this happening is extremely low, but use your common sense about drinking more when you've been drinking all day long. This condition is aggravated by being on restrictive diets, fasting, being sick, and taking medications.

SPORTS DRINKS

The electrolyte beverages will help you top off your fluid levels and, to some extent, your glycogen levels. Again, don't go overboard. A maximum of one quart of your favorite sports drink is my recommendation, consumed over the "awake" hours.

FOLLOW THE DIET THAT GOT YOU HERE

You'll probably be tempted, after walking through a pre-race expo, to try one of the "miracle foods" that you hear about there. Don't do it! Even if a food is the best in its category, if you haven't used it before, you'll probably have some significant negative reactions. To reduce the chance of food and GI problems, use the same eating plan as on your long runs: the same foods, the same amounts, the same timetable. If you had GI problems, reduce quantity and/

or consult a sports nutritionist. Since you're going to have some nervousness and stress, it doesn't take much of a nutritional change to produce intestinal misery.

EATING DURING THE MARATHON FOR BETTER CONCENTRATION AND...CELEBRATION

Your eating plan during the marathon will give you an amazing amount of control over your attitude at the end of the marathon and your ability to enjoy your accomplishment afterward. By eating some blood sugar-boosting snacks during long runs and the marathon, you can stay more focused and motivated. Even when your legs are totally fatigued, your spirit can soar if you manage the blood sugar level.

The long runs again serve as your testing ground for your stomach. I eat a PowerBar (around 230 calories) before long runs and find that my blood sugar remains stable for eight to 10 miles. It doesn't pay to wait until the level goes down to prop it up. About 60 to 90 minutes into a long run or marathon, start reloading with your snack of choice: PowerGel, PowerBar, etc. (always with water). If you didn't eat before the start, your blood sugar-boosters should begin at the 10 to 15-minute mark. The frequency and amount of gel or other snacks should be adjusted on long runs so that you know what to do on marathon day. If you got nauseous at the end of long runs, you probably ate too much at one time, didn't drink enough water, or overloaded the system with a sport drink, etc. Having a blood sugar drop at the end means that you need to increase the amount or frequency of your booster product all the way to the end of the run. It's usually better to take smaller amounts and take them more often.

When the blood sugar stays up, you'll be able to concentrate better, even at the end of the marathon. You'll not only avoid the concentration loss that accompanies a blood sugar crash at the end of your run. Such a crash is a major stress on your system and activates your left brain to release a continuous stream of negative messages. A good, stable BSL leaves you feeling under control at the end of the marathon so you'll want to celebrate afterwards.

If you're one of the few runners who have digestive problems with the smallest amount of gel during a run, try hard candies. Of course, you don't want anything so large that you could choke on it. Sucking on one hard candy per mile (with water) has not caused problems for anyone so far as I know.

WATER VS. SPORTS DRINKS

Electrolyte beverages can cause problems in long runs and marathons. The sugar in the drinks overloads the digestive system, slowing down the absorption of water, which the body needs greatly. Many runners who use sports drinks in marathons suffer from nausea during the second half—due to the residue of sports drink fluid which stays there causing trouble.

This differs greatly from the experience of cyclists. In running, the digestive system slows down dramatically—or shuts down completely. Cycling is not stressful enough to shut down digestion, allowing sports drinks to be absorbed. Much of the research on the sports drinks was done on cyclists and doesn't apply to runners.

71

Avoid the following:

Salt—Salt consumed during the 24 hours before the marathon will produce blood more concentrated in sodium. Fluid is then taken from muscle tissue and other areas, reducing your capacity for performance through dehydration.

Fat—The more fat in your diet the day before a long run (especially after 2 p.m.), the more sluggish your digestive system and the less effective the food will be in delivering nutrients that can be used during the marathon. Because it takes a longer time to process, a fatty meal often causes stomach or bowel problems the next day. Fat is not a good thing…in the long run.

Fiber—Too much loading up on fiber foods the day before the long run (or marathon morning) can lead to unloading during the long one. Not only is this embarrassing, it's dehydrating.

Large meals the night before long runs or marathons—The next morning, much of that food will still be in your intestines, drawing blood away from the exercising muscles.

Alcohol—This central nervous system depressant will leave you with less motivation the next morning. This will interfere with your goal, whether it be for a time or to finish. Alcohol is also a major dehydrating agent.

TIME GOAL RUNNERS NEED TO PRACTICE ON LONG ONES AND MILE REPEAT SESSIONS

Everyone should practice "eating on the run" during long ones. During their mile repeat sessions, time goal runners will also benefit from eating the booster snack they will use in the marathon. This not only prepares the stomach for the marathon, the boost will help you get through the speed session and recover faster.

CAFFEINE

If you are used to drinking a cup of coffee before running, there's no reason why you shouldn't have a cup before a long run or marathon (see the last section of the previous chapter). Only about half of the fluid in the cup of coffee will be available for use by the body so don't account for the whole cup in your hydration computation. Caffeine is a central nervous system stimulant that helps to get your mind and body up to speed from the beginning of a run. It promotes an early breakdown of body fat and has been shown to increase endurance capacity. And, yes, it can get one important personal detail taken care of early so that you don't have to spend time in the portajohn before the race (or wish you could).

INSPIRATION!

WHY DO WE TAKE ON THE CHALLENGE OF THE MARATHON?

COMMENTS THAT I HEAR, EVERY YEAR, FROM HUNDREDS OF SATISFIED MARATHON FINISHERS:

"The marathon date on the calendar made me highlight other activities in my life more than ever."

"I'm a CEO, am financially secure, but nothing in my life has given me the same internal satisfaction as finishing this marathon."

"Before I started training for the marathon, my friends called me 'Whiner.' Now they address me as 'Capt. Confident.' It's true."

"Once I learned how to pace myself, I received a great attitude boost after every run."

"The marathon training gave a purpose to my physical side, which I had neglected. I am hooked for life."

"There is no other activity in life that bestows respect, from inside and from the general population, as training for and finishing a marathon."

"The day I returned from finishing my first marathon, at age 42, my co-workers and friends had a subtle but definite new respect for me. That has continued for 15 years."

"Marathon training made me feel like a whole person—body and mind working together as a team."

THE SOURCE OF MOTIVATION

Just a few minutes each day will keep you motivated and will make you a more positive person.

*T*here are many quick fixes which can get you out the door or a mile down the road. I actually like to have, as a last resort, some of these "dirty tricks" (which will be noted later in the next section in this section) ready when the primary motivation elements are not working. But it's actually quite easy to stay motivated by expressing the positive thoughts, feelings and momentum you receive from your runs. Just a few minutes each day will help you understand the process of staying motivated and will make you a more positive person. In this section you'll find a range of concepts and techniques which have helped thousands of runners to find the spark inside to meet any challenge, starting with rolling out of bed when the alarm goes off.

Getting on the motivational track is as simple as saying out loud to yourself some of the positive things running does for you and others. It may take you a few weeks to set up your motivation routine, but once in place, you can stay motivated with a minimum of regular, fine-tuning exercises. You'll learn about developing a vision and how to transform this into a real and satisfying mission. Some quick and simple belief exercises are included which can help you mobilize your internal enjoyment of running and point you toward your mission.

Following are a series of tips for getting motivated, staying motivated, and breaking through barriers. Throughout, you'll discover successful strategies for maximizing use of the creative and intuitive right side of the brain. Once you realize how to keep the left side under control, you'll be able to do what you're capable of doing. All of us have much more potential than we usually allow ourselves to explore. It is my mission in the following chapters to help you tap into those strength areas inside you so that you can head toward the accomplishment you desire—including getting more enjoyment out of life.

Yes, you can train yourself to be motivated, staying motivated and, then, in the next section, breaking through barriers. The same principle applies: regularity of practice doing exercises which realistically simulate the problems you will face. But before we talk about the exercises, let's look at the bigger picture and, at the same time, find ways to have more fun as we run.

THE LEFT SIDE OF OUR BRAIN TRIES TO HOLD US BACK

Inside the left hemisphere at the top of your head is the center of logic. The left brain solves math problems, organizes and nitpicks, and conducts the structured cognitive activities during your workday. One of the primary missions of the left brain is to steer you in the direction of pleasure and away from discomfort. Any form of stress or perceived stress will stimulate this negative center of logic to produce a stream of messages to "slow down!" or "quit!" or to question your sanity: "Why are you doing this?"

Because we rely upon the left side for logical guidance, we listen to these messages. If we're weak or tired, we're very likely to give in to the messages and compromise our goal. Certainly we must always monitor the real dangers which could produce health problems (heat buildup, traffic, overfatigue) and take action when there is due cause. Most of the time, however, our left brain overreacts in warning us long before we are in real danger. Motivation training desensitizes us to the extraneous negative messages and the left brain's nagging style. You can also set up a positive mental response to the negative left side that will reduce its effect and allow you to head toward your goal at a speed that is within your capabilities.

THE RIGHT BRAIN

Your creative and intuitive center is in the right side of your brain. Running is one of the best ways to tap into your right brain, as long as you're running slowly enough to stay within your capabilities. This right side is a reservoir of creative solutions to just about any problem, challenge or obstacle. Through pacing, walk breaks and blood sugar-boosting, you can cut down dramatically on stress, reducing the negative left brain messages so that you stay on the right (brain) track. Later in this section, I'll go over some proven methods of stimulating right brain activity. To maximize time in the wonderful world of the right brain, become sensitive to the stress buildup of your runs and the marathon itself. Only you have the complete power to reduce the intensity and disconnect the negative speaker of the left brain before it makes your running seem like work.

FUN

Before we go any further we must bring in the magic ingredient which keeps you motivated under just about any situation. When you find ways to have fun during your run, you open the door for the right brain to take over and work its creative magic. You may start it rolling by reading a funny story before your run or visiting a coffee shop with interesting characters. Running with a person or group, going to a favorite trail. . . Don't stop with my suggestions. The best ones are those that allow you to enjoy parts of a run or the whole thing. Anything that makes your run special and interesting to you should be included in your bag of fun tricks.

VISION AND FOCUS

No one stays totally motivated all of the time. Those who are more successful sometimes seem to be always fired up, but they have down times like everyone else. By concentrating on the positive aspects of your run, several times a day, you become focused on something that makes you feel good. It only takes a few seconds every two hours or so and you'll be motivated to get out there and collect your endorphins.

THE VISION EXERCISE

You only need to spend a few relaxed moments each day to collect your positive thoughts about running and what makes you feel confident, looking forward to your next run. Do a quick reality check with your

"I'm looking forward to my run"

- The physical exertion will feel good.

- My legs want to run.

- The increased blood circulation makes me feel more alive.

- I love the way I feel afterward: relaxed and focused, with a great attitude.

- My family appreciates the way I am after a run.

- It's so great to run in the morning to get the mind and spirit mobilized and focused for the day.

- My afternoon run takes away the stress, getting me ready to enjoy my family.

- During the second half of my run and afterward, I'm in another world, swimming in endorphins.

vision to see how your present position relates to the larger vision you have for the next six to 12 months. Those who don't spend these few moments to stay focused often are guided by dreams and illusions which lead in one direction, and then, no direction.

THE DIFFERENCE BETWEEN A DREAM AND A VISION

A dream is not connected to reality. It's easy to dream that you'll run below two hours in the marathon. Yes, you can dream far beyond your capabilities and set yourself up for great disappointment. At the instant of your dream, you may be exhilarated. But without a plan and the reality checks along the way, motivation is lost very quickly. Even when dreams are within your capabilities, without a well-structured training program and regular mental contact with

your vision, dreams are seldom realized.

In contrast, a vision is a series of images that can be molded over several months into a realistic behavioral plan that is put into action every week. In effect, you're a sculptor who molds an elusive image into a series of real experiences that have all of the elements that prepare you for and lead you to a goal that is realistic, fulfilling and engaging.

A vision is a realistic future behavioral experience that you can prepare for by specific physical and mental exercises. To truly fulfill a vision, you must chart out these exercises, constantly adjusting and fine-tuning them to make the vision more complete and meaningful to you. Then, you end up with a final product that is much better than the one you started with. With each adjustment, you get more involved in the process and become more motivated.

77

TRANSFORMING THE VISION INTO A MISSION SUSTAINS MOTIVATION

Adding the behavioral elements to your vision is as simple as writing the date of your specific goal event (marathon, half marathon, etc.) on a calendar. But the process often starts weeks or months before. It may be the snapshot of an overweight friend finishing a marathon. "If Suzi can do it, I can too," you say. You enter a marathon and write the date on your kitchen calendar. The mission begins with your first run-walk, a three-miler. During each long one you will solve new problems, make adjustments and apply the revised vision to the mental rehearsal of the next long one. All the way through the program, you're making your vision more realistic as you keep the mission on track all the way to the finish, wearing a big smile.

The difference between a *Dream*...and a *Vision*

Dream: unconnected with reality

- often of fantasy as the dreams during sleep
- no direct connection to your past experience
- specific items or experiences you'd like to do but unconnected with current behaviors and/or plan of action

Vision: a series of images which...

- give a clear path to the final result including the behaviors
- directly attach to behaviors you want to change
- break down the grander goal into a series of behavioral changes
- give a vision of future behaviors at each step along the way
- start with a behavior that has been recently done
- lead you through a series of improvement experiences to the goal behavior
- fill in the future experience with the eating behaviors, the exercise behaviors, etc. which are necessary to make it happen or support the transformation
- leave you with a reasonably focused and detailed image of the final behavior...physically, mentally and spiritually

IT STARTS WITH A DATE ON THE CALENDAR

A significant mission, such as a marathon, will get your attention and motivate you to do things you haven't done in years. Instead of rolling over, you'll get out of bed an hour early and cover the miles, feeling better for it. After those "bad days" at work, you'll find a way to get on the roads because you have that race scribbled on your kitchen calendar. You're rewarded by an erasure of most of the stress of the day. There's

something powerful about the act of giving yourself a deadline that pushes you down the road on days when you'd just as soon cut the run short.

YOU MUST BELIEVE!

When you truly believe in your vision, you believe in yourself. At the same time, you make the mission easier. Look at the list below and select the ones that support your efforts. Then add items which help you believe in the success of the mission.

· I look forward to the creative challenges.

· I have the creativity to find fun in every run—and this fun will increase as I progress.

· I have the resources to realize my vision.

· I will develop increased resources which will help me complete my mission.

· I will develop the discipline to get in all of the runs that are listed.

· I will find a way to dig deeper, to keep going on those few occasions when I don't feel like it.

· I will do what is reasonable to support the goal (eating, sleeping, scheduling, etc.).

· I will look forward to the positive changes inside me through this mission.

· This mission will give me a more positive vision for my future in almost all areas of life.

REGULARITY IS IMPORTANT

While it is possible to miss several runs and still survive the marathon, most runners who try this drop out of the program. The longer you wait to return to exercise, the more negative messages you receive, which can keep you from getting out there. If this is your problem, put "regularity" at the top of your list of commitments.

AN EXTENDED FOCUS

As you notice changes in yourself, you extend the positive effects into other areas of life. You have a better attitude at home, enjoying the time with your spouse and the kids much more. Stress doesn't bother you as it did before. You can deal with problems more directly, and you maintain focus to the finish of your work projects. Everything in your life can be better when you run regularly.

Your own motivation notebook

Here's a simple tool that will help you mold your vision, revisit positive experiences, bring back the attitudes and behaviors that produced them, and remind you to improve certain things during your next mission. You can use the "Notes" section in Jeff Galloway's <u>Training Journal</u> or any basic school notebook. Tabs help you flip to the appropriate section quickly. Please rearrange the components listed below, and arrange the tabs and sequence in the most efficient pattern for you.

Vision: Here's what I want myself to be doing at the end of my marathon mission:

   Exercise:

   Eating:

   Choice of food:

   Attitude:

   Other:

Mission: Here's how I am putting my vision into action:

   Date:

   Event:

   Problems that worry me:

Mistakes made...and lessons learned

Reserve two blank pages. At the top of each lefthand page write "Mistakes" and on the right, "Lessons Learned."

Progress Report

On the lefthand page, write the following items:

      Overall focus improved

      Concentration improved

Responding to challenges

Am I digging down deep when under stress

Other:

On the righthand page, draw a series of vertical lines and make comments each month during your mission.

Successes

Leave a section of two to four pages to note the times when you overcame problems, went further than you thought you would, or discovered hidden strength that you didn't know was there.

Need Help

Leave a section of two to four pages for items you need to work on or situations in which you need more motivation.

My suggestions for staying motivated during my next mission

Whenever something comes up that you think could help you in the future, write it down!

79

GETTING MOTIVATED:
THE INSPIRATION MUSCLE IS THE
HARDEST TO FLEX

Inside of each of us is all the motivation we need to get going and stay motivated.

After six to 12 months of regular exercise, most runners have made the lifestyle adjustments which make exercise a scheduled and important part of the day. Before we get to that point, it's necessary to make an effort to reinforce the regularity of

exercise and maintain the daily run or walk as a top priority. Sometimes it's as simple as learning to appreciate the rewards, such as relaxing endorphins. You've been receiving them all along, but you didn't take time to enjoy.

But everyone will have to find some extra insertions of fun from time to time. Some runners look for different birds or flowers during a run. Others test the winter ice and look forward to the challenge of layering to meet the colder temperatures. A dip in the pool or a mid-run shower can get you out the door and keep you out there when the thermometer tops the 85° mark. Some of my college track teammates broke roadside bottles for entertainment. So let's talk about getting started, whether you're taking your first steps or trying to get out the door on a low motivation day.

Most of those who say they just need a little motivation to get into shape are only dreaming. Yes, they have a dream of being a stronger, firmer, more active person, but the dream is not attached to the behaviors which bring it into reality. Dreams are the illusive things that go through your head at night. An image without a series of weekly workouts will stay, merely, an image. If you really want to change behaviors, believing that you can is only the first step. It is the

Affirming the benefits of exercise

When you're tentative about your motivation to get out the door for a run, it often helps to read (possibly out loud) the following list of benefits you receive after running:

- Your attitude is better after every run.
- Stress is released, often completely dissolved.
- Natural body chemicals called endorphins relax the body, reducing or eliminating muscle aches and pains.
- Your spirit is engaged, leaving you with feelings of accomplishment, confidence and strength.
- Body and mind are connected, giving you the confidence that comes with being a more "complete" person.
- Your right brain is engaged, energizing your creative and imaginative resources.
- You're learning connections to hidden inner resources which kick in whenever you're under stress.

behavioral vision of moving the legs every other day which can change body shape and improve mental outlook. An idea or image is powerful only if it is practiced, refined and then changed into a vision of permanent lifestyle fun-running.

CONFIDENCE IN THE PROGRAM

To get motivated, runners at all levels need to feel that each day's workout and the program as a whole is doable. When in doubt, it's always better to err on the side of a less demanding program or one that has flexibility. It also helps to study the program before beginning to determine your level of confidence in the schedule and the designer before you get in over your head.

BE PREPARED TO BACK UP

Practically everyone who trains for a marathon has setbacks. You're going to be more motivated to stay on a program if you know that it's possible to add more walk breaks, for example, or reschedule the long runs. Since there's a wide range of abilities and fitness backgrounds, individuals will progress at different rates, and some schedules don't allow for this.

THE RIGHT GROUP WILL MOTIVATE YOU

If you can find a group of runners at your ability level in your area, join it. Because the group is waiting for you, you'll roll out of bed on mornings you wouldn't otherwise. The chemistry, fun and bonding that comes out of a group run will have you looking forward to the next run. You'll get as much out of helping others as being pulled along on your "dog days."

Choose a group that...

Is composed of people at your level—not the level you want to achieve

Takes walk breaks from the beginning of all long runs

Runs at a pace that allows you to finish long ones without breathing so hard that you can't carry on a conversation

Gives you a feeling of comfort and acceptance

Meets at a time and place which would fit into your lifestyle

WHAT IF THERE ARE NO GROUPS IN YOUR AREA

If you're having trouble getting out for a run, put on your running shoes and clothes and call a friend who will talk you out the door. There are a growing number of online running companions for the same reasons. For more info on groups in your area, see the Galloway Training Program page in the back of this book.

81

IT COULD BE LOW BLOOD SUGAR

You may be just half a PowerBar away from motivation. If your exercise time is midday or later and you feel tired and unmotivated, you may suffer from low blood sugar. Waiting for more than two hours to eat a balanced snack or meal (high sugar foods make the situation worse) will lower your concentration and motivation. Low blood sugar is a significant stress on your system, causing the left side of your brain to unleash a stream of messages, such as the following: "You'll feel better tomorrow, take the day off," "You have too much to do," or "You'll feel so much better on the couch." An energy snack, with water, about one

When I have a cup of coffee and a PowerBar, I feel that I can do anything!

hour before exercise, will often turn off the negative and get you off the couch.

REDUCE THE ANTICIPATED DISCOMFORT OF THE RUN

If you're scheduled for a four-mile continuous run and are experiencing left brain stress, tell that negative nagger that you're only going to go one or two miles and will walk most of it. Most runners who do that end up finishing the four-miler feeling great. Even if you don't feel up to doing a race but know that it would be a good conditioner for you, talk yourself down to an easier time goal or to merely running the first half of the race. With the pressure off, most racers run the whole race in a surprisingly good time.

MISSION: GETTING OUT THE DOOR AFTER A HARD DAY AT WORK

Even the most dedicated runner has days when the gravity that pulls one back to the bed or couch is much stronger than usual. Anyone can become successful at starting a walk or run by setting up a process similar to getting a model train moving when it is just short of the top of a hill. A few extra pushes or pulls to get the momentum started and you're moving down the road with that same momentum. Those who are successful in getting regularly out the door spend a little time at the beginning to set up a process with a reward system. After going through the series of steps that gets you going, over and over again, one step will lead automatically to the next one.

Whatever your challenge, the "scripted" approach has three components:

1. Lowering your anticipated discomfort—and telling the left brain to take it easy
2. Setting up a series of small steps, no one of which is difficult enough to produce stress or alert left brain radar
3. Rehearsing through the sequence of small steps so many times that you move from one to the next almost automatically

ONE TINY STEP AFTER ANOTHER...OUT THE DOOR

Let's say that it was a bad day at work and you really don't want to run. Your mission, should you choose to accept it, is to get the body in motion using whatever tricks, rewards, etc. are necessary. Here's a simple "script" that has helped thousands of folks get moving—and stay moving until the endorphins start flowing. You'll need to adapt the following to your situation and rehearse it over and over, especially when you're going home after work each day. The more you rehearse it, even on days when you don't need the motivation, the more likely you will move from one step to the next when you hit a low.

Scene # 1: You're driving home after a terrible work day, hungry, and your left brain has a dozen reasons why you shouldn't run.

The crossing of a street usually breaks the bond of the couch and signals that you're on your way!

Action:

1. Lie to the left brain, saying "I'm not going to run today. I'll take it easy around the house in some comfortable clothes."

2. You arrive home and immediately put on running shoes and clothes telling yourself, "I'm not going to run today, just going to be comfortable around here."

3. Eat a PowerBar or other energy snack and drink your beverage of choice (hint: caffeine helps if you're okay with it).

4. Put on some inspirational music and read some of the affirmations in this chapter and the last one.

5. Stick your head out the door to see what the weather is doing and then just step outside.

6. Walk to the edge of the block to see what the neighbors are doing.

7. Cross the street and you're on your way!

Scene # 2: From the bed to the street

Action:

Here's another challenge for many runners: getting out of bed early enough to do the morning run. Again, you should individualize this to your own needs and situation.

1. Look at your clock the night before. Tell yourself what time you will be getting up. Go through a quick mental rehearsal of yourself hearing the alarm and getting out of bed. Have your clothes laid out so that you can put them on without thinking.

2. The alarm goes off. Without thinking, your feet go on the floor.

3. Without thinking, stand up and head for the kitchen.

4. Prepare your beverage of choice: coffee, tea, juice, smoothie, etc.

5. Sip your beverage and put on clothes— as automatically as possible.

6. Walk out the door, not thinking about running.

7. Walk to the street, not thinking about running.

8. Cross the street and you're on your way!

83

STAYING MOTIVATED

A *body on the couch wants to stay there.*
But once a body is in motion, it wants to
continue in motion.

*J*ust as any motivated runner will have low
motivation to start some days, everyone
reaches plateaus. This chapter is dedicated
to helping you continue individual runs
when you want to stop. Also included are
some of my secrets for staying on a schedule when you hit the natural motivation
lulls.

FORWARD MOTION EXERCISE IS MOTIVATING IN ITSELF

If you start your run slowly enough, it only
takes a minute or two to be rewarded by the
flow of relaxing endorphins and attitude-
enhancing mental hormones. You may
need to walk very often, but moving
forward is naturally pleasurable to the body
and mind when done at an easy pace.

GET A MISSION AND WRITE IT ON THE CALENDAR

When you pick a challenge like a marathon
and write the date on your calendar, you're
more likely to be motivated on those hot,
muggy days or when looking at snowflakes
falling. Everyone knows that an event as
long as, say, 26.2 miles, requires preparation. This pulls you out of bed when the
temperature outside is in the 90s or 10
below, and it keeps you going when you get
the urge to cut the run short.

A MID-RUN MOTIVATION CRISIS IS ALMOST ALWAYS THE RESULT OF GOING TOO FAST, FOR YOU, ON THAT DAY

The more stress you place on yourself, the
more negative messages you'll receive from
the left brain, which will lead to a desire to
quit. Ease up, take more walk breaks, and
you'll get through most of these "walls." If
the weather presents you with too much
heat/humidity and/or you went too fast in
the beginning or the middle of the run, it
may be too late to do anything but walk.
Learn from this, and back off early the next
time.

BRING A POWERGEL WITH YOU

Your preferred blood sugar foods can pull
you out of motivational lulls. Everyone will
experience a blood sugar crash after about
12 to 15 miles. By consuming products like
PowerGel or PowerBar (with water), almost
all runners will be able to keep blood sugar
(and motivation) at a high level. These
products also help on short runs if you
haven't eaten enough prior to the run.

BE SURE THAT YOU'RE NOT HAVING A MEDICAL PROBLEM

It's extremely rare, but there are a few times when you should not push through barriers. If you have or suspect a medical emergency—stress fracture, cardiovascular problem, heat disease, etc., stop immediately and get help. In fact, this is approximately a million-to-one occurrence. Even though this is a very unlikely event, it's always better to be safe than sorry. If there are good reasons why your ache or pain can lead to significant health risks, it's always better to quit early and talk to a doctor.

A second level of medical alert relates to overtraining and injury. Some aches and pains are early warning signs of injuries or excessive fatigue. Experienced runners become very sensitive to the weak links, those knees, tendons, muscles that become injured most often. By backing off early or taking an extra day off, you may avoid weeks or months of layoff later—because you tried to push through an early-stage injury.

ON THE VERY TOUGH OR FAST RUNS

Almost every runner has at least one tough run every month. Whether it occurs during a tour around the block or during a 23-miler or speed session, here are my tricks for continuing:

1. Slow down and allow the body and mind to get a break. Take more walk breaks as needed, take more rest between intervals in a speed session, and start back into the run slower than before. The earlier you make an adjustment, the better quality you'll be able to salvage from that workout or run.

2. Break up the remaining distance into segments that you know you can do. Take a walk break (or a shuffle break) every three to five minutes. You know that you can go another three minutes, right? If three minutes is too long, try one minute. Your run or race is a series of these segments to the finish line.

3. Use distractions. Look ahead to the next mailbox, stop sign, fast food restaurant, water stop, etc., and tell yourself that you can take a break there. Make sure the segment is short enough so that you feel confident in getting there.

4. Focus on the person ahead of the person in front of you. By looking ahead, you can be pulled past the person in front of you if you're running in a group or a race. Stay mentally attached to that person, noting the outfit, the printing, the hat, etc. If you're only looking at details, you'll at least be preoccupying the left brain so that it won't zing you as badly or as often. See the following section on "dirty tricks" you can play on the left brain.

85

5. Use a mantra. There are various types of words and phrases which will do more than distract you. Practice these and develop your own to put yourself into a positive trance. See the sidebar below for more suggestions.

6. Don't give up. If you respond to each thought of quitting with the internal resolve that you are going to finish, you will! Positive mental attitude alone can pull you through many difficult situations.

Mantras for Staying Motivated (to be said over and over)

Strength mantras will connect into your hidden resources that keep you going when tired. The specific words you choose will help to make subconscious and intuitive connections with muscles and your inner resolve. As you learn to tap into the right brain, you'll coin phrases that continue drawing on mental or spiritual resources. The following have been used when under physical and mental stress, but use these only as a primer. The best ones will be your own mantras that relate to your experiences with words that work. Action phrases not only keep you going but also help you perform as you find ways to dig deeper into your resources.

Feet—stay light and quick, keep moving

My legs are strong

My heart is pumping better

More blood in the muscles

Lactic acid, go away

More oxygen, lungs

The strength is in there, I'm feeling it

Talk crazy to me, right brain

I'm feeling creative—I'm making adjustments

I feel comfortable—I'm in control

I feel good—I feel strong

I'm floating

Come to me—endorphins

I'm having fun

Distraction Mantras start by preoccupying your left brain so that it won't send you so many negative messages. After saying these over many times, you may be able to shift into the right brain.

Look at that store, car, building, sign, etc.

Look at that person, hair, outfit, hat, T-shirt design, etc.

One more step, one more step

One more block, telephone pole, stop light, etc.

Baby steps, baby steps, baby steps

Vision Mantras help you feel that you're getting where you want to be.

I can see the next mile marker

I can feel the pull of the finish line

I can feel being pulled along by the runners ahead

I can feel myself getting stronger

I'm pushing through the wall

I'm moving at the right pace to finish with strength

Funny Mantras get you to laugh, which is a right brain activity.

I'm running like a clown, ballerina, football player, stooge

Float like an anchor, sting like a sponge

Where's the bounce, glide

Creative Mantras

I'm building a house, railroad, community, bookcase, etc.

What type of novel could that person ahead of me have written?

What type of crime could that person on the sidewalk be plotting?

What type of movie could be staged here?

86

IF YOUR GOAL ISN'T MOTIVATING ANY MORE

Having gone through more than 120 marathon training programs, I've experienced many motivation letdowns. On most of these, I've rebounded, but on a few, I didn't. Burnout and dropout are mental injuries. If you back off and adjust early, you can avoid major burnout later.

Getting Beyond the Mid-Goal Wall

1. Reduce mileage and cut your running days to three. Put a lot of walking into those.
2. Run and walk in scenic areas, places that really motivate you to run—to even schedule a run.
3. Schedule a social run with a friend or a group of friends. Tell him, her or them that you need help. Have a good time and meet afterward for a snack or meal.
4. Do anything necessary to add more fun to your program: after-run rewards, special outfits or shoes after specific long runs, etc.
5. Adjust your goal event so that it is more motivating. Stay at a special hotel, get some friends to meet you there, or schedule weekend activities with your family (at events such as the Big Sur Marathon or the Walt Disney World Marathon).
6. Sometimes it helps to choose another goal event and adjust your training accordingly.

87

BREAKING THROUGH BARRIERS

STAYING FOCUSED ON THE BIG DAY

A Mental Tour Of The Marathon

A thorough mental rehearsal of one of life's challenges will mobilize all of your resources and bring mind and body together.

*B*efore attempting something challenging like a marathon, wouldn't you love to have the confidence of having done it—without the fatigue, sweat, aches and pains? Thanks to the wonderful world of visualization, this is now possible. So lace up your mental shoes, and let's start reducing the effect of the negative left brain messages.

In this chapter, we're going to rehearse the marathon so that you can totally immerse yourself in the experience. The better your rehearsal, the more prepared you'll be for the marathon itself. Draw upon your experience from the long runs to construct your mental marathon. The more challenges you rehearse, the less effect they will have should you encounter them in the marathon itself.

REHEARSE!

We're going to take a mental tour of the marathon. By doing this over and over again, you'll develop a confidence in finishing which is similar to that of veteran marathoners. Even more significant, you'll be gradually adding realistic details and situations to positively overcome the physical and mental challenge experiences of the marathon. This mental *conditioning* will make you tougher and will build the

specific confidence needed to confront the same problems in the 26-miler itself. Your long runs help you to 'desensitize' to most or all of the possible items which *could* go wrong. You can then anticipate and find solutions or inner strength to get the job done.

89

Rehearsal Benefits

Fast forward Mentally rehearsing the marathon gears up mind and body for the sequence of events. The more times you're able to rehearse, the more smoothly you'll mentally prepare for each segment of the marathon and the better you'll anticipate your need for resources and adjusting for success.

Left brain garbage The negative messages released under stress are reduced because you've desensitized yourself to them. In other words, there's less stress, therefore less garbage.

Mind-body teamwork develops better in mental rehearsals because you can edit and improve responses in a short period of mental rehearsal time. This doesn't get you out of doing your long runs, of course. Once you've had two to three runs over 15 miles, you have an experience base that will allow you to convert

Continued on pg. 90

> **Rehearsal Benefits (cont.)**
>
> 15 minutes of mental rehearsal time into months of training experience.
>
> **You gain** control! Instead of waiting for things to happen or taking what comes your way, rehearsal allows you to set up the steps you'll take to get through each stage and challenge of the marathon.

Probably the greatest benefit you'll receive from rehearsal is the opportunity to mold your experience in advance, setting up a blueprint for the challenge of the marathon. At the same time, you gain insight into the series of possible challenges facing you. Each long run will teach you a few more lessons as it tosses up problems to solve. By the time you've done your 26-mile run, all of the major challenges will have been encountered (except for changes in weather). As you rehearse yourself through the next long run and the marathon, make the adjustments which you didn't make the last time. The process gets easier and easier even though you're dealing with a greater number of rough edges, components and anxieties.

The object is not to solve every problem. Many of the doubts, anxieties, aches and pains just go away as you make a few minor adjustments, dig down a little deeper and keep going. By setting up every possible problem you could have in your rehearsal, you'll start the right brain looking for solutions.

As you're being realistic, unleash your creativity. Include in your rehearsal a few unexpected situations that you haven't faced yet. This will reduce your shock and stress if and when these occur in the marathon itself. Be sure to insert some fun rehearsal elements, such as strange people along the way, interesting conversations

with your fellow travelers, and landmarks. I want you to enjoy your marathon, and mental rehearsal will increase the likelihood of this.

PRINCIPLES OF MENTAL REHEARSAL

- Break down the experience into a series of small events:

1. None of which is challenging in itself

2. Each of which leads directly and automatically to the next

- Desensitize yourself to the uncomfortable parts:

1. By mentally experiencing them, they aren't as bad when you *run* into them.

2. The more you rehearse problems, the more solutions you may find for them.

3. When you mentally "tough it out" in rehearsal, over and over, it's easier to "gut it out" in the marathon itself.

- Rehearse every possible "problem" you could have in the marathon itself:

1. When in doubt, rehearse it—it's better to be prepared for anything.

2. Rehearse each to be worse than you expect it to be in the marathon.

   - Problems which are less intense than rehearsed are less likely to engage the negative left side of the brain.

- Rehearse often!

1. Rehearse parts of the marathon every day.

2. Concentrate on those aspects which make you the most apprehensive.

90

3. Go through each segment, dealing with each problem and getting through it.

4. Mentally, you can find several solutions to the same problem.

5. At least once a week, do at least a quick mental rehearsal of the marathon, as we are doing now.

THE MENTAL MARATHON... STEP BY STEP

First, let's talk through the night before. You've had a full day of walking around the expo,

♦ drinking four to six ounces of water each hour,

♦ snacking on PowerBars and other low-fat (low-salt) snacks all day and all evening, and

♦ sharing good experiences with friends and with other marathoners from around the country.

Now that it's bedtime...what's going through your mind?

"I'm not going to sleep a wink."

"It's going to be rough tomorrow."

"What have I gotten myself into?"

Yes, all of these are legitimate questions which will come....and pass through. These negative thoughts will come from your left brain, which is programmed to respond to stress. The more you frame the marathon as a stressful experience, the more negative messages you'll receive. But it's just as easy to frame it as a positively challenging journey.

THE BATTLE: LEFT BRAIN VS RIGHT BRAIN

♦ An inner-brain conflict will occur every time you put yourself to the challenge.

♦ The left side has a million logical reasons why you can't do something.

♦ The right side won't try to argue; it will just try to get the job done using its unlimited supply of creative, spontaneous and imaginative ways of steering you in the direction of that which you are capable.

♦ In most cases, it's easy to get out of left brain control by relaxing, taking the pressure off yourself, and engaging in a right brain activity, such as laughing, story-telling, or low-level physical activity (walking, for example).

Okay, now, how about some positive thoughts about the marathon?

"Knowing it's over"

"Having my psychiatrist tell me that I'm okay—even if I want to do a marathon"

"The satisfaction of finishing with the medal around my neck"

On the first two, your left brain is still in control. Now the medal...the medal around the neck...That's the bottom line! Let's start there—you're wearing *your* medal! Sure, there are aches and pains, but overpowering it all is the feeling of accomplishment and personal satisfaction. This is a significant achievement which you did with your own resources. You had to pull from the various sources of your inner strengths and you did. No one can ever take this achievement away.

When the Left Brain Bothers You.....

*Diffuse the stress by saying that you're **not** going to push yourself:*

- It's going to be a walk.
- You have all the time in the world to finish.
- This is your day to smell the roses.

Focus on the positive effect of your marathon experience:

- You feel more invigorated.
- The training has improved your attitude.
- Your focus is better.
- You're positive because you're doing something very positive for yourself.

Gain a vision of yourself crossing the finish line:

- Sure you're tired but you're satisfied.
- The sense of accomplishment is unlike anything you've ever experienced.
- You've found new sources of strength inside.
- The medal around your neck symbolizes all of this—bestows a wonderful glow.

Walk around or jog around:

- The forward motion creates positive momentum.

- Your body is designed for forward motion and responds positively when you move.
- Natural endorphins relax you and settle you down.
- This gets the right brain connected to the body, allowing you to bypass the left brain.

Tell a joke:

- Laughing helps to engage the right brain.
- It bestows a gutteral confidence.
- Collect a few funny thoughts and jokes which you can call up with a key word.
- Even if you tell it to yourself, learn how to laugh with yourself.

Have a number of positive success stories:

- The best ones are the many little successes you've had in marathon training.
- You can also draw from the success stories of others.
- Trade stories with the runners around you.
- Positive behavioral experiences build a positive attitude and inspire positive behavior.

This glow will color every other part of the experience. When you start to feel unequal to the task, you'll come back to this very powerful inner feeling which you receive from finishing.

THE NIGHT BEFORE

Yes, you're nervous, but it's normal to feel this way. You've got everything laid out for the morning according to your checklist [see the Practical Advice section]. You may be so nervous that you won't sleep at all. That's also okay because you don't need to sleep the night before a marathon. The crucial nights are the two before the last one. Sleep deprivation may be a good thing when it's limited to the night before the marathon. Many marathoners, including some world-class performers, have run their best times after a sleepless night. The important concept is that lack of sleep is not going to bother you. In other words, it's not the lack of sleep, it's the worrying about not sleeping the night before which will engage the left brain and produce negative messages.

So you're resting, thinking about all of the things that are about to happen to you. You may decide to read or you may just lie there resting. If it's an out of town marathon, be sure to bring a magazine, book or something which can keep your interest in those hours of darkness. Positive, interesting concepts or stories are best, but anything that has worked in the past is fine. I bring along the newspapers which pile up on my doorstep between trips.

WAKE-UP CALL

You're motivated to get going and begin a water-drinking routine: four to six ounces every half hour. As you collect the items on your checklist (see Practical Advice), you develop a vision of the positive, successful feeling you're going to have with the medal around your neck. When the negative side of your brain, the left side, starts to send negative messages, think of the medal around your neck and move into some productive activity.

THE LINE UP

Hopefully, you'll be connecting with friends as you go to the start. It helps to know, in advance, about the area of the start, how you'll get there, the problems, etc. In New York City, for example, you must board a bus quite early and sit under a tent for several hours. At the Marine Corps Marathon, you will be walking or taking the Metro to the start, in all probability, and it's a fairly long walk.

You're joking with friends or folks as you walk to your starting position and wait for the gun. You've spent a little time preparing for this with some interesting stories and jokes, which you will be sharing. As you're laughing, you realize that the left brain is kept under control and can't unload many negative thoughts.

Trying to overwhelm the left brain with distracting left-brain activity: *it doesn't work*

Some folks try to counter the negative left brain activity with logical challenges. For example, to counter the message "This marathon is going to hurt," some will mentally work on a math problem or construct some business situation or analytical exercise.

While this may distract your left brain for a while, it keeps you under its control. It is only a matter of time until a major or continuous stress wave will overwhelm this temporary distraction. When your stream of mental messages is hooked to the left hemisphere, you'll tend to get increasingly more persistent messages of a negative nature.

The greatest drawback of this approach is that you lose the intuitive capacity to reach toward that which you are capable. By shifting into the right side, you have the opportunity to search for hidden strengths and find spontaneous motivation, inspiration and even entertainment which you didn't know were there.

93

It's natural to feel nervous and to be excited. Settle yourself down by saying things such as "I feel relaxed and ready to glide" and "I've prepared and have plenty of power." When you receive even the hint of a left brain message (and you will), squelch it with a positive behavioral thought, such as the vision of yourself going across the finish line. Take a few jogging steps as you mentally rehearse those good thoughts.

THE START

You begin to get uneasy when the announcer calls everyone to the start. But as you share energy with the people around you, tell jokes, or mentally revisit some very successful experiences, you're feeling comfortable and secure. The gun fires and you gently move with the people around you. You're all in this together, moving forward towards a positive goal. It's a mass migration in which you're destined to triumph!

At times, you'll be tempted to go faster to express a few hidden, competitive urges (which you may not know you have). But you hold back. Realizing that there is plenty of time and distance to run the pace you wish, the first few congested miles don't bother you as you continue to go with the flow. Several times you find yourself feeling good and starting to run faster than you know you're ready to run so you return to a realistic pace (or better, a conservative one).

You're tempted to not take the first few walking breaks, pushed forward by your left brain ego. But at each place for a walk break, you walk. As people go by, and you're tempted to cut the break short, you resist the temptation. Soon you're into the flow of the breaks—mentally segmenting the distance.

If the left brain tries to insert a stress message about how far you have left to the finish, you immediately focus on your next walk break, saying out loud 'just ____ more minutes' (fill in the number of minutes you'll run before walking).

Many of you will be walking a minute every mile. After a few miles you'll make it a game to focus on a few individuals who are running at your desired pace. You follow them with your eyes as they get ahead on walk breaks, and you playfully catch up with them by the end of each running segment. By the 15-mile point, you'll have to choose another set of people because your original group has dropped off the pace by running continuously.

CHALLENGES

It is better to know the course you will be running (see the specific course descriptions in the race flyers). But if you're unsure of exactly which course you'll be running, you can rehearse a generic marathon. It's even better to over-rehearse the challenges; if you're prepared for a more difficult experience, then a less demanding one won't engage the left brain as much.

Hills present a variety of challenges. In the early stages, you may have a tendency to run a bit too hard going up so you hold yourself back. When you reach a difficult uphill, a slight shortening of the stride will relax the legs again and keep you moving with strength. When hills get difficult later on, you continue to shorten the stride, even as short as tiny 'baby steps,' if needed. This allows you to keep moving and get the job done. It's always better to rehearse hills that are longer, steeper and more frequent than those actually on the course. If you over-rehearse the difficulty of the last six miles of the marathon, you'll be in a better position to enjoy the end of the marathon itself.

The most significant challenges will come during the last six miles when the left brain is going to be activitated by a variety of stresses: fatigue, blisters, aches, fatigue, low blood sugar, dehydration, *fatigue*. Your greatest enemy at any point in the marathon is not the stresses or even the negative left brain messages which are generated by them: it's the internal doubt which your left brain promotes and upon which it feeds. By focusing on magic words and phrases which feature your past successes, you'll have a great tendency to ignore the alarmist negativism and earn your success.

GUTTING IT OUT

Most of the problems, insecurities, and resulting negative messages can be managed and overcome by digging down a little deeper into your reservoir of intestinal fortitude. This source of strength comes directly from your spirit, which has the capacity to continuously generate positive momentum. By rehearsing yourself through these low points, you not only become stronger but also you develop the intuitive paths which can connect you to these resources in the future: for fitness, work, personal challenges, and other areas of life.

ON TO THE FINISH

And so we end where we began. The positive flow of energy toward the finish line is your destiny, pulling you past the challenges, through the doubts, and out of the depths of uncertainty itself. You've done this yourself, and you've developed a lot more than physical capabilities along the way. That medal symbolizes a significant internal journey which has unlocked treasures that will continue to enrich you.

95

MAGIC MARATHON WORDS

Magic words distract you from the discomfort, while they connect directly to the extra horsepower that all of us have hidden inside.

*B*y using a few special words, you can pull yourself out of the downturn of motivation and physical energy that usually happens at some point during long runs. I've heard from several runners who, when the fatigue settled in, started to feel sorry for themselves and slow down but, through liberal magic word use, ran a personal record or close to it. Even when your conditioning and weather conditions stop you from a fast performance, the use of these words can mentally reframe any experience into a positive one.

POSITIVE BRAINWASHING

Magic words give you another means of taking control of your performance. They allow access to the internal patterns of dealing with stress and pulling up strength which you or others have used in the past. I like to compare the network of inner connections to a mass of tangled wires, some making strength connections, some going to insecurity and negativity, and a lot of loose ends. The association of experience with words trains you to make the right connections to stay positive, deal with real problems, and pull the strength available when needed. But when used in a negative way, this ancient process is called "brain-washing."

YOU CAN USE MY WORDS, IF YOU WANT

My three magic words are *relax, power* and *glide*. I started using them during my competitive career to deal with three problems I encountered during difficult runs and races.

Relax: Usually at the end of a hard run, when I feel my resources slipping away, I have a tendency to tense up under the misunderstood anxiety that things are going to get worse. With the increase in negative left brain messages due to the stress, I used to slow down and obey these messages. Now, I know that the left brain is really bluffing, making the conditions seem much worse than they really are. When I feel the first sensation of tightening, I focus on pushing beyond the stress, by saying the word "relax" to myself. After two decades of use, I now receive an instant while subtle relaxation.

Power: When I start to slow down, the left brain tells me that my strength is almost gone, bringing on a new set of brain messages from the left side, such as "You may not finish," or "Stop now before it gets worse." By merely saying the word "power," I feel a rebuilding of my strength, with the sensation that everything is going to be all right.

You don't have to give in to any negative message that hits you when you're under stress. By focusing on the positive, you maintain control. It's what you put in the forefront of your thoughts that counts.

Glide: During the latter stages of any long or hard run, my form gets shaky. To counter this trend, I say the word "glide" and instantly I feel smoother (even when I don't look any smoother). I've now associated this magic word with hundreds of runs when I started to get the "wobbles" but finished with a feeling of good form and efficiency. Now, when I say "glide," I'll receive a bit of the same sensation I felt at the end of some of my best lifetime efforts, while my pace is sometimes twice as slow.

When you say the magic words

· You instantly feel a sense of control.

· The words first confuse and distract the left brain, cutting off the negative messages for a while.

· A surge of confidence eases in as you apply the words.

· A series of positive memories flood the subconscious and sometimes the conscious, further cutting off the left brain.

· Sometimes this series of events will jump-start the right brain, helping you find intuitive solutions to current problems.

· You relive (and are energized by) the past experiences during which you started to "lose it" but were able to focus on the positive, collecting all available resources.

· On a few occasions, you may set a personal record, finish an impossible run, or pass a competitor you haven't beaten before.

· More likely, you'll be able to do what you were capable of running on that day.

· With each use, you become more confident and effective in using your own magic.

HERE'S HOW TO MAKE YOUR WORDS MAGIC

As in any program, you must have a continual training program to develop and fine-tune these responses.

♦ Start by listing the problem areas where you could use some inner strength: relaxation, motivation, continuing under adversity, digging deeper.

♦ Go back in your memory bank and list beside each problem area, as many specific experiences as possible in which you overcame the problem.

♦ Attach a key word or phrase to each experience. The more experiences you have "cataloged" under one of these keys, the more powerful their effect.

♦ Each time you overcome one of these problems again, add a new experience to the category and attach the key word to it.

As you add more experiences, the magic of the words becomes more powerful. You're training your organism to set in motion the same complex set of reactions which produced the success in the past. Not only does this help to mobilize the elements which can get the job done. Intuitively, you set in motion a search for the many little connections inside which give you a realistic feeling of control and power.

Use these as needed to take off the pressure and bring back the confidence. Add more key words and the accompanying thoughts which make sense to you. Subtract items which don't engage you. You are molding this to fit your needs like a glove.

97

> **"*I know I would have run 15 minutes slower, at least, if I hadn't used the magic words you told me about.*"**

RELAX

- There's no pressure on me; I'm here to have fun.

- I'm going slow. If it gets tough, I'll just slow down more.

- From the first step, I'm going to relax and enjoy the endorphins.

- I feel comfortable, supported by all of the energy.

- I'm part of a very positive movement.

POWER

- I feel good about myself and what I'm doing.

- This experience gives me control over myself.

- I know what I'm doing when I'm out here.

- This is my heritage; the power of the human migration spirit is with me.

ACHIEVEMENT

- I've developed great self respect through this marathon and the training.

- I created this level of fitness, and I'm very proud of it.

- Each step is giving me benefits.

- This achievement builds upon a long series of successes.

I'M STORING ENERGY

- I've got all day—enjoy!

- Slow down and savor this moment.

- Store this energy away.

WALKING EXTENDS RESOURCES

- The walk breaks push back my wall.

- Every person who passes me is pulling me along.

- This side of the road is my walk break lane; I own it.

- Walk breaks give power.

- Walk breaks are my heritage.

- I only have _____ more minutes (until the next walk break).

- Walk breaks hold back the energy tide so it will surge at the end.

NO PROBLEMS WILL GET TO ME

- I've got all the resources I need.

- Everyone feels discomfort.

- I'm hanging in there.

- I'm working through this.

- The problem is easing; it's going away.

- I can slow down and feel better.

- I can shorten my stride and relax the muscles.

> *The words aren't magic in themselves. They come alive and make better connections as you associate each with experiences in which you overcame specific problems. The more experiences, the more magic.*

MUSCLES—LISTEN TO ME!

- I'm shortening stride and shuffling.
- Movement pulls out the cramp.
- The muscle is loosening up.

I LOVE HILLS!

- All the power is there to zoom up this hill, but I'm going to save it.
- I'll shorten stride down to "baby steps," if needed.
- I'm low to the ground and feeling light on my feet.
- My muscles are relaxing; I've got the strength.
- The hill is working with me to pull me up.

SHORT (STRIDE) IS BETTER

- I'm shortening stride and feeling more power.
- Just a little stride-shortening makes the muscles relax.
- This shorter stride gives me more control.
- Every time I shorten stride, I decrease my chance of injury.
- With a shorter stride, I can turn over my legs better.

I'M GETTING THERE!

- I'm tired but strong.
- I'm feeling better.

- I'm tired but proud.
- There's plenty of strength left.
- The reward is coming.
- What wonderful accomplishment!
- Less than one tenth of one per cent of the population can do this—I'm doing it!
- Tight legs are a sign of accomplishment; I'll shorten my stride and run smooth.

WARNING: YOUR WORDS WILL LOSE THEIR MAGIC, IF YOU USE THEM IN A LEFT BRAIN WAY.

Some runners can get a quick fix by using the word "power," for example, to pick up the pace for a hundred meters or so in the middle of a race. This will almost always lead to a significant slowdown at the end of the run.

Magic words gradually program your internal systems to pull together in an instant the complex series of internal connections which produced success in past experiences. The invoking of an isolated word to dramatically turn around the natural effects of fatigue can increase speed for a short distance, while using up valuable resources that you need...in the long run.

DIRTY MARATHON TRICKS

"When I was feeling at the end of my re-sources, at mile 24, I tried one of your dirty mental tricks. It gave me a sense of... control, and I ran the last mile with a smile on my face".

A really good rehearsal (with good pace judgment) will pull you most of the way through the marathon. By adding your magic words, you'll push two to five miles further, sometimes all the way to the finish line. But there are moments in every marathon, usually near the end, when the magic seems to have gone out of your words, and worse, your legs. This opens up a big microphone into which the left brain shouts its messages. You've probably heard most of them:

"It's over. Just walk to the finish."

"Slow down; it'll feel much better."

"Stop now and feel great."

"Oh, do I feel bad."

"I can't do it today."

(And the worst one of all) "Why am I doing this?"

It's time to play some dirty tricks on your left brain, After all, it does the same to you all the time. Almost anyone gets these messages. You're only in trouble if you listen to them. Dirty tricks distract the left brain so that you can get further down the road. But they can do so much more.

As you find a series of creative images which get you into your right brain, you'll trigger other imaginative thoughts. These may entertain you, but they are most effective when they jump-start right brain activity, which produces intuitive solutions to problems. When you get it working, the right brain acts like a hacker trying to break through Pentagon security codes. It keeps probing, hitting dead ends and trying again until it finds the direct connections to the centers that get the job done. In addition, right brain activity improves motivation and keeps your organism working all the way to the finish.

If you've trained according to the schedules in this book and pace yourself realistically in the marathon itself, you will be physi-cally on the express train to the finish. There is, however, a very real mental wall which most marathoners must push through to get within sight of the finish line. By doing your mental training home-work, you'll push the wall back closer and closer to the finish.

♦ Mental Rehearsal:

If you've really immersed yourself in regular and effective mental marathon rehearsals for at least 12 weeks leading up to the marathon, you'll cruise through most of the problem areas during the first 18 to 20 miles. An increasingly effective mental rehearsal will keep you on track and off the beam of the negative left brain for most of the marathon. [See the marathon rehearsal section of this book.]

♦ Magic Marathon Words

After the mental rehearsal loses its effectiveness and stress causes the negative messages to increase, it's time for some magic words. By attaching an increasing number of successful experiences to your "magic marathon words," you can flood the brain with positive memories and renew subconscious performance connections which got the job done before. This positive brainwashing will push back the mental wall, usually, to the 23 to 25-mile mark. [See the "Magic Marathon Words" section in this book.]

Just as leg and overall physical fatigue is delayed by regular shifts in running form, mental freshness is maintained by shifts back and forth between the left and right brain. Mental strength is developed through rehearsal and use of your magic words. As you increase the ease of shifting into the right brain, you'll delay even further the point in the marathon where your attitude won't respond.

Dirty tricks are reserved for that aggravating place, late in the marathon, when a growing stream of mental E-Mail bombs from the left brain are invading and attacking your will to go on.

Almost everybody gets these messages or worse. You're only in trouble if you listen to them and believe them. Dirty tricks help by distracting the left brain for a few moments so that you can get further down the road. As you find a series of creative images

which activate the right brain, you will trigger other imaginative thoughts. These can become visions which will entertain you and may unlock creative solutions to problems, activate motivation, and keep you exercising to capacity all the way to the finish line.

Dirty tricks are merely crazy ideas which can't be grasped by the left brain because they are not logical. Let's go through one of these so that you can see the dynamic aspects of their effects.

Even without this marvelous performance enhancement band, we have the capacity inside to run faster. Because we're under maximum marathon stress at this point, the left brain is in control. Dirty tricks allow you to break free for a while.

TWO MAJOR ROLES FOR DIRTY TRICKS

♦ *Sneak down the road while the left brain is confused*

The left brain, in all of its logic, doesn't know what to do with "a giant, invisible rubber band." While it is befuddled, you have a window of opportunity for avoiding negative messages and moving toward your goal. The more you get into the vision of the dirty trick, the more time you'll have before the negative side starts spewing its venom again. You may get 100, 200 or 400 meters down the road. But the finish line is only a series of dirty trick segments away.

♦ *One crazy thought can unlock another*

Even one imaginative dirty trick can start the creative side of the brain working on other interesting images, visions, and notions which will entertain you and get you closer to the finish.

More significant, a series of these "tricks" can unlock inside you the creative process itself, which can mobilize all of your resources in overcoming challenges and getting you to the finish line feeling good.

The best dirty tricks are the ones that work for you. Only you will respond to the unique chemistry of specific images and crazy concepts. Start concocting these during your right brain runs and remember the ones that work. The more

you use them, the more effective they become.

Almost any imaginative idea will distract you for a while. To engage the performance components inside, it helps if the "tricks" are related to behaviors which help you in the marathon. Here are a few ideas that have worked for me:

◆ Oxygen molecules

The night before a marathon, I collect several million oxygen molecules in a sandwich bag and pin it on my shorts. During the latter stages of the marathon, when the oxygen doesn't seem to be as abundant, I take off the bag and squeeze it out in front of my mouth or nose. Before squeezing, I exhale completely every third or fourth breath. Just one or two squeezes last about 100 to 200 yards. The best part of this trick is seeing and hearing the reactions from the people around you in the marathon. If you're a real salesperson, you may try to make some money from the severely oxygen deprived folks who went out too fast. Just bring along some extra bags.

◆ Ball Bearing Atoms

This is a high-tech right brain invention which will send you gliding to the finish. As the legs lose their resiliency near the finish, you can shake off of your hair millions of atoms which normally act to help it shiny. As they drop on to your shoes and feet, you'll find that you don't need to stretch out your stride any more. You glide better through the air and stay economically more efficient by staying closer to the ground. When you're losing this effect, shake your hair again. Balding people, like myself, will always appreciate some strategic head shakes from others. A downhill portion of the

102

Jeff Galloway's Giant Invisible Rubber Band

On all marathons, I carry with me this device, which is mounted to my shorts in the small of my back. When someone passes me in the late stages, my left brain explodes with a stream of negative messages, such as "Look how smooth he/she is running, and how ragged you are." It's easy to listen and give in to those logical messages which are trying to reduce my effort and slow me down.

But instead of believing this source of lazy and distractive ideas, I attack by throwing the giant band over the head of the individual who had the audacity to pass me. For a while, the lead may grow. During the next few hundred yards, I fill in a great number of details, such as imagining how the tension on the rubber band is increasing, cutting off oxygen supply to the brain of the person I "rubber banded." The hope develops that he or she will have to slow down.

At some point I must laugh at myself for believing in such a ridiculous device. But laughing helps to send me into the right side of my brain, and I relax. Limber legs turn over quicker, and I usually catch up with, or pass, the person that passed me.

The giant invisible rubber band worked again!

course will enhance the effect of these virtually invisible ball bearings.

- A Giant Hand

The ancient Greeks often imagined that Zeus or another god was helping them in difficult situations. When it becomes tough to go up a hill during those last six miles, call for the giant hand to come in and gently push you up. Most folks find that the hand comes in gently as you get your posture upright. The support increases as you shorten stride, keep feet low to the ground, and let the feet gently lift off when they are directly underneath you.

- Your "Inspiration" Shoes

If logistics permit, you might consider changing shoes during the last six miles of the marathon. Both shoes must be broken in, of course. Save your "inspirational" pair for the last part. Just putting them on sends a jolt of invigoration into your feet, up your legs, then through your body and into the right brain. At that point, all types of crazy and innovative things can happen.

- The PowerBar Boost

For the marathon journey, you're not bringing just any PowerBar. Pick the ones with the greatest energy potential from your most powerful stash of bars and infuse them with even more energy. Handle the pieces of these bars with care as you don't want to infect everyone around you. As you chew on each piece and drink water you feel the energy move from your mouth to your right brain. Then, instantly it unlocks other pockets of energy which have been hiding until that point.

Have fun with these dirty tricks. Since your only constraint is the imaginative power of your right brain, there are no limits to what you can unleash.

103

RECOVERY AND BEYOND

RACE RECOVERY

*E*ven if you've run twice as far as you've ever raced before in your life, you can be back to your normal running routine very quickly by following a few simple steps, before and after your race. By mentally and physically preparing for the morning after, you can reduce the negatives, while emotionally riding the wave of positive momentum from even the toughest of races.

THE POST-RACE LETDOWN

Even with the best preparation, however, there will be a natural motivational lull. When you've spent months working toward a specific event and you've reached the finish line of a significant physical test, even the most focused athletes experience a psychological letdown. The challenge has motivated you to be regular with your exercise, to keep pushing your endurance limits on long runs, and to reach down deep for motivation and the strength to go on. Like any almost unique lifetime accomplishments, the day of achievement is an emotional peak day, followed by a downturn. As soon as you fully grasp the reality that the "accomplishment doldrums" will occur, you can prepare for them and desensitize yourself to the negative effects. Talk yourself through this: "It's natural, after six months of preparation for the big day, to miss the focus, the commitment,

and the reinforcement of others who supported me in my mission." But you can also tell yourself with honesty that in a few days you can be shrugging off the blues as you strike out in a new direction. So...let's get another mission started, NOW!

SELECT ANOTHER "MISSION" BEFORE THE BIG DAY

Write the date of your next project on a calendar, journal, etc. The farther ahead of your first goal, the better. It's best to shift gears in selecting a different type of mission: a scenic trail run, a weekend trip to a big festival event, a group run with friends you haven't seen for a while, etc. If you've trained in a group, schedule an easy group run three to four weeks after the race, and you'll look forward to the reunion. It's okay to shift missions in midstream, but be sure to have a specific event always written on the calendar. If you wait until after your first "mission day" to choose another goal, your letdown will be more severe.

THE BODY FOLLOWS YOUR MENTAL VISION

The more you embrace your new mission in advance, the quicker you'll lose the aches and pains of the big race. Instead of wallowing in your misery, tell yourself that your muscles have achieved their "good tiredness" by overcoming a great challenge—and you're still glowing from it. The positive mental momentum from your accomplishment will pull you through the few days immediately after when you may (or may not) feel that the legs don't want to run a step. Read this section several times before your event, mentally rehearsing each of the elements.

A FEW SECONDS OF PATIENCE...

If your pace in the early miles is conservative, you'll recover a lot faster. You'll also run faster at the end of the race than you would have. When the first few miles of a race are run even 10 seconds too fast, you'll often slow down 30-60 seconds/mile at the end. By going out 10-20 seconds slower than you could run in the first few miles, you'll pass more runners at the end, pick up the pace, run a faster time and recover in at least half the time.

HYDRATE AND AVOID SALT AND ALCOHOL

During the 36-hour period before your big race, look at the labels of products you eat and avoid those that have any significant salt content. It's also best to watch the food you eat in restaurants because most kitchens put significant amounts of salt in almost everything. Drink six to eight ounces of water or electrolyte beverage every hour you're awake, until you hear sloshing in your stomach. I like to drink up to a quart of the event's electrolyte drink on the day before a marathon. Rehearse this hydration plan on the long ones leading up to your event, and you'll have your program set for your goal event weekend.

AT THE FINISH LINE

Even if you don't want to, keep walking after you cross the finish. Grab two cups of water, drink and keep walking. Get two more cups and pour them on your legs and two more on your head if you feel hot. Walk to the food area, pick up your carbohydrate snacks of choice, and eat, while you continue drinking water or electrolyte beverage. Keep walking for a mile or so—your legs will recover faster because the walking pumps new blood in there, pushing the waste products out.

THROUGHOUT THE AFTERNOON

After a meal and a shower, walk for two to four more miles very easily—just keep the legs moving. Drink water, electrolyte beverages, citrus juice and eat some lowfat protein with other carbohydrates. You've earned your food rewards, and you'll reload most effectively when you've eaten a good small meal within 30 to 60 minutes of the finish. You don't have to be a pig, just keep snacking all afternoon and evening. For the next few days, you may want to increase your consumption of vitamin C to speed up healing of little micro-tears in your muscles and tendons.

THE NEXT DAY

Walk for 30 to 60 minutes or more. The pace can be as slow as you wish, just keep moving. If you have soreness, the walking will work it out quicker than sitting on a couch.

TWO DAYS AFTER—YOUR RETURN TO RUNNING DAY

Start by walking for five to 10 minutes. Then, insert a one-minute run break every three to five minutes. Stay out there for 30 to 60 minutes, adjusting the walking and running so that you feel comfortable and are not straining. The return to short segments of gentle running will speed up even more the recovery of race-weary muscles.

CONTINUE TO ALTERNATE RUN DAYS WITH WALK DAYS

Over the next two weeks, continue to walk 30 to 60 minutes one day, followed by a day of walk-running for 30 to 60 minutes. Gradually increase the running portions as you feel. Four days after the race, for example, you could try walking three minutes and jogging two to three minutes. Two days later, you may be back to running three minutes and walking one minute. Don't push yourself and you'll recover faster.

TAKE ONE WEEK OFF FROM RACING AND SPEED TRAINING FOR EVERY SIX MILES OF THE RACE

After a marathon, don't race for at least five weeks. You could schedule a short race three weeks after a half marathon. Even if you're feeling great, a 5K race run too soon after a marathon or half marathon can leave you more fatigued than you felt after your big race.

WEEKEND RUNS CAN GRADU-ALLY INCREASE IN DISTANCE

For races between 5K and 15K, you may resume long runs either the weekend after the race or the one following. A race longer than 15K up to 30K, such as a half mara-thon, will require a two to three-week vacation from long runs. From the 30K distance and beyond, the long one can be done three to four weeks after the race and

every third week thereafter. As you resume long runs, be sure to pace them at least two minutes per mile slower than you could run that distance on that day. Most runners will speed recovery faster if they run even slower on the long ones.

Marathoners have the option of waiting three or four weeks before resuming long ones. The distances recommended for the other weekends is 8 to 13, then 10 to 16, followed by either a long one of 12 to 21 or an easy five to 10 (if your long run is to be run the following weekend).

IF YOU'VE RUN A MARATHON AND WANT TO RUN ANOTHER ONE IN THE NEAR FUTURE...

First, make sure that you're recovered (consult the table in the sidebar at the end of this chapter). Once you've run 18 miles or more, you can maintain this level or increase your limit by running long every third weekend for at least 18 miles. Those who will run a marathon six weeks later would have a 23 to 26-miler three weeks after the first marathon. If there are more than six to seven weeks between mara-thons, count back from marathon day. Three weeks before the second marathon, run 23 to 26 miles; three weeks before that, run 20 to 23, etc.

THE GROUP WILL PULL YOU THROUGH

After every goal-oriented event, there are a few who are unmotivated to run by them-selves. The fun and the bonding that occurs inside a training group that runs at a very comfortable pace for you will keep you running and can make running fun. When you have a choice, pick a group that runs at a pace that is slower than you usually run. By running totally within yourself, you'll be able to tell jokes and even remember some of the better ones. On the back page of this brochure, you'll find an 800 number and website which can connect you with training groups or a "web-group" for those whose schedule or location prevent running together.

THE "MARATHON A MONTH" CLUB

A growing number of marathoners are choosing to do their training run in a different city's event each month. The self-proclaimed members of this fictitious club enjoy the travel with a mission and the different personality of each marathon. By doing these at least two minutes per mile slower than they could run on that day, inserting all walk breaks, there is little risk of injury.

ABOVE ALL...

Don't get carried away. Enjoy your accomplishment and have fun with your running. If you run slowly enough, you can recover quickly and receive all of the satisfaction of long runs and long races.

108

Before and during: The little things which speed recovery

- Start conservatively. Time goal runners should start the race 10 to 20 seconds slower than you feel you could run on that day for at least the first 15 to 20 percent of the race (three to six miles in a marathon). First-time marathoners should slow down by one to two minutes per mile. At best, during the second half you can choose to speed up or to finish within your capacity for a faster recovery. Even if it happens to be a hot, humid, bad day, you won't slow down as much at the end if you've started conservatively.

- Avoid alcohol, salt, and limit caffeine during the 36 hours before the big day. In addition, drink six to eight ounces of water or electrolyte beverage until you hear sloshing in your stomach.

- Take every walk break, from the beginning, and pace yourself conservatively accounting for heat, humidity, hills and other factors.

- Don't overstride at any time. Without knowing it, many runners are so exuberant in the beginning that they lengthen their stride too far, overextending the muscles. More damage occurs from overstriding at the end of long runs and races—especially marathons. Try very hard to rein in your stride as you go downhill. Studies continue to show that you'll run faster and recover faster when you keep your feet low to the ground, have a short stride and stay light on your feet.

- Eat PowerGel, pieces of PowerBars, etc. all the way to the end, during the second half of a run that will last 90 minutes or more. Most runners should start taking these "boosters" after 60 to 80 minutes on all long runs to find the frequency and quantity of product which you need during the long events. Be sure to drink water when you take these products.

- Drink at every water stop unless you hear sloshing in your stomach.

How soon after a marathon can I realistically think of doing another one?

It depends upon how close you ran to your potential, or maximum effort, in the most recent marathon:

If your pace was...	& your legs felt good in...	you can run the next one...
At least 2 minutes per mile slower	3-5 days	4 weeks later
At least one minute per mile slower	3-8 days	8 weeks later
At least one minute per mile slower	6-14 days	12+ weeks later
At least 30 seconds per mile slower	8-18 days	16+ weeks later
At least 30 seconds per mile slower	19-24 days	20+ weeks later
As fast as you could have run	NA	26+ weeks later

109

THE BIG DAY

YOU STILL HAVE A CHANCE
TO ASSUME CONTROL

RUNNING FASTER
WITHOUT TRAINING

YOU CAN STILL IMPROVE YOUR PERFORMANCE DURING THE LAST 48 HOURS

While the physical training has been done, you can significantly enhance 1) the way you feel afterward and 2) the quality of your performance by choosing certain behaviors and avoiding others during the final two days. Graduation day is near; don't let your vision get cloudy.

FOCUS

Because of nervousness, the excitement of the expo and the distractions of another city, the marathon, friends, etc., it's easy to lose concentration on a few key items. Be sure to read this section over several times during the last few weeks so that you're more likely to keep the mind and body on track.

YOU'RE IN CONTROL

You need to be in charge of your behaviors during the crucial 48 hours before the marathon. In this way you can control your attitude, your eating, your schedule, etc. This doesn't mean that you should stay by yourself in a hotel room eating salt-free pretzels and PowerBars and drinking water. Being with friends is positive. You have veto power over what goes into your mouth, where you go, and how late you stay out. Being in control of your destiny is the primary step in running faster without training.

BE POSITIVE

Have a list of statements, similar to the ones in the "Magic Marathon Words" section of this book, which you can repeat as necessary. You're going to have negative thoughts slip out from the left brain so we'll work on a way to bypass them and move into the world of the positive.

- I have no pressure on myself.

- I'm going to enjoy this.

- I'll start very slowly.

- The people are great.

- Because I started slowly, I'm finishing strong.

- The satisfaction of doing this is un-equaled.

- I've developed a great respect for myself.

DRINK!

During the 48 hours before the marathon, drink at least four to six ounces of water every hour you're awake. If you're sweating, drink more. If you prefer to drink juices or electrolyte beverages, then do so. Try to avoid drinking too great a quantity of fluids which are loaded with sugar. Even apple juice and orange juice have a high sugar content so take this into consideration as you watch your blood sugar level. Your best positive attack against dehydration is to drink water continuously until you hear sloshing in your stomach.

AVOID THE DEHYDRATING ELEMENTS

Alcohol: During the 48-hour period before the marathon, it's best to avoid alcohol completely. Your exercising muscles and kidneys will thank you especially for abstaining the day and night before the race.

Caffeine: For those who dearly love their cup of coffee on race morning...go ahead. But make it just one cup, and drink a glass of water before the coffee and at least one glass of water afterward. Throughout the rest of that 48-hour period before the big event, just say NO.

Salt: This is probably the leading dehydrating agent for most marathoners. Because it's used so widely in the preparation of most restaurant food, you're likely to consume large amounts of it when you're away from home without realizing it. For this reason:

1. Try to avoid restaurant food during the 24-hour period before the marathon.

2. Eat foods which you know do not contain salt (or are very low in salt).

3. Drink a little more water than normal if you've consumed food which you suspect has some salt in it.

Even one salty meal the night before a marathon will leave you significantly dehydrated for the marathon itself—no matter how much water you drink. So if you go to the pasta-loading party the night before, watch out for the sauce and the garlic bread! (Just nibble on the pasta, and digest the conversation.)

MEDICATIONS:

Most medications (especially those for colds, flu, etc.) have a dehydrating effect. Be sure to consult with a doctor (who supports and knows the various effects of running) to adjust your medication accordingly.

EAT!

The best eating plan for the 48-hour marathon countdown is the best eating plan for life in general: keep eating low or non-fat snacks continually, all day long. Avoid eating a large solid-food meal the afternoon or evening before the marathon.

So if you want to snack on PowerBars all afternoon or have a series of carbohydrate snacks which you know will get through your system quickly, do so. Concentrated forms of sugar (frozen yogurt, syrup, candy) are not recommended.

CHECK OUT THE STAGING AREA

If it is possible, go over the staging area the day before. As a guide, you can't beat someone who has run that marathon before: he or she will know where you'll be arriving, where you can keep warm and relax, and the best way to get to the portion of the road where you'll be lining up. If you

112

get a clear idea of all this ahead of time, you'll feel more in control and will tend to receive fewer left brain messages.

REST

You don't have to sleep, but you must rest. Settle into your home or hotel room and relax in the best way you know. Read, watch TV, listen to music, talk with friends...but relax. Again, take control of your environment and mold for yourself a positive and cozy atmosphere. Don't worry if you don't sleep at all, but lay that head down and store up some energy.

WAKE UP

Set your wake-up call so that you have plenty of time to get moving, gather your gear together, and go through your usual eating and drinking timetable which worked for you during the long runs.

DRINK UNTIL YOU HEAR SLOSHING

From the time you wake up, drink four to six ounces of water every hour until you hear sloshing in your stomach. Whenever the sloshing stops, start the drinking again. It's always better to have water in your stomach, or in your system, than to suffer the devastating effects of severe dehydration and heat disease. During the race itself, drink at every water station—unless you hear the sloshing.

EAT—TO HOLD YOUR BLOOD SUGAR UP FOR THE FIRST HALF

One of the reasons I've advocated eating before all of your long runs is to discover the foods and the pattern of eating which will work best for you in the marathon itself. While about 70 percent of those in our various training groups find that

PowerBar digests most quickly and provides the best blood sugar stablizing effect, you should use what has worked best for you in your food countdown before long runs. Eating about 200 to 250 calories of high quality carbohydrate about an hour before a long one has helped many runners to stablize their blood sugar level for the first half of the marathon.

GO SLOWLY IN THE BEGINNING

Almost everyone who performs a personal record in the marathon runs the second half faster than the first. Slow down by 10 to 20 seconds per mile (from your projected marathon pace) during the first three to five miles, and then follow the guidelines in the "Pacing Tips" chapter which follows this one. Many marathoners report that by starting out 15 seconds per mile slower, they have the resiliency to run 20 to 30 seconds per mile faster at the end of the marathon.

113

TAKE WALK BREAKS

A high percentage of those who didn't achieve the time goal they desired in the marathon by running continuously have been able to significantly improve finishing times by walking for one minute each mile—from the beginning of the marathon. See the section which follows on "Pacing Tips."

EAT DURING THE SECOND HALF OF THE MARATHON

Eating small carbohydrate snacks during the second half of the marathon has helped marathoners improve time goals by boosting the blood sugar level. This maintains mental concentration, sustains a positive mental attitude, and reduces the opportunity for negative left brain messages to creep in. Be sure to re-read the "Food and

Fat-burning" section in this book—especially the "blood sugar boosters" section.

HAVE FUN!

By staying within your physical capabilities throughout the first 20 miles, you can enjoy the people, the joking, the sights, and the overall experience...as you are rewarded with the feeling of accomplishment. Be gentle on yourself throughout the marathon and the enjoyment will flow. For sharing purposes, don't forget to bring with you the following: a joke, an interesting story, a controversial issue, and/or some gossip. Of course, bring along anything else like this that doesn't weigh much and will add to the fun.

114

MARATHON DAY
CHECKLIST

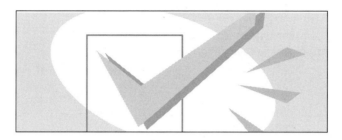

IN GENERAL

- Drink four to six ounces of water every hour.

- Mentally rehearse the marathon, feeling good, overcoming challenges, recovering.

- Eat small carbohydrate snacks constantly.

- Relax with friends or family.

THE NIGHT BEFORE

- Drink four to six ounces of water every hour.

- Eat light carbohydrate snacks like PowerBars.

- Relax, laugh, enjoy the moment.

- Go over the procedure, route, etc. for getting to the start.

- Do a very relaxed mental rehearsal of the marathon, concentrating on the positive.

- Pack your bag.

YOUR MARATHON BAG SHOULD CONTAIN:

- Race number and pins

- Race instructions, map, etc.

- Copy of "Marathon Morning List" (below), and a copy of "Magic Marathon Words"

- Prepare to bring a controversial issue, at least one interesting story, and at least one joke

- Shoes, socks, shirt, shorts, and warm-up suit

- Other clothes if it's cold: tights, polypro top, long-sleeved T, gloves, hat, ear covering , etc.

- Water (about 32 to 64 oz.)

- Bandages, Vaseline, etc.

- $20-30 for reserve funds (rapid transit tokens, etc.)

- PowerBars or your chosen carbohydrate source (enough for start, second half, and after)

- Fanny pack or plastic bags, pins

- Some extra "give away" shirts and/or pants as extra layers in case staging area is cold

- Garbage bags as an inexpensive water-proof top and ground cover

"MARATHON MORNING LIST"

- Drink four to six oz. of water every 30 minutes until you hear "sloshing."

- Eat—according to the schedule which has worked for you in the long runs. (example: one PowerBar with 8 oz. water, one to two hours before the start)

- Bring your bag, car keys, etc.

- Leave at least 30 minutes before you think you'll need to leave...in case of traffic, etc.

- If you have several hours at race site before start, stay warm, get off your feet and relax.

- Sixty minutes before the start, walk around the staging area to mentally rehearse lining up.

- Thirty minutes before the start, walk around for 15 minutes to get the legs moving.

- Jog for three to five minutes (very slowly) just before lining up.

- Keep the legs moving, in place if necessary as you stand waiting for the start.

- If going for a time goal, get to the starting area early enough to secure a good place.

- Most of us with the goal "to finish" should line up in the back of the crowd.

- Joke around; enjoy the energy and personalities of the folks nearby.

- Go out slowly. If it's hot, go out even slower!

- Get over to the side of the road and take every walk break, from the beginning.

- Drink at every water station until you hear sloshing in your stomach.

- If you feel warm, pour water over your head at each water stop.

- Each walk break gives you a chance to appreciate and enjoy each mile.

- When tired, shorten stride.

- Don't stretch during the run or immediately afterward.

- You may cut out the walk breaks after mile 18 if you're feeling good.

IMMEDIATELY AFTERWARD:

- Grab water and carbohydrate food(s).

- Walk, eat and drink, for at least a mile.

RECOVERY:

- If possible, immerse your legs in a cold bath, as soon after the finish as possible.

- Walk for 30 to 60 minutes later in the day.

- Eat carbohydrate snacks continuously for the rest of the day.

- Drink four to six oz. of water or electrolyte fluid (at least) every hour.

- Walk for 30 to 60 minutes the next day.

- Run/walk for 30 to 45 minutes two days after the marathon.

- Continue to alternate: walk 30 to 60 minutes and run/walk 30 to 45 minutes.

- Wait at least a week before you 1) schedule your next race and 2) vow never to do another marathon.

116

PACING TIPS FOR THE MARATHON

- For **the first three to five miles,** run marathon pace during the running parts and take the walk breaks.

- A one-minute walk break (for the average person) will slow you by 15 to 18 seconds.

- A slightly slower pace will allow the legs to warm up before pushing into race effort.

- Remember to adjust your pace for heat, humidity and hills.

- **Between three and eight miles,** shift to running faster in the running por-tions *and* take the walk breaks.

- You will gradually pick up the pace so that by eight miles, you're running at goal pace when you average the walk breaks and the running segments.

- If it's a struggle to pick up the pace, stay at an effort level which is comfortable.

- Don't even think about cutting your walk break short to speed things up.

- **Between eight and 18 miles,** run at marathon goal pace (run faster to compensate for walk breaks).

- Run each mile about 15 to 18 seconds faster than your goal pace, then walk.

- Stay smooth as you ease down to walk and ease back into running.

- Compute your pace each mile.

- Uphill miles can be slower, and downhill miles can be faster than goal pace.

- **After 18 miles,** you can cut out the walk breaks if you're feeling strong (and want to).

- An alternative: walk for 30 seconds for several walk breaks before eliminating them.

- If you need the breaks but legs are cramping, shuffle instead of walking.

- **After 23 miles,** you can keep picking up the pace if you feel up to it.

A FASTER MARATHON

BEFORE YOU ATTEMPT A TIME GOAL MARATHON...READ THIS

THE MANY WAYS TO "WIN" A MARATHON

There are an almost unlimited number of different marathon "missions." Each can enrich your life in a different way, while delivering about the same exhilaration as received the first time.

Over the past 20 years, I must have compared notes with over 50,000 veteran marathoners. A few continue to focus exclusively on running the fastest time they can run, every event. But almost every veteran, even those with over 100 completion medals, will put at the top of the rewards, the unique feeling of satisfaction experienced every time you cross the finish line.

The most important concept you can grasp as you get into the running lifestyle is that you are the captain of your ship. You'll get a lot of advice about how you should run and what you should do next. Pick a good, conservative program, like the ones in this book, and learn to have fun following it. When you take too many elements from too many different types of programs, you can decrease your chance of success and enjoyment. At the same time, a "combo" program will increase your chance of injury.

WHY RUN FASTER IN THE MARATHON?

Good question! When the benefits are few and the challenges significant and many, you must answer this question before and throughout the program to maintain consistent motivation. Every person needs to dig down and come up with his or her own answer. I'll give you mine.

While most of the enduring and life-changing benefits from the marathon experience come only from finishing, there are a few unique life-enhancing capabilities to be gained from testing yourself in a time goal marathon program. It's possible to get all of the benefit from this test, even if you don't do the marathon. It's also possible to have the good genes and or luck to run a fast time and receive none of the good internal engineering.

Finishing a marathon forces everyone to bring mind and body together and to reach for extra resources from the power of the human spirit. A time goal marathon program goes one step farther than finishing, putting you on the edge of endurance and strength almost every week. In this process, you will invariably find weakness and setbacks. As you pull yourself out of the rut, you must question your resolve and your spirit, readjust, and come back stronger. Almost every one of the time goal runners I've communicated with has been re-charged by the challenge with a better understanding of who they are, as people. And many of these apply the lessons to other areas of life.

DON'T ATTEMPT A TIME GOAL UNTIL YOU HAVE RUN AT LEAST ONE MARATHON

Even veteran runners will learn some very important lessons in their first marathon. Everyone can have a really good experience in their first marathon if they start out slow and keep the pace comfortable throughout. A good first-time goal should be a marathon that is about an hour slower than you could run the same distance when racing.

SO WHAT IS A REALISTIC GOAL?

Run several 5K races throughout the training program on non-long-run weekends. Look at the Predicting Race Performance Table in the back of this book and see what your 5K time equivalent is in the marathon. Add 10 to 20 minutes to the time because this prediction assumes that 1) the course is perfectly flat, 2) the temperature is below 51° F, 3) there is less than 25 percent humidity, 4) there is no wind, and 5) there are no turns on the course. Having attended over 600 marathons, I've never experienced those conditions.

If it's your first marathon, add an hour to the adjusted prediction time. If you have run a marathon before and want to finish feeling good, add 30 to 90 minutes to that adjusted time. But everyone, including trained competitive athletes, should add at least 10 minutes of adjustment to the predicted time.

LIMIT YOUR TIME GOAL MARATHONS

There are many negative consequences to setting a goal on each marathon that is too challenging. If you enjoy the competition and the satisfaction of achieving a specific goal, then one or two marathons a year (at most) could be set aside for this purpose. The best reward for this hard work is the Boston Marathon.

Qualifying for Boston is one of the greatest accomplishments in a runner's life. The experience of that special weekend, during which over a million people cheer you with unique intensity, will be something you'll remember for the rest of your life.

Before committing to a time goal program, be sure to evaluate the risk-reward ratio. To finish a marathon requires very little interruption in your lifestyle. The extra time required for a time goal, however, can take its toll on family, career, and other areas of life. Training "to finish" takes about one-third to one-half the time required by most time goal marathoners. The extra mileage and speed training will also produce more aches, pains, doubts, negative messages, and, possibly, injuries.

There is a high burnout rate among time goal marathoners. They often become so focused on the goal that they miss the joy of the body responding to an early morning run or the glow of a trail at sunset. If the satisfaction is derived solely on the clock at the finish, most of the joys of running slip by, underappreciated. One reason for the high rate of failure of marathoners in hitting a specific goal is that they have no control over several of the primary reasons for slowing down in a marathon: temperature, humidity, course difficulty, and congestion of a crowded event.

Jeff Galloway's Experience

From a 2:38 marathon to a 5:10 marathon in one year....and happier!

A few years ago, I trained to run a marathon faster than 2:40. In spite of my eight to nine minutes per mile pace on daily runs, I believed that my 45+ year old legs could average six minutes per mile (if I could add some regular speedplay to my program). A session of mile repeats every other week (building up to 13, running each at 5:40) seemed to be doing the job. My longest run, three weeks before the race, was 29 miles (at 8:30 pace). Despite pushing the pace too fast in the middle of my target race, the Houston-Tenneco Marathon, I achieved my goal, with two seconds to spare!

Several months later, I was asked to help someone run his first marathon. He guessed his performance potential to be just over four hours, but stomach problems pushed us over the five-hour barrier for the first time in my marathon life.

The 5:10 marathon was a much better experience than the faster one. I received the same satisfaction from finishing the slow one as I did from finishing the fast one. An even bigger benefit was revealed during the recovery.

Three days after my five-hour marathon, I was running smoothly, easily and as fast as I wanted to run. There were no aches or pains and no lingering problems. Quickly and easily resuming my normal running program, I enjoyed the glow of satisfaction from having re-established marathon endurance.

Four weeks after my 2:38 marathon, the pride of time goal achievement had worn off, yet my running muscles were still stiff. For several weeks, I continued to feel regular bouts of lingering tiredness. During those many weeks, I longed for the day when I'd feel smooth and fluid again.

I've articulated a pattern from analyzing many other slow and fast marathons, which have been run by me and thousands of the folks with whom I work. The slower you go, particularly in the beginning, the faster you'll recover from the marathon. I believe very strongly that the satisfaction is identical whether you register a personal best, a personal worst, or anything in between. Finishing a marathon bestows great personal achievement and accomplishment. Period!

Certainly there is significant meaning in training for and realizing a time goal in the marathon. I recommend, however, that this be reserved for very few occasions (once every 12 to 24 months).

When you enjoy a marathon and recover quickly afterward, you'll reinforce all of the positive behaviors and internal connections you've developed in the training. I believe that one should have at least three very slow and enjoyable marathons for every fast one—to keep the balance.

I'm not denying that our egos are important sometimes and that some runners need to feed them with an occasional accomplishment. Don't give up the pursuit of a time goal if this is what you want. Just realize that focusing too exclusively on speed and time has led to burnout for many runners.

I want you to enjoy running for the rest of your life. So...take it easy!

If you include running fun, every week, and you're flexible about your goal, you can usually have your time goal...and a life too. At least two of your long runs could be done in other marathons, gradually building up to the fast one (observe the Two-Minute Rule!). If the weather or your body doesn't cooperate on goal day, don't thrash yourself. Drop out before mile 18 and you can usually recover fairly quickly.

THE ROLE OF THE SLOW MARATHON

I've run over 50 marathons the recreational way. By running slower than I could run, from the beginning, the marathon becomes enjoyable. I ran Boston with my father in 1996, after having run it four other times.

Since I was going along comfortably I enjoyed the course and was surprised to recognize very little of it. Each of the other efforts were fiercely competitive. I hardly noticed anything but the clock, my competitors, and how I felt. It was so much better in '96, savoring the landmarks, the people, and the time with my Dad.

The more significantly you back off from what you could run, the better you'll feel during the marathon and the more likely it will be that you'll remember what went on. You'll expand the number of possible running companions and open yourself up for a number of "fun" missions, listed below.

122

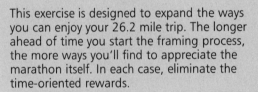

Framing the Marathon

This exercise is designed to expand the ways you can enjoy your 26.2 mile trip. The longer ahead of time you start the framing process, the more ways you'll find to appreciate the marathon itself. In each case, eliminate the time-oriented rewards.

If you haven't already done so, you should start a "Mind Power" notebook. This will be your mental guidebook which will help you fine-tune your mental training. As you discover patterns of rehearsals which inspire you, write them down. As you collect positive experiences, write them down. This helps you to catalog a more formidable experience "resource library" and gives more magic to the words and phrases you attach to specific experiences.

In the section on mental rehearsal, you'll begin with an outline. As you fill this in with specific advance experiences, you are molding the way you'll feel in the marathon. You can significantly carve out enjoyment, in advance, which will influence the race itself. By 'framing,' I mean setting up a process which will open you up to a wide variety of

experiences during the marathon and enhance your enjoyment and growth.

1. Write down what you will look for and seek out as you run the marathon:

- getting to know some of the folks around you

- picking up on the energy of the spectators along the way

- getting a feel for the personality of the city

- looking for places along the course where you'd like to return

- other items which are meaningful to you

2. Write down how you'd like to feel as you run your relaxed marathon:

- enjoying the confidence of running within yourself

- appreciating the glow bestowed by exertion

- feeling the support of the spectators

- gaining strength from the others around you...you're moving through the challenge together

MISSIONS

Time goal variations: Time goals don't have to be gut-wrenching. Here are a few that have energized myself and others. Don't stop with these ideas. Be creative and you'll look forward to every one.

- **Set up a predicted time**, one that you know you could do. Tell your friends about it and see if they want to have a pool. The winner and the marathoner, you, get a free celebration dinner.

- **Beating a younger you** Every 10 years, I go back to the event where I started my marathon career in 1963—the Atlanta Marathon. My mission is to beat the time that I ran as an 18-year-old. So long as this is a realistic goal, I'll continue to do

it. When it stops being fun, I'll shift to another version.

- **Running no faster than**... This is particularly a good idea for those who find it hard to slow down. Put a penalty on speed by punishing yourself for running faster than a certain time. This has helped hundreds of runners to learn how to hold back and enjoy the company of those farther back in the pack.

OTHER MARATHON MISSIONS

Helping a charity A growing number of runners find it fulfilling to raise money for a charity that means something to them. Many charities have programs that allow donors to deduct the contributions, while

- bouyed up by the sense of meaningful purpose of completing the marathon
- other feelings

3. Write down how you will feel after the marathon

- having enough left to talk to people and enjoy the refreshment area
- enjoying a great shower
- walking around with a friend or two, with no major aches, pains or fatigue
- enjoying the meal you've earned and sharing the experience with others
- feeling a little tired but having plenty of energy since you've stayed within yourself
- feeling a great sense of accomplishment
- continuing to enjoy the sense of achievement while recovering quickly afterward

4. Be Creative!

- imagining you're writing a detective novel and seeking clues and venues for your story
- planning how you would paint the

interesting areas you're running through if you had a canvas

- training yourself to snap a mental photo of specific scenes...with details
- designating people along the way as characters in your novel: what are they up to?

■ Write these down into the margins of your outline.

■ Go over them every week (every day or so, if possible).

■ Add other items in each area as you go through the program.

■ The experience becomes more alive and fun...with each rehearsal.

■ This leads to the same pattern in the marathon.

■ Use this evolving 'story line' as you move from marathon to marathon.

123

the runner earns a free trip to a great marathon.

Running with a relative I've heard it said numerous times that there's no better way to see relatives in a positive light than to train with and then run a marathon together. The bonding is impossible to describe. When you live in different cities, the phone contact throughout the training keeps you in touch and your relationship alive.

Mentoring someone who really needs it
At every marathon expo, I talk with folks who are reunited by training for and running a marathon together. Maybe you want to reconnect with a college roommate going through a divorce or introduce a high school best friend to your marathon training buddies. It could be a former mentor of yours who has lost fitness and focus and is looking for both. Marathon training helps people restart their lives (or reconnect) in a positive way.

50-staters After running five to 10 marathons, some new marathoners like the challenge and the travel. So they set out on a five to 10-year goal to run a marathon in every state. This has been extended to all continents, Canadian provinces, etc. Whatever makes sense to you is an appropriate mission!

Revisit a special place It could be the town where you or your father grew up, went to college, started your career...whatever is interesting to you.

A scavenger hunt If someone in your group knows the course, you can set up a scavenger hunt. Buy souvenirs from certain parts of town on the course, wear pieces of clothing from distinctive stores, or take a "throwaway" camera and get pictures of yourself with landmarks on the course for proof. Your imagination is your only limit.

Siteseeing, with a list Carry a little notepad and pen in your fanny pack and note the historical and scenic points on the course. Try to find something about each area that most people would overlook. This gives you a creative task during walk breaks. Compare notes with friends at your victory celebration afterward.

THE "MARATHON A MONTH" CLUB

A growing number of recreational marathoners informally identify themselves under this banner. Their long run, every three to four weeks, just happens to be in a marathon, in different cities. Club members must run at least two minutes per mile slower than they could run that distance on that day. Here are a few other items which become treasures later as you revisit your marathon victories:

1. Must write down at least five (and hopefully 10) positive aspects of the trip

2. Must have at least one funny or interesting story about the trip, the marathon, the people, etc.

3. Must share the stories and other feedback in their social run the following week

QUESTIONS ABOUT SLOW MARATHONS:

"I've tried to run a marathon slowly, and I became more sore than I was after a fast one."

If you're getting sore or feeling more effort when going slowly, then you're running inefficiently. By shortening your stride and keeping the feet low to the ground, you incur very little exertion. In this very efficient running mode, your main running muscles are mostly resting.

I've talked to several fast runners who seem to be running correctly, yet still became sore after a marathon. After a few more questions, however, I learned that they went into the marathon with a long run of only 19, 16, or, in one case, 12 miles. Whenever you ask your body to go that much further than you have gone in the recent past, you can predict that there will be some muscle retribution afterward.

To reduce the chance of soreness under any long run mileage increase, don't run with the same form every step of the way. By taking walking breaks early and often you'll accomplish this.

"Why should I waste a marathon by running slowly?... I don't understand how you can run a slow marathon. You have to train for six months and I want to make the most of this once, or twice, a year, challenge."

I understand where you're coming from. For my first 60 marathons, I was the competitor. When the gun fired, the force of my being was directed at reaching the finish line as I would in any race: with nothing left. While I ran some fast times including a 2:16, I did not enjoy these experiences. When I placed well, such as a win at Honolulu and fifth and seventh place finishes at Boston, the afterglow was compromised by weeks of healing: soreness, tiredness, blisters and ego (which always told me, even when I ran well, that I could have run faster).

To Run Faster...you must run faster

*Y*ou can't run all of your runs slowly if you want to run fast in the marathon. But you can't go too fast either. By running the speed play too fast, for example, you will prepare your muscles to go out too fast in the marathon and pay dearly for that later. The best type of speed is that which simulates the marathon experience. This will encourage the exact type of endurance/speed adaptations necessary to go faster on race day.

Strength and coordination are developed simultaneously with the other improvements generated by speed sessions.

The cardiovascular system adapts:

- The heart pumps more blood into the exercising muscles.

- Waste products are withdrawn more quickly from those muscles.

Your oxygen processing system becomes more efficient:

- Oxygen is absorbed more efficiently from the air.

- Oxygen delivery to the muscles allows you to burn fat longer.

Adaptations occur inside the muscles due to the challenges of speed play:

- Fat-burning makes you more efficient.

- You also become more efficient when burning glycogen.

- Waste product removal gets more effective.

- Individual muscle cells work at a higher capacity for a longer period.

- Muscle cells learn to work together, in systems.

You develop the mental strength to go further:

- You develop instant and continuous mind-body feedback.

- You learn how to dig deeper and push through doubt.

- You learn the difference between real problems and the lazy messages of your left brain.

[For more information on the changes in muscles, see Galloway's Book On Running, pp. 38-43.]

But every time you run fast, you increase the chance of injury, you stress and fatigue the main running muscles, and you increase the chance that you'll not recover before the marathon itself. To do your best in the marathon, all of your components should be ready for top performance, working together, and trained to make further adaptations under stress. The stress of speed play is necessary for you to run faster, but you need to monitor fatigue to avoid injury or overtraining.

RECOVERY! RECOVERY! RECOVERY!

THE theme of a time-goal program is *recovery*. If you build enough rest into your program before you need it, your body will be continuously recovering, rebuilding and adapting for the performance demands of your goal. By preventing extra fatigue and taking extra rest even at the first hint of slower recovery, you can maintain a steady performance increase without taking a week or more off due to injury or overtraining.

MONITORING OVERSTRESS

Keep a log book next to your bed and write down your pulse rate before you get out of bed each morning. Do this before you've had a chance to think about anything stressful, like getting up, work, etc.

Why? When your exercising muscles are over-fatigued, they don't have the resiliency to help move the blood through the system in the smoothest way. The heart must work harder and registers this with a higher heart rate.

When to take a day off: After several weeks of listing your heart rate, you'll be able to tell what your lower baseline levels are. When you see a five percent increase over your low baseline, you should take an easy day. When the heart rate is 10 percent above baseline, just take the day off from running.

Recovery Enhancers

- Enough days off from running each week

- Long runs which are slow enough— with walk breaks

- Walking the rest interval between mile repeats

- Starting out every run very slowly (at least three minutes per mile slower than you could run the distance you plan to run). You can speed up later in the run if everything is okay....*just start very slowly.*

- Making sure that you are recovered enough from the weekend sessions before you do any tempo running, accelerations, etc. during the maintenance runs on weekdays.

Remember that heart rate is also affected by stress, elation and other emotions and thoughts. Try not to think about anything before taking your pulse.

MILEAGE HELPS—BUT AT GREAT RISK

By adding mileage to your program, you'll improve overall conditioning and improve the chance that you can achieve your time goal. But higher mileage dramatically increases injury risk: it is *the* leading cause of injury by a wide margin.

There are some ways to increase total mileage and reduce the chance of injury:

- By increasing mileage very gradually

- By adding a short additional run to a running day

How many days per week?

Almost every marathoner, including most of those training for the Olympic Trials could benefit from two days off from running per week. Age will determine, and ultimately dictate, how many more days off you will need.

- Those in their 30s can get by with two days off per week.

- In your 40s...better take three days off from running per week.

- If you're over 50, it's best to shift to every other day.

If you've been running six or seven days per week, I'd start by cutting back by one day per week. As the long runs reach 15 miles and beyond, cut one more day out of the schedule. You can actually increase mileage to running days by adding an additional run (if recovery is proceeding well). Alternative exercise can be done on non-running days, but take it very easy the day before:

- your long one,

- races and

- your speed play day.

Example: The late Dr. George Sheehan improved by reducing from six days to three days.

As he approached the age of 60, Dr. Sheehan's marathon times slowed down. For years, he had been running five miles a day, six days a week. Admitting that his competitive days appeared to be over, the running cardiologist cut back to three days a week, while increasing his daily mileage to 10 miles. In other words, weekly mileage held steady at 30 miles per week, while he gained three extra rest days.

After about three years of this schedule, at age 62, George ran the fastest marathon of his life: 3:01. He gained more training effect from one 10-miler than he did from two successive five-milers. Even more significant was the recovery he received by taking a day off between runs.

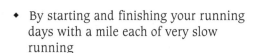

- By starting and finishing your running days with a mile each of very slow running

(at least three minutes per mile slower than current 5K pace)

Be aware of all the early warning signs of injury or over-fatigue and back off at the first indication of trouble.

AS WE GET OLDER

Since it is possible to continue to improve times at any age, many runners over 45 are elated when they run personal records or high age-group performances...and forget that they're over 45. The exuberance of

achievement will push marathon improvers at any age into over-fatigue before they know it; the older the runner, the longer he or she has to pay for the excessive training.

Unfortunately, there are few early warning signs of overtraining in a marathon program. Most of those who get into trouble are increasing gradually enough; they just don't have enough recovery time built into their program. The progessive buildup pushes the muscles beyond their limits so gradually that the effects are usually masked by internally produced stress hormones. Once the resource reserve has been used up, older runners must endure a long recovery period.

PAST THE AGE OF 35:

- Fatigue comes on more quickly but is usually masked by stress hormones.

- It's easier to push into overtraining without warning signs.

- The worse the overtraining, the longer the recovery.

Fatigue takes twice as long to recover from (compared to the below age 35 group).

Over-fatigue takes five to six times longer to recover from (compared to younger groups).

THE FATIGUE-PRODUCERS:

- too many days of running per week

- too many miles per week

- too many races

- speed sessions

- the very long, long runs

The volume of miles which most time goal marathoners put into their program is enough to produce overtraining among the over-45-year olds. It's so easy to push just a bit too hard on races, speed sessions, or any of the other components, but the recovery from stepping over the line is significant.

REDUCING INJURIES FOR 35+ MARATHONERS

- Add an extra day off from running (to a minimum of three running days per week).

- Slow down long run to a pace of three minutes per mile slower than you could run that day.

- Add walk breaks to long runs, from the beginning.

- Walk for two to three minutes (minimum) during the rest interval in speed sessions.

- Carefully monitor resting heart rate.

LONG RUNS CAN IMPROVE MARATHON SPEED

By increasing beyond 26 miles, you'll build reserve endurance which will boost performance in many ways:

- You'll push your "wall" past 26 miles.

- You'll have the strength and stamina to maintain a hard pace during the last three to six miles when most competitive folks slow down.

- With reserve endurance, you can often get away with a few small pacing mistakes.

129

YOU MUST RUN SLOWLY OR YOU'LL LOSE THE BENEFITS:

- You get the same benefit from a long slow one as you do from a long fast one. You'll just recover faster from a long slow one.

- Going beyond 20 miles in the long one helps marathon stamina dramatically but you must run slowly. By pacing these long ones at least two minutes per mile slower than you could run that distance on that day *and* taking walking breaks, you'll get the job done!

- Running slower will help you recover faster and therefore keep the legs ready to do speed sessions on the following weekend.

- Liberal walk breaks will also speed recovery from the long ones. Remember that these one-minute walks must be taken early and often to give your legs the relief needed.

* Make sure the maintenance runs during the week are done slowly enough. Sometimes a slight bit of fatigue will appear on the second or third day after a long one or a speed session. Take it very easy if that happens.

ACCELERATION-GLIDERS

To improve running form and efficiency, accelerations can help you greatly. When your form improves, a speed increase will occur naturally.

BENEFITS OF ACCELERATION-GLIDERS

- They warm up the legs before speed sessions, hills or races.

- By focusing on these gliders, you teach yourself efficient marathon running form.

- They help you develop the capacity to glide or "coast" for segments of 50 to 200 meters, resting the major running muscles so that they will perform better later.

ACCELERATION-GLIDERS MUST BE DONE

- regularly—at least twice a week

- with no sprinting—no major effort used

- low to the ground to minimize effort

- using quick turnover of the feet and legs

HOW TO DO THE ACCELERATION-GLIDERS:

1. It helps to have a slight downhill to get momentum going, using the last 20 to 30 meters of the downhill as momentum to get right into gliding at an increased pace.

2. Keep the legs and body relaxed throughout, but particularly at the beginning.

3. If no downhill is available, pick up your leg rhythm by shortening stride length and gradually increasing the turnover of your feet and legs. (Turnover is simply the number of steps you take per minute.)

4. When you feel comfortable at the faster rhythm, let the stride lengthen out naturally, but don't let it get too long. (Avoid any feeling of tension or over-stretch in the back of your legs.)

5. You're now up to speed so just glide...keeping feet low to the ground, using very little effort.

6. Let this gliding continue for 50 to 200 meters.

7. Rest by jogging between accelerations. You may also take walking breaks as needed.

YOUR ACCELERATION-GLIDER PROGRAM:

1. Work on the marathon form mentioned in the form chapter later in the book. Keep your feet low to the ground, body upright but relaxed, and maintain a smooth, quick turnover while using little effort.

2. Warm up before each session with one to two miles of easy running (with walking breaks if you wish).

3. Keep the legs relaxed throughout the warm-up, the gliders themselves, and afterward.

4. Ease into the gliders, using downhills as noted above to get you started on each. In this case, the downhills act as the accelerations. If you don't have a down-hill available, accelerate by shortening the stride, picking up the turnover rate of the legs, and then gradually lengthening out the stride as it feels natural. The "gliding" will follow.

5. Start with three to five gliders and increase by one or two each session to a maximum of 10 or 12.

6. Two of these sessions per week will help to mechanically reinforce form improvements, which will help you in the marathon itself.

7. You can use these as a warm-up before hills, speed sessions or races. You may also do them during your recovery/ maintenance runs each week.

HILLS BUILD STRENGTH

*E*veryone can benefit from doing some hill accelerations. Hill training provides a gentle and effective transition between very slow running and the faster speed play needed by veteran marathoners for faster performance. If you're just starting to run, you shouldn't jump into hill play. But those who've been running regularly for six months or more can benefit from the strength increase which only hill training can give. You don't have to have a time goal to benefit from play on the hills.

HILLS: THE BEST STRENGTH TRAINING FOR RUNNING

Hills provide resistance to the main running groups, primarily the calf muscles; the regular but gentle uphill stress encourages these muscles to develop strength in the act of running. Weight training, in contrast, builds static strength in only one range of motion at a time. Since weight work can strengthen some leg groups more than others (and knock your running motion off balance), it is not recommended for runners. Hill training strengthens as it coordinates the dynamic action of running and can bestow all the running power you need.

When runners of all ability levels run hill sessions regularly, they develop the lower leg strength to support body weight farther forward on their feet. As the foot rolls forward in the running motion, greater support strength will allow the ankle to be loaded like a strong spring. The result is a more dynamic lift-off of the foot as the ankle releases its mechanical energy. Due to the incredible efficiency of the ankle, more work is done with less energy expended by the muscles. Such conservation of muscle resources allows one to run further or faster or a combination of both.

IF YOU'RE DOING HILL TRAINING FOR THE FIRST TIME...

Beginning hill runners should be conservative. It's too easy to run too fast in the first few sessions without realizing it. DON'T PUSH THE EFFORT! Run at a comfortable and non-fast pace on each incline during the first few hill sessions. The grade of the hill will be enough of a challenge to bestow a training effect. After three hill play sessions, you may run the hills a little faster.

HILL TRAINING RULES:

- Never run all out!

- Never go to the point that you're huffing and puffing and can't talk.

- Don't run so hard that you feel significant tension or extreme exertion in any of the muscles or tendons in the back of your legs. If this happens, slow down immediately and shorten your stride. (The lengthening of the running stride out of its efficient range can cause injury, extra fatigue and long recovery.)

BENEFITS OF HILL TRAINING:

- Strength from hill training helps runners shift his or her weight farther forward on the foot and gain a more efficient "lift off" with each step.

- It strengthens a set of muscles which are used as back-ups for the main running muscles.

- It helps the cardiovascular system adapt to faster running without going into oxygen debt.

MARATHON HILL TRAINING:

- Take a very slow one to two-mile warm-up and warm-down.

- Pick a hill that is 200 to 800 meters long.

- The grade of the hill should be very gentle.

- Run up; walk down.

- Run with a smooth, continuous effort over the top of the hill.

- Never sprint or run all out. Just maintain an increased turnover rate over the top.

- Start with two or three hills, and increase by one or two hills per week until you can run eight to 12 hills.

- Don't feel like you have to increase the number each session. Back off if tired or sore.

HILL TRAINING FORM:

- Maintain upright body posture.

- Feet should stay low to the ground.

- Keep your stride short at first; pick up the rhythm until you feel comfortable.

- Keep your rhythm going quickly and smoothly over the top of the hill.

- When the incline increases, shorten your stride to maintain turnover rate.

The length of the hill segments is longer in a marathon program than in a 10K or 5K training routine. These longer inclines develop *endurance muscle strength* as opposed to *explosive muscle strength*. Due to the distance increase, each should be run slower than you'd run hills of shorter length.

As in the other elements of training, it's important for hill sessions to be done regularly, in order to produce the adaptations desired from the legs and muscles and to improve overall running efficiency. Since hills will prepare the running muscles for a higher level of performance, the greater the number of weekly sessions, the more you will benefit from the added strength and running efficiency when you shift to speed play. When speed sessions begin, hill training is terminated.

REMEMBER TO PUT THE PLAY IN HILL PLAY

By picking an interesting hill, you can improve your motivation and fun. You may vary the cadence or turnover of your legs in segments of the hill. When you have a hill play group, there is always the potential for more fun. (Just be sure that you aren't running faster than you should.)

HILL PLAY

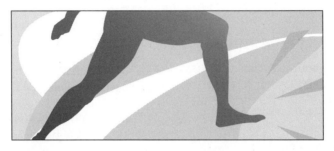

HILL PLAY SESSIONS

WHEN?

On non-long-run weekends, before marathon speed play begins

WARM-UP AND WARM-DOWN

A good walk of five minutes gets the blood flowing and the tendons and muscles warmed up. Start running very slowly, and jog for at least .5 mile before doing any hills. The warm-down should reverse the warm-up. Runners and competitors could add four to eight acceleration-gliders just before the hills and could increase the warm-up and warm-down to at least one mile.

HOW STEEP

The incline of the hill can increase to the maximums listed: one to two percent for both beginner groups, three to four percent for runners, and five to six percent for competitors. The grade is measured from horizontal being zero percent and perpendicular being 100 percent.

HILL PLAY ORGANIZATION

DEFINITIONS

Beginners have been running for less than three months and have never done any kind of speed play.

Advanced beginners have been running for more than three months but have never done speed play.

Runners have been running for more than six months and have done some speed play.

Competitors have been running for years and have done regular periods of speed play.

BEGINNER HILL PLAY

Grade: (one to two percent) so easy that you barely feel the incline

Distance of hill segment: 50-60 meters long (about half of a city block)

Pace: about the same speed as your easy running on flat land (no huffing or puffing)

Recovery: walk slowly down the hill, and walk at the bottom for as long as needed

How many hills? Repeat the hill, as before:

Hill Form

The resistance of the hill will strengthen the lower legs through repetition. Bouncing, high push-offs and long striding are counter-productive to marathon hill form. Many runners aren't reminded about their form imperfections on the flat, but the extra effort required going up will aggravate form flaws. Your goal is to find the way of running which is easier, lighter on your feet, and which requires less effort. By increasing leg and foot turnover, you can often run faster while you run easier.

Run relaxed: Don't contract the muscles or strain to keep the right alignment.

Posture upright: Head is over shoulders, over hips, and all are lined up over the feet as they assume the weight of your body. Your alignment should be perpendicular to the horizontal and not the incline of the hill. In this way, you're most efficiently distributing the weight of your body as it interacts with gravity.

Short stride: Keep shortening the stride until you feel a slight relaxing of the hamstring muscles (back of thigh). If your stride is too short, you'll feel that you're slowing down due to choppy steps and loss of fluid motion. Too long a stride is noted by tightness in the hamstring and/ or the quadriceps muscle (front of thigh) and significantly more effort required for only a small increase in speed.

Feet low to ground: The less you have to lift your feet, the more effort you'll conserve.

Quick turnover: Those who want to improve speed and strength can gradually increase the cadence or turnover of your legs and feet.

As the hill gets tougher: Keep reducing stride length, while trying to maintain or increase turnover of the legs and feet. Remember, stay light on your feet and keep feet low to the ground.

two to three hills on the first session, with an additional hill each week until you reach a comfortable number (maximum eight to 10 hills).

ADVANCED BEGINNER HILL PLAY

Grade: (one to two percent) easy so that you barely feel the incline

Distance of hill segment: 50-80 meters long

Pace: a little faster than the speed of your easy running on the flat, but no sprinting

Recovery: walk slowly down the hill and walk for threre to five minutes at the bottom (more if needed)

How many hills? Repeat the hill, as before, starting with two to three hills and building to eight to 10 hills,

RUNNER HILL PLAY

Grade: (three to four percent) easy for the runner but greater than that for the beginner

Distance of hill segment: 150-300 meters

Pace: no faster than 10K race pace and usually slower

Recovery: walk slowly down the hill and walk for three to five minutes at the bottom

How many hills? repeat the hill, as before, starting with two to four and building to eight to 10 hills

[Note: The distance range is longer in hill play for marathons than that for shorter distance events. Make sure that you keep stride length short to maintain turnover without tension in leg muscles. Avoid overexertion, and avoid extending your lower leg too far in front of you.]

COMPETITOR HILL PLAY

Grade: (five to six percent) pick a grade which will allow you to maintain a steady speed and turnover over the top. If that means less of a grade, that's fine.

Distance of hill segment: 300-600 meters

Pace: about 10K race pace, adjust to maintain smoothness, relaxed leg muscles, and turnover

Recovery: jog and walk down the hill, walk for two to three minutes at the bottom

How many hills? Repeat the hill as before, starting with three to four and building to eight to 10 hills.

[Note: The distance range is longer in hill play for marathons than that for shorter distance events. Make sure that you keep stride length short to maintain turnover without tension in leg muscles to avoid overexertion and to avoid extending your lower leg too far in front of you.]

NO COMPETITION!

Competing is not allowed during hill sessions. (Legs in varying stages of conditioning, which are not warmed up as they should be, can be pushed to injury when individuals try to stay with someone who is feeling good and in better condition than he/she is.)

LONGER HILLS FOR THE SPEED DEMONS

- Run longer hills
  - Run hills which are 30 to 50 percent shorter

- Run the hills with no strong push off
  - Run smoothly, but hard

- Maintain a quick, smooth cadence
  - Run up with more strength

- Feel that stride length is a bit short
  - Maintain a stride which feels normal

Q- Won't these longer hills keep you tired?

A- Not if you run them with the short stride indicated above. Through practice, you'd be amazed how fast you can turn your legs over when going uphill. By not overextending the hamstring or calf muscles, your legs feel reasonably fresh, even at the end of the session.

Q- How do you pick up the turnover?

A- Don't expect it to happen all at once. First, ensure that the hamstrings are loose and ready to respond to a quick turnover.

- The difference between the shortened stride and a stride which feels like it is giving full extension may be only an inch or so.

- You only need a slight stride shortening to relax the main running muscles.

- Relaxed muscles are more resilient, can respond quicker, and return to do it again quicker. This means quicker turnover.

Jeff Galloway:

Short uphill stride helped me run my fastest marathon...at age 35

The 1980 Houston-Tenneco course had several significant rolling sections, and this worried me. I had strained my hamstring eight weeks before the race and had to lay off from fast running. As the time closed in on the marathon date, I discovered that the only speed sessions I could do were hill repeats with a shortened stride. While the injury was not fully healed, I picked up the turnover and jokingly told myself that I was the fastest "short strider" in the U.S.! The hill's resistance gave me the quality of speed play needed to run a high-performance marathon. The stride reduction released the tension on the hamstring and allowed it to continue healing. Not only did I recover while doing quality work, I passed about two dozen competitors while going up hills in the race itself. They were huffing and puffing, and I was zooming by at my normal respiration rate. I ran strong to the finish in a lifetime best of 2:16.

137

SPEED PLAY

THE RIGHT TO HAVE FUN

Let me introduce you to a new type of speed session...one which offers the invigoration of going fast and the satisfaction of knowing you're getting better. You'll be able to joke with friends or yourself throughout the session and provide games which keep the experience interesting.

Starting now, we have abolished the old, archaic speed work and replaced it with a clean, upbeat and uplifting speed play. You're going to like it so much that you'll finish each session wanting to do more. And because you don't do more than assigned, you'll look forward to the next session.

Set up your speed session in an interesting area. You can also change the venue if variety helps make it more interesting. Bring music, a clock (if possible), and banners which are funny, inspirational or instill pride. Some runners bring along a few posters with uplifting graphics.

Many runners like to read something before the speed session. Humorous, entertaining, informative...any reading will offer the chance that the left brain will be preoccupied so that it won't bother you with negative messages and excuses.

Running with a group will improve morale, increase and maintain motivation, and make the session more fun. The requirements of the group are as follows:

* You can start together,

* But don't run the pace of someone who is faster than you.

* When in doubt, take more rest between repetitions, even if the rest of the group is not.

DO THINGS THAT ENSURE FUN

* Require each member to bring to each session 1) a joke, 2) a controversial viewpoint, and 3) some spicy news.

* Set up games in which runners of all abilities can run the same repetition, with the winner being the one closer to his or her assigned pace.

* Alternate the jokes, etc. so that there is a continuous flow of entertainment.

* Use the walking between repetitions for other fun activities.

WHERE

A track is not necessary. Road segments, a park, well-packed trails or other safe venues are just as good. Wherever you run, make sure that the mile is accurately measured. During the first few sessions, a track can help by giving regular timed feedback, usually every quarter mile. This helps to set the internal pace clocks more quickly. Also important is the ability to hear music as you make the loops of the oval. When choosing a road segment, avoid downhills that are too steep or give you too much advantage. Likewise, avoid uphills which are too steep and will force you to either slow down or overwork to maintain pace.

SPEED AND ENDURANCE... SIMULTANEOUSLY

Running faster in the marathon requires that you develop a special type of speed-endurance. This means that the actual pace of the speed segments is only slightly faster than marathon goal pace. You're developing the capacity to maintain a moderate pace over a long distance. Compared with speed sessions for shorter distance racing goals, those for the marathon emphasize building endurance by

- running longer repetitions (usually mile repeats)

- increasing the number of repetitions: up to eight, 10 or 12 mile repeats (Faster marathons require more repetitions.)

LEARNING HOW TO PACE YOURSELF

You'll gain a sense of pace at the same time you're developing the capacity to run mile after mile in the time you need. It's actually detrimental to run the mile repeats faster than your schedule prescribes (20 seconds faster than goal pace). If you exceed this speed limit, even in the beginning of the speed session, it becomes difficult for your

internal pace clock to acquire the pace judgement needed in the marathon itself. A fast start will either leave you struggling at the end of the session or produce tired muscles which require a long recovery.

RECOVERY, RECOVERY, RECOVERY!

Finally, the need for recovery cannot be overemphasized. Because the long runs and the speed sessions are long and fatiguing, everything possible should be done to speed up this important process.

- Strict adherence to the pace of the speed repetitions to avoid going too fast

- Lots of walking as rest between each mile repeat—when in doubt, walk some more

- Enough easy days (and easy running) between the weekend sessions

139

HOW OFTEN?

To encourage the adaptations and improvements in form, rhythm, etc., speed sessions must be done regularly, that is, on most of the non-long weekends starting about 16 weeks before the marathon (see the schedules for specific frequency). By adding some other innovations to your program, such as tempo or pace runs during the week, you'll maintain and extend the faster running form and performance benefits gained from mile repeat sessions into all of your runs.

PICKING YOUR GOAL

The most important part of the speed development process is the very first step: picking a goal which is realistic for you. It's okay if your goal is slower than you are capable of currently running. This is a strategy which has led to many personal records. By setting yourself up for a performance that has some challenge but is realistic, you will take pressure off, stay in

Time-tested, realistic goal prediction:

1. Run at least three 5K races on non-long-run weekends.

2. Take two or three of your fastest ones and average them.

3. Chart your equivalent performance on the Predicting Race Performance in the back of this book.

your right brain longer, and often achieve at a much higher level.

If your goal is too far ahead of your ability level, then you set yourself up for disappointment and fatigue. By overestimating your capacity, you'll force yourself to run the speed sessions too fast. You just won't recover between speed days and long runs.

You'll be fine-tuning your racing form and technique after you've run two or three 5K events. If the courses were hilly or the weather conditions were adverse, you may conservatively estimate the time you honestly believe you could run under better conditions. The prediction table gives equivalent performances for many race distances, including the marathon, which have been very accurate.

What a great reality check! If your 5K performances don't predict the time you'd like, swallow your pride and select a less ambitious time goal. This means that you'll be slowing down the pace of the mile repeats and the early pace in the marathon.

Always be conservative in choosing your goal. If the 5K performances predict a 4:30

marathon, shoot for 4:40 or 4:45. It's always better to finish the marathon knowing that you could have run faster: you've already started the momentum and motivation to do it.

WARM-UP

Whatever speed play format you choose, get the blood flowing through the muscles in a gentle warm-up. This introduction to exercise allows the tendons, ligaments and muscles to warm up together and begin working as a team. A good warm-up will decrease the chance of injury and increase the intuitive cooperation of components within the muscles.

* Walk for five to 10 minutes.

* Jog VERY slowly for five to 10 minutes.

* Jog another five to 10 minutes at a comfortable pace.

* Do four to eight acceleration-GLIDERS.

* Walk for five minutes.

STRETCHING

If you can't resist doing a gentle stretching routine before running, be very careful. Research has shown that stretching before running doesn't help you for that run, and it may increase your chance of injury. It's easy to overstretch a muscle that hasn't been engaged in much activity. This will leave the muscles tighter than before and more open to injury.

Don't make the most detrimental stretching mistake of trying to "loosen up" a tight muscle by stretching the heck out of it. A slow walk followed by very slow running and walking for 10 to 15 minutes will allow the muscles to relax and warm up better than any stretch routine. Tight muscles tell you that you need to ease off on them until they feel loose.

On these days some runners require three to five miles of super easy walk-running to warm up. As we age, we need more slow warm-up distance at the beginning of every run. When it comes to the warm-up, slower is always better.

The best time for stretching is probably just before bedtime. If you must stretch before running, do so very gently. Above all, never push into a tense or tight muscle but maintain a relaxed extension.

[For more stretching information and specific stretches, see GBR, pp. 158-169.]

REPEAT MILE INTERVALS

The most popular form of marathon speed play is that of "interval training," used by world-class athletes for most of the 20th century. In this format, measured segments (repetitions) are run at a pace that is slightly faster than marathon goal pace, followed by a rest interval. This process is repeated many times. Shorter distance goal races, such as the 5K and 10K, use shorter repetitions of 400 to 800 meters. The longer repetitions, such as mile repeats, have been overwhelmingly the most successful distance in the Galloway program. Thousands have used mile repeats to improve their marathon times.

While 800-meter repetitions can give a significant training effect for the marathon, the mile distance helps to mold together the components of marathon form and exertion at one time.

LONGER REPETITIONS, SUCH AS THE MILE:

- force your legs and feet to find more efficient ways of running, by eliminating or significantly reducing extraneous motions and getting the most efficient "lift-off" from each step

- develop better pace judgment, teaching you not to start races (and speed play) too fast

- help the internal systems to work together and become more efficient: muscles, pacing, intuitive connections, and instinctive efficiency adjustments

- fine-tune the components of performance, such as energy sources to the muscle, waste removal, hidden resources to keep going, etc.

- develop the mental strength to continue running at a good pace even after fatigue sets in

- teach you when to keep going and when to stop to avoid damage

PACE OF REPEAT MILES

Each mile should be run about 20 seconds faster than you want to run in the race itself, followed by a walk of at least 400 meters. If you feel much more comfortable with shorter distance repetitions, go ahead with 800-meter or 1200-meter reps. Your pace on the shorter reps can be increased to an average of 25 to 30 seconds per mile faster than marathon goal pace. It's still better to do repeat miles or to alternate between miles and reps of shorter distance.

ADJUST FOR HEAT, HUMIDITY, ETC.

Even during the extreme heat of summer, you can continue doing speed sessions, but be careful. If you notice yourself or anyone in your group having symptoms of heat disease, stop the session and get medical attention immediately.

The best time of the day to do speed sessions on warm days is very early in the morning, before the sun rises. Be advised, however, that when the temperature is above 65 degrees, you *must* run slower (and may also cut the distance of the reps to 800 or 1200 meters). Instead of 20 seconds faster per mile than goal pace, make adjustments as follows:

When the temperature is 65 degrees, run mile repeats 18 seconds per mile faster.

When the temperature is 70 degrees, run mile repeats 15 seconds per mile faster.

When the temperature is 75 degrees, run mile repeats 12 seconds per mile faster.

When the temperature is 80 degrees, run mile repeats 9 seconds per mile faster.

When the temperature is 82 degrees, run mile repeats 5 seconds per mile faster.

When the temperature is above 85 degrees, don't do the session; wait for a cooler time.

* Note: when you feel that there is any possibility of heat disease or a cardiovascular problem, abandon the exercise, cool off and get help.

WALK BETWEEN EACH MILE REPEAT

It is better to walk between the repetitions to minimize fatigue and recovery. Most runners should walk 400 to 600 meters between each of the repeat miles. Walk more if you feel the need. The extra walking will not reduce the training effect of the speed session. You receive the same conditioning from speed play of 8 x 1 mile with a 800-meter walk as you do from 8 x 1 mile with a 400-meter walk. If you have a heart rate monitor, keep walking until the heart rate goes below 70 percent of your maximum heart rate.

HOW MANY MILE REPEATS?

If you haven't done any speed play before, start with only one or two mile repeats. Veterans can begin with four to five repeats, and others can pick a starting number somewhere in between. On each session, increase the number of repetitions by one or two until you reach the upper limit for your respective goal:

Time Goal	# of Mile Repeats
4:01 and slower	6 x 1 mile
3:30-4 hours	8 x 1 mile
3:15-3:29	10 x 1 mile
3:00-3:14	12 x 1 mile
Below 3 hours	13 x 1 mile

PRACTICE *GLIDING* DURING EACH MILE

As you alternate between the prime running motion and your gliding motion, you'll save the muscles which do most of the work. The reduced demands of the gliding motion allow the main running muscles to regain a small amount of resiliency even as you are moving at a significant speed. By gliding early and often in speed sessions and in the marathon itself, you'll feel stronger at the end and will recover faster from each speed session.

Most importantly, you'll develop the teamwork between muscles which will bestow great performance benefit in the marathon itself.

142

The gliders should be a natural part of your running, but be sure to start them within the first 500 meters of each mile rep. A glider of 50 to 100 meters, done about every 400 to 600 meters, is often enough to help you integrate gliding into your racing routine at the same time that it helps you fine-tune your running technique. Be sure to go back and re-read the section on acceleration-GLIDERS to reinforce the concept.

FARTLEK

Literally meaning "speed play," this free-form method of speed development can accomplish all of the objectives of interval training and add a mental strengthening component to your training. Used as a substitute for interval training or other speed play, fartlek is usually performed on non-long-run weekends instead of mile repeats.

- The "speed" part of fartlek should equal the total distance equal to the number of mile repeats you would have done on the track, according to the time goal schedule you are following.

- Make sure that you're resting the legs by walking between the speed segments.

- By shifting back and forth between use of muscle groups, you'll develop greater performance capacity. For example, instead of running the same pace throughout a fartlek session, you can alternate between pace running, accelerations, gliding and speed-effort.

EXAMPLE:

The speed segments should be at least 3/4 mile long but give better marathon conditioning if they are one mile or longer (1600 to 3000 meters). Let's say that you choose a segment that is 1.2 miles long (about 2000 meters).

1. Start the segment at marathon pace.

2. Several times during the first .6 mile (1000 meters), put in some acceleration-gliders which would vary between 100 and 200 meters, each time going back to marathon pace. In other words, start at marathon pace, accelerate for 50 meters and glide for 50 to 100 meters, returning to marathon pace. Repeat this process two or three times.

3. From about .8 mile to 1.1 mile, shift into "speed effort" and pick up the pace to about 25 to 30 seconds per mile faster than marathon goal pace, and then glide during the last .1 mile.

4. Walk for three to five minutes between each fartlek session.

5. Four of these fartlek segments may be done in place of a 6 x 1 mile marathon speed session.

6. The three other segments may vary between 1.3 and 1.8 miles (2200-3000 meters).

FARTLEK RUNNING MODES:

- marathon pace—running smooth and natural so that you feel comfortable at that pace

- accelerations—picking up the turnover for a short distance, not spending much effort

- gliders—relaxed and quick turnover motion which follows an acceleration with practically no effort expended

- speed effort—picking up the turnover for a longer distance, running faster than goal pace. You'll spend some effort doing this, but try to stay smooth and comfortable for the duration of the pick-up.

MENTAL STRENGTH

The mental tenacity you receive from fartlek training is enhanced by not setting specific limits on where you'll end each segment, each acceleration, each glider, etc. By going beyond artificial barriers, you'll learn to intuitively coordinate the performance demands of the running body with available resources. In so doing, you reduce the chance of negative messages from the left brain when things get tough in speed sessions and in the race itself. You'll still get those "pings" from the left side, but they just won't bother you as much.

Fartlek desensitizes you to the discomfort and uncertainty of pushing, gliding and pacing beyond your current limits. As in other training components, fartlek must be done regularly to force the systems to work together, to coax out adaptations from the exercising muscle cells, and to develop the intuitive capacity to become more efficient in every way. By pushing through mental and physical barriers at the same time, you'll find yourself continuing to run when tired or uncertain. Fartlek develops a sense of focus and resource coordination not found in other forms of training.

[For more on fartlek, see Galloway's Book On Running.]

TEMPO TRAINING—AT MARATHON GOAL PACE

During the week, time goal marathoners can run parts of the easier runs at marathon pace. As long as the legs, feet and cardiovascular system have all recovered from the weekend's long or speed sessions, this race-pace running gives you a chance

to lock into the exact cadence "clock" you need for your goal.

After a warmup, which includes a few acceleration-gliders, run one to two miles at marathon pace. Your goal is to make marathon pace seem "normal." If the paces and effort levels of hill training and speed sessions are adjusted to your current ability (and you've recovered from the long or speed runs on the weekend), you should feel "at home" with marathon pace after a few repetitions.

Ease into each of these "marathon goal miles." As you get up to speed, you want to feel smooth and efficient at the pace you've chosen for the marathon. Even doing one or two of these every other day can help further your "pace education."

A walk of 400 to 800 meters between these "paced miles" (or a jog slow jog of 800 meters or more) should leave you completely recovered. It's important to remember that this is not supposed to be a stressful speed session: no significant effort required to do each mile and no significant fatigue afterward. If you're working hard to maintain your marathon pace in these sessions, jog for the rest of the session. This either means that you're just not ready for the chosen pace or you haven't recovered from the runs of the previous week.

TROUBLESHOOTING SPEED SESSION PROBLEMS

Q: *I can't finish a speed session*—my legs just can't keep going at the pace needed. What's wrong?

A: If you're having trouble maintaining pace on the mile repeats, there are several possibilities:

144

1. Your goal is too ambitious for your current fitness level—adjust to slower repetitions.

2. You went out too fast in the first part of the speed session—slow down in the beginning.

3. Fatigue from other sessions is still there—you need more rest days or easier rest days.

4. You need more rest between mile repeats—double the walking between each mile.

Q: *I feel great on the repeat mile sessions* and have no trouble running them 40 seconds per mile faster than my goal pace, *but my legs don't 'have it' in the marathon itself.* Won't running the mile repeats faster help me run faster in the marathon?

A: No! You're actually hurting yourself by running the mile repeats faster than your assigned time (20 seconds faster than goal pace). The 20-second pace increase will develop the perfor-

mance capacity and the pace judgement which has a proven record of marathon success. The effort required to go faster than this can keep you tired for many days and compromise the other quality sessions in your program. Stick with the schedule for your best chance of success.

Q: *Between the mile repetitions, I've been jogging instead of walking* because I've heard that I'll get in better shape. Is this true?

A: No. By doing more walking between the hard repetitions, you won't lose any of the conditioning of that speed session. The extra rest during each repetition or speed segment will help the legs start recovering from that speed session while you're doing it. Walking between mile repeats performs the same function as walking breaks during the long run, keeping the running muscles from getting overextended. If you've been running at the pace that you *should have* on the mile repeats, liberal walking breaks in mile repeat sessions will allow you to recover within a day or two in most cases.

145

[For more on the practical aspects of speed play, see the "Mile Repeats" chapter.]

MILE REPEATS

REMEMBER THE PROBLEMS OF BEING TOO EXUBERANT:

- Running the first two to three mile repeats too fast

- Going too fast during the first 400 to 800 meters of each mile repeat

- Trying to stay up with someone who is faster than you (or is showing off)

- Overstriding, especially when you start to get tired

Walk more than you think you need between the mile repeats. This helps your group to stay together and will speed your recovery.

YOU DON'T GAIN ANYTHING FROM RUNNING FASTER THAN ASSIGNED PACE!

By running the mile repeats faster than your schedule says, you actually hurt your chances of achieving your goal.

- Even 15 to 20 seconds per mile too fast on the track can lead to extra tiredness and slow recovery. Such fatigue is cumulative and is often carried into the marathon itself. When you reach the last four to six miles of the marathon, this

tiredness will come back to haunt you. your legs will lack the rebound to maintain or increase speed to the finish.

- Your pace clock is messed up when you run too fast on the mile repeats. Running 20 seconds faster than goal pace prepares you to run that pace in the marathon between walk breaks. Your muscles and cardiovascular performance system are gearing up to do exactly what they need to do in the actual marathon. By going faster than this, you train yourself too fast in the marathon itself. This usually leads to an early pace that tires you quickly causing you to slow down at the end of the marathon.

START THE SESSION, AND EACH MILE, SLOWLY

It's always better to go out a little *slower* than you expect to average in the session. This helps the muscles gradually adjust to marathon pace, instead of sending shocks to the system. You're also teaching the energy system to be as efficient as possible.

WALK BETWEEN MILE REPEATS

You can speed up the recovery between each mile repeat and enhance overall recovery from the speed session by extending the walk break between mile repeats. When in doubt, walk an additional 100 to 200 meters. The extra walking can help the pace groups start each mile together. There is no advantage in cutting the rest interval short (unless you're planning to break the world marathon record). You receive the same benefit from the speed session with lots of walking between miles, as with taking a little walking or jogging between. When you're fully rested between each repeat, you not only recover faster, you're better able to focus on the important aspects of 1) running each mile in the time assigned and 2) running the number of mile repeats listed for that session.

MARATHON RACE FORM

Using your running muscles in the same way will cause them to fatigue quicker. If you regularly change your running form modes, even during a mile repeat, you'll allow the calf and the hamstring to relax. Even a slight relaxation like this, when done regularly during the mile repeat, is often enough to infuse a little leg resiliency. By the end of the speed session, you'll still feel strong, even if you're getting tired, and you'll experience a faster recovery between this exercise and the next long run or race. This process teaches marathon muscles to automatically shift usage during the 26-mile journey itself.

It's crucial to shift early and shift often. You don't have to go more than 50 to 100 meters when gliding, etc., but you must start early and do it regularly on each mile repeat to receive the benefits.

SHIFTING GEARS INTO VARIOUS FORM MODES:

- *Race form*: About 90 percent of your running in the speed sessions and the marathon will be done using this form.

This is a very efficient running motion at a pace that is 20 seconds per mile faster than goal marathon pace. There is little effort required when running in this mode, if you're actually in condition to run the pace you are predicting.

- *Gliding*: Every 300 to 600 meters of running at race form, let your feet shift lower to the ground and glide for 50 to 100 meters. You'll feel very little effort when you glide correctly, as you use mostly momentum and mechanical efficiency to move. When gliding correctly, you'll lose only two to three meters every 100 meters. Practice gliding on all of your runs to develop the most efficient motion, using the least effort while moving at the best speed. Practice will teach you how to glide very quickly.

- *Efficient rhythm accelerations (ERA)*: These are very short (10 to 20 yard) leg turnovers. While maintaining race form, pick up the rhythm or cadence of your feet and legs. This will gain back the two to three meters you lost when gliding. Don't lift your knees, don't extend your lower leg out in front of you, and never sprint (run all out). This is meant to be a very short pick-up which shouldn't cause you to "huff and puff." The only change to your running form will be an increase in the rhythm of your legs.

Combining modes: You are the captain of your running ship and may choose the rotation of running form desired. Here's a suggestion of how to arrange the modes during a one-mile repeat: Start with race form for 300 to 600 meters, then glide for 50 to 100 meters, return to race form for 200 to 300 meters, put in an ERA for 10 to 20 meters, then glide, and ERA, shifting back to race form, and gliding in.

FUN INNOVATIONS

The greatest benefit of the shifting process is the opportunity to transform what used to be a *work*out into a *play*out. By finding at least a few ways to divert yourself and/or the members of your speed group, the session becomes an event to look forward to. You're taking an experience which gives significant challenge and satisfaction and combining it with incidents of fun generated by the chemistry of individuals. Here are a few suggestions of how various groups have helped speed become playful:

- *Diversions*: Brief, improv "skits" in which individuals will do something to entertain the others. By planning these, the members of the speed group stay in touch during the week and build a sense of community.

- *Controversy*: It only takes two individuals in a group to have a different viewpoint on an issue for the whole group to have some fun with it.

- *Games*: Even silly children's games like "tag" can lighten up the end of a difficult session. Avoid the temptation to overextend the stride length, etc.

PACE JUDGEMENT

One of the very best lessons to be learned in mile repeats is how to intuitively sense your pace. This will help you conserve resources in the marathon, as well as in other distance races and workouts. Even with the shifting of form modes, you'll learn pace judgement as you increase the number of mile repeats.

148

Setting up the group mile repeat session

- Groups are organized according to marathon time goal so that there are at least three to five runners in each one to a maximum of about 15 (with an ideal size of eight to 10).

- Timing: It's ideal to have a digital display clock so that each runner can see his or her time each lap. The next best situation is to have a volunteer reading out the time each lap. This job can rotate among the runners who are walking between mile repeats. In each case, the continuous time is read out. Each runner could track his or her pace by noting the time at the start of each mile and subtracting it from the total time at the finish. Example: A runner waited for the clock to click over to exactly 30 minutes as she started her fourth mile repeat. She finished in 40:40, doing the mile exactly in 10:40 (for an 11 minute per mile time goal pace in the marathon).

- Each group starts together, with some "straggling" throughout each mile. Within each group there will usually be three to five different pace goals represented, requiring individuals to be very aware of his or her goal pace from the beginning of each mile.

- Each pace group should have a group leader who helps to infuse fun, holds back those who are going out too fast, and encourages more walking between repeats for those who aren't resting enough.

GETTING BETTER AS WE BECOME MORE MATURE

Age Issues

"I feel better, at age 78, than I have felt in my 45 years of running. Slower, yes, but much happier with my running."

I met a runner recently, after a 10-mile race, who was 93 years old. He was mentally alert and just as fired up about finishing as any of the other runners. The number of runners is growing, but the segment of those over 80 is growing faster. I'm proud to say that my father is one of them. These folks are clearly showing that the joys of running continue at any age if you're more conservative and use walk breaks.

Yes, you must add more rest, run slower and put strategic walk breaks into your runs. But the endorphins are the same at 80 as at 20. And the benefits of extra vitality and a positive attitude cannot be derived from any pills or any other activity I know. An 86-year-old man who ran 30 miles a week told me that his sedentary wife got on him constantly for not settling down and acting his age. He said the problem was mostly solved when he started running during her regular naps. His mileage actually increased and she didn't know any better.

No bone and joint damage after more than 40 years of running!

Twenty five years ago, many well-meaning doctors (who didn't run) told me that if I

continued to run I could expect to be using a cane to walk by the time I reached the age of 55. I'm proud to say that I've passed that barrier now and am averaging over 60 miles a week, enjoying every one of them.

I'm actually part of a study. In the early 70s, the labs of David Costill, Ph.D. (physiologist) and Dr. Kenneth Cooper (Aerobics Institute founder) joined resources in a landmark study of world-class athletes. I was proud to be invited as a subject of this study. Over the past decade, these two labs have started bringing us back to see how much we've deteriorated. After doing bone scans, CAT scans, and X-rays of all major joint areas, I received a clean bill of orthopedic health.

I'm not alone. Two studies have been done on runners over 40 and 50-year periods. Both showed less incidence of arthritis and other joint problems among the runners. Other experts have told me that runners who are genetically predisposed to arthritis will get it but later in life and with less severe symptoms.

If running could destroy joints and cartilage, I would have done it. During my competitive years, I pushed the edge, going over it into injury about every three weeks. I was so obsessed with performance that I continued to run, as hard as possible, until

I could not. In dozens of cases, I had to take weeks or months off from running because I refused to take a day or two off at the first symptoms. Needless to say, I've had hundreds of injuries.

Fortunately, our bodies are programmed to adapt to running and walking and make adjustments. One X-ray specialist told me that I had the knees of a healthy 18-year-old. So now I want to pass on the adjustments I've made which not only have made running more enjoyable but also have kept me from having an overuse injury for over 14 years.

VITALITY AND ATTITUDE

For a fit person, age is not a factor. Sure, my muscles don't feel as good as they did even 10 years ago—but that doesn't matter, as long as I check my ego at the door as I leave the house. It was a wonderful revelation that slowing down allows you to feel great—just about every day. I'll also describe two other factors which speed recovery and make the exercise fun: running every other day and walk-breaks.

The quality of my life has been based upon two factors: vitality and attitude. Running maintains both at the highest possible level. For most marathoners over 50, attitude is often maintained at a lifetime best level.

I believe that we become more introspective as we age. Running provides a positive outlet for this continuous inward journey and more time to oneself to organize the brain and get things on track.

For runners over 50, fatigue is related to the number of running days per week and only indirectly the number of miles per week. For example, many runners have improved by taking an extra day or two off per week, while maintaining the same weekly mileage.

Our recovery rate slows down each year. By taking more days off from running, we speed up the rebuilding process. At the same time, a higher level of performance can often be achieved by increasing the number of miles run on a running day. Speed and endurance sessions which are specifically designed for the marathon, for example, have allowed many runners to improve as they have pushed up to the next age group.

ALTERNATIVE EXERCISE

On non-running days, an alternative exercise will boost performance without pounding. The exertions which produce the most direct improvement are water running and cross-country ski machine exercise. Walking, rowing and bicycle sessions are great for recovery and bestow some indirect benefits. Swimming and weight training help to balance the muscle development of the body but don't help to improve your running. Stair machines, high impact aerobics and leg strength exercises are not recommended and can slow down the recovery process.

How Many Days Off Per Week?

40 year-old marathoners need three days off from running.

Over 50-year-old marathoners should shift to every other day running.

Over-60 folks should run three days per week and monitor for fatigue.

The over-70 crowd can maintain a significant level of performance by running three days a week and taking walk breaks on every run.

Performance Tips for the Over-40 Crowd: getting better as you get older

Run twice a day on the running days:

Usually the first run is very slow.

Accelerations or hills can be done on the second one—but be careful.

Accelerations maintain a high leg turnover:

Marathoners in their 50s can do accelerations on each of the afternoon runs.

Marathoners in their 60s can do accelerations twice a week on the afternoon runs.

Marathoners in their 70s can do accelerations once a week on an afternoon run.

Remember that accelerations are merely increased turnover drills and not sprints.

If your legs are tired or too tight, don't do the accelerations.

Long Run Pace: Three minutes per mile slower than you *could* run that distance on that day.

Yes, this is a minute slower than younger runners would go, but it will give you the same endurance, based upon the mileage covered. Remember to account for heat, humidity, hills, and other factors as you set your pace. I start my long runs about four minutes per mile slower than I could race the distance, and I not only feel great at the end of the run, but in two or three days, I'm almost always recovered, even from a 26-miler. I know, I can see the looks on some of your competitive faces. Yes, it will take a longer time to cover these long runs, but this just gives you more time to brag about your grandchildren. In our marathon training groups, grandparents have a priceless opportunity: a captive audience for several hours!

Increase the length of the long run beyond 26 miles:

The purpose of the long one is to build endurance only. The slower you go, the quicker you'll recover. By having at least one long run beyond 26 miles, you can boost your endurance limit, which will allow you to maintain a hard marathon pace for a longer time in the marathon itself. When you go the extra distance, it is crucial to take the walk breaks and adhere to the pacing guidelines. For maximum performance, the longest run should be 28 to 29 miles. Again, you must go extra slowly on these extra long ones.

Take walk breaks every mile, from the beginning, to reduce fatigue:

Put one to two-minute walk breaks every three to six minutes of running from the beginning. This will reduce fatigue while you increase endurance through the long one.

Walk breaks do not reduce the endurance value of the run.

Walk Break Schedule for experienced conditioned marathoners:

40-49-year-olds—Walk one minute every five to ten minutes.

50-59-year-olds—Walk one to two minutes every five to eight minutes.

60-69-year-olds—Walk one to two minutes every four to six minutes.

70-75-year-olds—Walk two minutes every three to six minutes.

76 and over—Walk two to three minutes every three to five minutes.

Alternate long runs with other weekend runs:

Until the long one reaches 18, you may run it every other weekend. After that point, run long every third weekend. When the long run reaches 26 miles, you have the option of taking four weeks between. On non-long-run weekends, you may run a slow one of half the distance of the long one or race a 5K—but no longer than a 5K.

Accelerations:

Keep your feet low to the ground—stride short. While staying light on your feet, pick up the rhythm after about 100 to 150 meters, glide by reducing the effort while maintaining the turnover.

AGE MAGNIFIES THE DAMAGE

Even young athletes will suffer from the following mistakes. Because recovery rate slows down each year, the negative effects of "stepping over the line" are more dramatic and longlasting in those of us who are... challenged by age.

Junk miles

Running a few miles on a day when you could be resting keeps the muscles from fully recovering. You're better off not running at all on an easy day and adding those miles to a running day—either as part of an extra warm-up or warm-down or as a separate run.

Starting too fast

Whether on a slow training run or in a race, a pace that is too fast in the beginning will cause a slowdown at the end and/or damage to the muscles, requiring a longer recovery time. It is always better to start out at a slower pace than you think you can maintain. Practically all personal best (over 50) performances are accomplished by running a negative split: the second half faster than the first.

Overstride

When runners of all ages err with the length of their running stride, they tend to overstride. The negative consequences are greater for those over 50 in terms of tendon and muscle damage and the recovery time required for healing. Runners are most likely to overstride when tired at the end of long runs, races or speed sessions. To avoid this problem, work on a lighter step with a shorter stride. The primary sensation is a lowering of tension in the hamstring muscle.

Overstretching

When there is tension in the running muscles, many runners mistakenly try to "stretch it out." Massage is a better treatment mode in this situation. But there's hope. When you feel that you've overdone it, don't stretch the area for an extended period of time, talk to a therapist about massage, and ask your doctor if anti-inflammatory medication is okay.

As in the other situations mentioned above, the damage takes longer to heal when you're past the age of 50. The best strategy is, as always, prevention.

Overexertion in speed or hill sessions

Young or old, every runner pushes too far when doing higher performance sessions.

Again, it is the older runners who have to pay dearly with a longer "down" time when this happens. Be particularly careful when doing faster running than in the recent past.

When increasing the number of speed or hill repetitions, do so very gradually. By taking more rest between repetitions, you'll reduce the chance of overuse injury and speed up the recovery time after each session. When doing a repeat mile session, for example, 40-year-old marathoners should take at least a 400 meter walk between miles. Fifty-year-olds need at least an 800 meter walk between, 60-year-olds at least a five-minute walk interval, and those over-70 folks five to 10 minutes of walking.

153

My favorite marathon companion

Before I started running, I had been a fat and inactive kid. Like many boys, I wanted to be like my Dad. In the eighth grade, I tried the sport in which he had achieved "all state" status: football. At first I sensed that my temperament wasn't quite right for the sport ("Hit 'em harder, Galloway. Make 'em feel your impact."). By the end of that season, I *knew* that my temperament wasn't right for that sport that was supposed to "make a man of you."

My dad steered me into cross country, where I felt instantly at home. I'm only guessing, but any parent would tend to want his or her child to hang out with the type of kids that choose to run distance events. Then, as today, at just about any high school, these athletes are better students and leaders of many school activities. I found them to be interesting and fun to run with. When my progress seemed to stagnate, my dad brought me some reading material about various training programs, including those of the great New Zealand coach Arthur Lydiard. These readings gave me the principles which I use to this day.

As I moved on to college, I became more fit as my sedentary Dad increased his fat. By my mid-20s, continuing to read about fitness, I became concerned about my father's health as he tipped the scales above 200 pounds. Not aware of the way our health is influenced by such factors, he complained about aches and pains and displayed an increasingly more negative attitude in general. He read the book <u>Aerobics</u> and other readings I gave him, but his sedentary behavior didn't change. On one occasion, when I suggested walking around the park in front of his office, he explained how his varicose veins and allergies prevented him from exercising. I stopped arguing with him.

A high school reunion, at the age of 52, changed his life. At this gathering of the Moultrie, Georgia class of '37, it was discovered that out of 25 boys who had been on the football team from that class, 13 had died of lifestyle, degenerative diseases. Out of all the activities of the weekend, this fact weighed on his mind on the three and a half hour ride back. By the time he turned into his driveway, Elliott Galloway realized that he could be the next one to drop from the roster, and he was determined to do something about this.

Starting at a particular telephone pole he set off that first day, determined to run the three-mile loop across the street from his office. Reality was harsh. He had to settle for only the next telephone pole, about 100 meters away. On each successive run, the goal was one additional pole, until he made it completely around. Almost two years later he was running 10K races. Seven years later, and 55 pounds lighter, he was running marathons, including one below the three-hour mark.

Having had an irregular heart rhythm for years, he decided, upon receiving doctor's orders, to finish his marathon career in 1996 at the 100th running of the Boston Marathon. He consented to letting me tag along with him. It would be my 100th marathon finish and the one I will remember for the rest of my life.

As we started, the thought hit me that the Boston Marathon had only been run for 23 times when my Dad was born. I forced him to walk at each mile mark—as best I could. You see, he doesn't listen to what I say. I had run Boston four other times, trying to do my best time in each. As we shared the scenery, the energetic crowd and the landmarks, I hardly remembered any of it. Oxygen debt must erase your memory cells. This was a day for savoring, and we did.

As we turned the corner and saw the finish structure, my Dad took off. We were zooming down the final straight as the clock ticked away towards a time barrier which we were determined to break: six hours. We did: 5:59:48. He told anyone who asked about the race that he would have run much faster if I hadn't slowed him down.

Now that I've pushed past the 50-year barrier, my Dad is my hero again. I hope I can be like him when I grow up.

154

PRACTICAL ADVICE

ACHES, PAINS AND INJURIES

By taking a day or two off from running, at the first sign of an injury, you can avoid two to three weeks, or months, off later.

WEAK LINKS

Everyone has them. Each of us, due to unique biomechanics and structured patterns of motion, tend to aggravate specific areas over and over. When we exercise too many days per week or increase intensity or mileage too rapidly, these sites are usually the first to be aggravated. This can be very positive, giving us an early warning signal to back off before we push into injury. Marathon training is more likely to reveal the weak links than most forms of exercise.

MOST COMMON SITES OF WEAK LINKS

1. Knee

2. Foot

3. Achilles Tendon

4. Ankle

BE AWARE OF AREAS WHICH

* get sore first

* are repeatedly sore, painful or inflamed

* take longer to warm up

* have been sites of injury before

* are not functioning in their usual way

As you become more sensitive to these areas, you'll take time off for recovery and treatment at the earliest of warning signs. Quick and early action will cut down on the chance that you'll have to spend weeks or months of recovery later.

IS IT AN INJURY? WHAT ARE THE SIGNS?

* Inflammation: look for swelling around the injury site

* Loss of function: the muscle, foot, tendon, etc. doesn't work the way it should

* Extended pain which increases or hurts consistently for a week or more

INFLAMMATION

This is the body's attempt to immobilize an injured area to keep you from damaging the injury further. The excess fluid around the injury notifies you that there is a problem in the weak link. Your range of motion is thereby reduced, which normally limits the extent of further damage to the area.

External swelling is usually apparent, such as the swollen area around a sprained ankle.

Internal inflammation is harder to spot. At joints, tendon connections, and in small areas of muscle, it only takes a little bit of inner swelling to reduce the capacity of the muscle and produce pain. Be very sensitive to the possible minor muscle (or tendon) pulls or strains in areas such as behind the knee, at the insertion between hamstring and butt muscle, the adductors, the abductors and the lower back muscles.

Repair and rebuilding of the muscle will be speeded up dramatically as you reduce or eliminate the inflammation around the injury.

LOSS OF FUNCTION

If the tendon, muscle or other injured part is not doing its job, then several negative forces can be working against you. By ignoring it and continuing to run, you're very likely to injure it further. If you take a day or two off from running at the beginning of an functional injury, you may avoid having to take weeks or months off later due to abusing it.

Running with an injury can produce a new injury by compensation. When the muscle, tendon, etc. doesn't function to capacity, the workload of running shifts to other components which are not designed to handle the stress. In many cases, this produces a series of "compensation" injuries.

PAIN THAT DOESN'T GO AWAY

Temporary aches and pains will come and go throughout a marathon program. These will usually be gone after a day or so, indicating that you probably don't have an injury. But if you sense an increase in pain or the pain continues for five to seven days, you should treat it as an injury (at least two days off from running, ice and other treatments as necessary). Continued pain, even without loss of function, can be an early sign of internal inflammation.

DON'T TRY TO "STRETCH OUT" A TIGHT MUSCLE!

It's a mistake to push a muscle to its stretch limits when it feels tight or is fatigued. Stretching is actually the third leading cause of injury because well-meaning runners stretch when inflammation gives the sensation of tightness. Muscles which are tight during exercise can benefit from massage, walking and a shortening of the stride length—but not stretching.

The fatigue of long runs and speed sessions will tighten the muscles and reduce strengthand range of motion. Stretching fatigued muscles will not improve their performance. It will tear the fatigued fibers, producing injury and increasing recovery time.

Don't be fooled if at first the extra stretching makes the muscles feel good. This is probably due to the endorphins released to kill the pain of the many little "rips" in the muscle or tendon caused by stretching a fatigued muscle.

You're almost certain to overstretch a tired muscle and engage the stretch reflex. This protective mechanism tightens the muscle up in order to protect it. Even while the endorphins are telling you that the muscle is feeling great, you may be tearing them

157

Moral: Stretching when you're fatigued will usually lead to some kind of stretching injury.

into a serious injury. At the end of long runs or speed sessions, fatigue will loosen the connections, allowing you to easily stretch the muscles into an overextended position.

ANTI-INFLAMMATORY MEDICATIONS CAN HELP, BUT ASK YOUR DOCTOR!

Many runners have reported that taking anti-inflammatory medications (ibuprofen, etc.) immediately after a difficult run can significantly reduce the chance of inflammation and injury and speed healing. Be sure to talk to your doctor, even before taking over-the-counter medications because all have some side effects. Taking any medication before or during a run (or the marathon) is not recommended. Whenever taking medications, follow the advice of your doctor and the instructions on the medicine, and discontinue their use at the first sign of potential problems.

INJURIES: HOW TO TREAT THEM

- **Get a doctor** who knows running and stay in touch with him or her. Getting a good diagnosis can speed the treatment and get you back on the roads quicker. A good doctor's advice and treatment can speed recovery by several weeks. It can often mean the difference between whether you will get to the starting line of your marathon or not next year.

- **Don't stretch** the area until it heals (unless you've injured the I-T band—ask your doctor).

- **Stop activity** that could possibly use the injured site for at least one to two days. In most cases your doctor will tell you that the injury doesn't have to heal completely before you run again, but you must get the healing started and con-

tinue a program that doesn't re-injure it. Again, talk to the Doc.

- **Ice!** If the injury site is near the surface of the body, ice massage will usually help. Be sure to use a chunk of ice and rub it directly on the injured area until it is numb (usually about 10 to 12 minutes). This is particularly helpful for all tendon and other foot injuries. Be sure to ice at the first sign of injury, ice as soon as possible after exercise, and keep icing for at least a week after the pain goes away. The regularity of the ice treatment is very important so do it every day! In deeper tendon or muscle injuries, ice treatment may not have any effect but should cause no harm.

- **Compression** will help to restrain further inflammation. Wrapping a sprained ankle soon after injury will reduce the inflamation. This is another area where your running-oriented physician should advise you. (You must release compression regularly.)

- **Elevation** can help to reduce inflammation. An injured leg, for example, would be elevated on a pillow or two as you read or watch TV in bed.

- **Massage** can dramatically speed up the healing of muscle injuries. A massage therapist or physical therapist, who is experienced in working with runners, should be able to advise you 1) whether your injury will heal quicker with massage and 2) when it's time to work on it (immediately after injury is not usually a good time).

GETTING BACK TO RUNNING

- If the short (one to two day) layoff from training allowed the healing to start, then easy running on the injured area is usually okay, if it's not causing further injury. Run no more often than every other day and listen to the advice of an experienced doctor who knows running injuries.

- **Choose alternative exercise** which will not aggravate the injured area and ease into it.

- **Continue with your injury treatment** as advised by the doctor. (Ice for at least one week after all symptoms go away.)

- **Gradually ease back** into your normal running routine as the healing takes hold.

[For more information on injuries, see Galloway's Book On Running, pp. 198-227.]

159

THE COMEBACK:
STARTING BACK AFTER INJURY, SICKNESS, VACATION, ETC.

*D*o you have to start all over if your marathon program is interrupted? Probably not. Most of us are not in a position to quit our job, leave our family and other responsibilities to train for a marathon and must steer our aerobic ship around the obstructions. There are as many ways to rebuild from a layoff as there are problems which cause the interruptions.

INJURIES

◆ At the first sign of an aggravated "weak link," take an extra day or two off.

◆ If it's an injury, see a doctor and get treatment immediately: the sooner treated, the sooner healed.

◆ Start alternative exercise immediately: the sooner started, the more fitness retained.

COMING BACK FROM AN INJURY

◆ Make sure the healing is continuing as you get back into running.

◆ Stay in touch with your doctor or physical therapist to limit the risk of re-injury.

◆ Continue to treat the injury as prescribed by the doctor.

- Ice massage, for example, should be continued every day for two weeks after the disappearance of all symptoms.

SICKNESS

◆ If Doc allows you to do some low level exercise (30 min, 3 x a week), do it!

◆ Always avoid the chance of lowering resistance to disease and getting sick again.

◆ Return to running conservatively after sickness.

TRAINING INTERRUPTIONS OF LESS THAN 14 DAYS DUE TO BUSINESS, TRAVEL, VACATION, ETC.

◆ You can come back to your normal weekly mileage in two to three weeks.

◆ But every run must be done slowly: follow the "two-minute rule."

BRING BACK THE LONG RUN

◆ You may increase the length more rapidly than usual by slowing down and taking more walking breaks.

◆ The longer your layoff from exercise, the more conservative your "comeback."

STARTING LONG RUN WHEN ON THE "COMEBACK TRAIL"

To designate your long run starting distance after a layoff from exercise, start from your longest run, three weeks before the day you plan to re-start the long ones and:

- take off 20 percent per week if you did no exercise at all,

- take off 10 percent per week if you did 30 minutes of alternative exercise, three times a week, or

- take off five percent per week if you did alternative exercise which simulated marathon schedule.

For example, a runner named Chris ran 23 miles three weeks ago. Three days after that, he ran too hard on the mile repeats and injured his Achilles tendon. He did no running for three weeks, then he ran easy every other day for 10 days.

Today his Achilles felt secure enough for a long one. He would have had the following options, in terms of long run distances:

- a four to five mile long run, if he had done no exercise at all during the layoff,

- 10 to 13 miles if he did 30 minutes of alternative exercise three times a week, or

- 15 to 17 miles if he did alternative exercise which simulated his marathon schedule.

Chris had either run in the water or exerted himself on the XC ski machine about every other day but for mostly minimal amounts. He decided that 15 miles would be his target for his first restarted long one.

HOW DO YOU PACE THE LONG ONES WHEN YOU START BACK?

- The first two miles should be three to four minutes per mile slower than you could run that distance.

- You could settle into a pace that is three minutes per mile slower or maintain original pace.

- Take walk breaks twice as often:

  - Before injury, Chris was taking a one-minute break every eight minutes of running. When he started his comeback, he took a one-minute break every four minutes.

  - A runner who runs three minutes and walks one minute would run one minute and walk two minutes.

HOW QUICKLY CAN YOU INCREASE THE LENGTH OF THE LONG ONE——AND GET BACK INTO "MARATHON RANGE"?

- Four to five miles per long run: when running more than three minutes per mile slower than you could run

  - and taking walk breaks twice as long and twice as often as before the interruption

- Three miles per long run: when running two and a half to three minutes per mile slower than you could run

  - and taking walk breaks twice as often as before the interruption

- Two miles per long run: when running two minutes per mile slower than you could run

  - and taking walk breaks as often as before the interruption

THE BEST SHOE

The best advice in choosing a running shoe is to get the best advice . . . at an authentic running store.

Most runners collect a closet full of bargain shoes until they find a real running store. The good advice of a trained staff can cut through the conflicting information, match you up with current helpful technology, and help you find a shoe that becomes an extension of your foot.

Except for computer components and internet software, and, of course, the latest in women's fashion, there are few areas in life that change as rapidly as running shoes. A tiny portion is fueled by new technology. Unfortunately, most of the flux is generated by the sales hype of companies competing to get on the feet of a growing army of new and addicted runners.

For efficiency you need an expert at a true specialty store. While rare, the authentic running stores are managed and staffed by adult runners who make it their life to test shoes, learn about the action of the foot, and collect continuous feedback on what shoes really work.

That's why I opened my running store, Phidippides, in 1973. I still own the store but my other activities keep me away most of the time. So now, I consult my staff each time I need a new pair of shoes. They haven't been wrong yet! If you're in Atlanta, please drop by.

The Top Five Reasons Why You Need Shoe Advice

1. Even the better running companies are using gimmicks in their design: some of the gimmicks work, and some don't.

2. There's always a reason why the catalog offers a dramatic discount on a given shoe.

3. The same shoe may be made in different factories—making each significantly different in the way it fits and in the many subtle ways it works when you run.

4. Only people who are really into running shoes can keep up with the gossip on running shoes—due to constant feedback they receive from hundreds of customers each week who really use the shoe for exercise.

5. Only experienced running staff people can look at you running in a shoe and tell whether it really fits—and works with your foot in the right way.

IF YOU CAN'T FIND A RUNNING SPECIALTY STORE...

The following procedure will help you sift through the maze of running shoes. It's not as good as getting the advice of Phidippides, but if you follow the steps below and use your best instincts, you're more likely to choose a shoe that will work for you. You'll also save time instead of listening to the pitch of commission-driven sales people, or high school kids, at stores that sell all types of sport shoes.

BRING WITH YOU: YOUR WORN SHOES, THE SOCKS YOU USE, FOOT DEVICES, ETC.

You need to bring to the fitting process everything you would use on a run. If you forgot to bring the socks that you use, buy a pair in the store that closely matches the thickness of your favorite ones. A good shoe expert can "read" the wear pattern on your shoes, which is the best indicator of how your foot functions. If you don't have this resource available, look at the diagram below.

YOU'RE IN CHARGE

Sure, you want the best advice available. But you are the only one who can feel how the shoe works on your foot. Narrow down the selection and then run in each shoe. Finally, you'll decide which works best for you as you run. Don't let anyone tell you that a specific shoe is the shoe for *you* if another shoe seems to feel better as you run or feels more natural on your foot. Get the best advice and then make up your mind.

BE PREPARED TO SPEND A LITTLE TIME

By spending at least 45 minutes (if you need it), you'll be more likely to try out the various shoe choices. Rushing in and grabbing the same shoe you got last year usually doesn't work at all. There are production changes with all shoes within a four-month period so the same shoe isn't

the same shoe. Besides, there's very likely to be a better one for your needs. Try out all of the options and then decide for yourself.

TELL YOUR SHOE EXPERT...

In case you get a good staff person, be prepared to tell the following: the terrain of your routes, your running schedule, injuries (particularly chronic ones), goals in the next six months, etc. The staff person should ask you about those items, but if this doesn't happen, tell him or her.

RUN IN EACH SHOE

Ask the salesperson to define the word "over-pronation." If they pass the test, ask him or her to watch you run in each shoe. As you feel how each one works, get feedback from your expert. While the input is beneficial from knowledgeable staff persons, you are still the person who will make the decision.

163

FIRST, LOOK AT FUNCTION AND THEN GO FOR FIT

Once you've found two to three shoes (at least) that seem to function well on your foot (rigid, floppy), adjust the lacing to fine-tune the fit of the shoe.

THE BOTTOM LINE: WHICH ONE WORKS BEST WHEN YOU RUN?

Look carefully at the two crucial factors listed immediately below. As you run in each one of your final candidates, determine which one fits your foot naturally and functions as an extension of your foot. If both shoes seem to be equal, ask the shoe expert which one lasts longer and whether the store has any customer feedback about how well they work a month or two down the road.

The DON'Ts of shoe selection

1. Don't get a shoe because it has worked well for someone else.

2. Don't select the shoe that best matches your outfit.

3. Don't take too seriously the advice of someone who can't give you a good definition of "over-pronation."

4. Don't buy from a shoe store that won't let you run in the shoe before purchase.

5. Don't pick the first shoe offered— especially if the salesperson says "Trust me, I know that's the best shoe for you."

6. Don't buy from a store where the average age of the staff is a non-voting age.

7. Don't buy from a salesperson who tells you about his or her running, best times, etc. and doesn't ask you about your foot problems, past shoe successes, and special needs.

8. Don't buy a shoe only because it's the most expensive.

164

DEFINITIONS: PRONATION, OVER-PRONATION AND SUPINATION

Pronation is the normal rolling in of the foot to a flat or neutral position as you walk or run, to absorb shock. Most of us land on the outside of the heel and roll quickly to the forefoot. Your foot pronates, or rolls inward, to a flat and stable position before rolling forward off the toe.

Over-pronation is rolling beyond the flat or neutral position of the foot, which can produce injury (but not always). Due primarily to the structure of leg and foot bones and tendons, the foot continues to roll to the inside as you push off. This usually over-rotates the knee but can also produce damage to the hip, shin, ankle and forefoot. When the force of your body weight presses down on a support structure that is out of alignment (as is the case with over-pronation), the weak link in your body will become injured. If there is any wear on the inside of the forefoot, you are an over-pronator.

Supination is rolling to the outside of the foot, which is usually okay because the bones on the outside of the foot are designed to support body weight. This motion only causes a problem when the foot continues to roll outside excessively, stressing the tendons of the ankle and sometimes the outside of the knee. This over-supination motion is noted by excessive shoe wear on the outside of the shoe and little wear elsewhere.

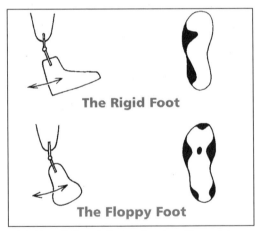

The Rigid Foot

The Floppy Foot

printed from Galloway's Book on Running with permission from Shelter Publications, p. 252.

FUNCTION: ARE YOU FLOPPY OR RIGID?

Imagine that your foot has hinges, like a door. The floppy foot is hinged so that the foot rolls easily from side to side. In contrast, the rigid foot moves forward and back.

Floppy feet often strike the ground first on the outside of the heel but roll to the inside as the body moves forward. This type of foot usually shows wear in spots, including some that are on the inside of the forefoot.

Rigid feet tend to push off strongly forward on the ball of the foot, showing wear on the outside of the forefoot, as well as the middle. Sometimes runners have one foot that's floppy and one that's rigid. Whatever type of foot you seem to have, there's no need to worry if you're not having aches, pains or injuries. Most feet make adaptations so that runners don't get injured due to their specific motion pattern. Increased stress due to mileage increase, speed training, or not enough days per week off from running can all tip the scales toward injury.

Runners with floppy feet that get injured should get a stable shoe, one that provides the foot with a good platform (this usually means minimal cushion in the forefoot). There are shoes specifically designed for motion control and orthotic and other foot devices that reduce the chance of excessive rolling to the inside as the foot pushes off. Talk to a doctor before putting anything in your shoe, but they can often help over-pronators who have chronic problems due to alignment.

SHAPE: ARE YOU CURVED OR STRAIGHT?

The "last" is the mold around which the shoe is built. If you look at a curved lasted shoe from the bottom of the sole, not only does it have a noticeable indention on the inside middle of the arch, but it actually curves so that the forefoot is supported more on the inside. When you look at a straight last shoe, however, the left shoe looks very similar to the right. Actually, most of the shoes today are mixtures of a curved and a straight last.

If a shoe puts pressure on the outside of your foot and there's extra room on the inside, you are trying on a shoe that is too curved for your foot. Ask to see a straighter one. But if a shoe seems to put pressure on your big toe and joint, you need a shoe that is more curved.

Your shoe should feel comfortable, naturally surrounded and protected—but not pushed up or pressured. The support of the shoe should be offered naturally so that you barely feel it. Never buy a shoe if it pinches or rubs parts of your feet when running. You know you've got a great fit when you run in the shoe and don't feel the shoe at all. Don't expect to get this perfect fit every time.

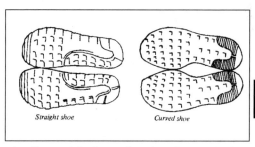

printed by permission from Galloway's Book on Running from Shelter Publications, p. 253.

BE SURE TO LACE YOUR SHOE SECURELY AROUND THE ANKLE

Many runners don't pull the laces tight when they try on a shoe. A loose fit at the ankle mistakenly seems to have an ill-fitting heel. If there is excessive heel motion, pull the last few laces snug and tie the lace together so that there is not a gap right at the knot. This may take several attempts because a new nylon lace is slick and resists being tightly knotted.

DON'T GET LOCKED INTO SPECIFIC MODELS OR BRANDS

After trying on one or two shoes of a brand that didn't fit, some runners assume that all of the shoes of that brand, until eternity,

165

are made the same way. All major brands have various lasts and shapes, which can fit most runners, and they introduce a new batch about every six months. Be open to the suggestions of your shoe expert, if you have one available, who will sort through the hundreds of running models currently available to find the best match for your foot. (Ask about the magic word "over-pronation.")

WHEN TO BUY ANOTHER SHOE

As soon as you know that a shoe fits and feels good when running, get another pair before the company discontinues it. Each week, at the end of a run, break out the new pair and run around the block. Over the weeks, you'll break in the new pair. But this is also a reality check on shoe support. After a month or so, you'll know when the original shoe needs to move on to greener pastures—as a lawn-mowing shoe. On that day, the new shoe gives support, while the old one flips, flops and wobbles.

Note: for more information, see Galloway's Book on Running, pp 248-260.

RUNNING FORM

Running form is most efficient when you don't feel any noticeable effort, when running is almost automatic.

Over several years, your running form becomes more efficient—even if you still feel "clunky." In fact, when runners get injured or fatigue themselves excessively due to bad form, they have often changed their form in the attempt to "run better." It's almost always better to go with the natural flow of your legs and body—even if you don't look like a star. In other words, if nothing seems to be wrong with your form, don't try to fix it. But if you're experiencing some of the form-related problems noted at the end of this chapter or others, I'll offer my prescription for moving easier.

ONCE A BODY IS IN MOTION...

Distance running is not a strength activity. Instead of overcoming gravity, we're trying to minimize its effect by staying low to the ground and reducing extraneous body motion. By going slowly in the beginning, it's easy to get moving, and, once in motion, the body wants to stay in motion. There are three components I use to monitor and fine-tune running form: posture, bounce and overstride.

How to Run a Marathon Efficiently

Marathon form is most efficient when you don't feel any noticeable effort, when running is almost automatic.

- Feet should stay low to the ground— no noticeable knee lift.

- Upright posture—Your body should be balanced with head over shoulders, over hips, so that no muscle power is needed to keep the body in position.

- Stay light on your feet. Those who want to improve times should increase turnover rate instead of stride length. (Turnover is the number of times your feet touch each minute.)

- The feet do not spring dramatically off the ground; they gently "lift off" in a reflex action as the body rolls forward.

- During most runs, concentrate on eliminating discomfort and noticeable effort in the exercising muscles. Strive to feel relaxed, comfortable and smooth.

POSTURE: RELAXED AND UPRIGHT

Don't try to be a Marine at attention. The best posture for running, walking or cruising is just good posture, with all elements relaxed and balanced as the foot comes underneath. A forward lean forces you to shorten your stride and creates extra tension on the lower back and neck. A backward lean is unusual but will also produce a shorter stride, loss of power from the running stride and possible tension in the lower back.

Some will argue that a forward lean will help you run faster, but I've found this to help only for a hundred yards or so. It forces you to work harder and therefore spends resources which are not available later in the run – causing you to lose more time than you gained during the short burst. The only exception I've found to this rule is when running on a gradual, downhill grade. A slight forward lean can help you run faster, and the boost from downhill gravity will offset the decrease in stride length. By having this slight monitor on downhill stride length, one can help counter the negative effect of overstriding, a temptation when running downhill.

CORRECTING FORWARD LEAN – by becoming a puppet on a string

Create a mental image during the form drill of yourself suspended from the very top of your head by a giant string (as if you were a puppet). The effect is to lift you upright – head in line with shoulders and hips and everything lined up with each foot as it assumes the body's weight. A good puppet image also helps you to stay light on your feet.

The first effect of being a good puppet is to have your body line up without any tension – you're in balance. Walk around with the image of the puppet on the string until you

feel relaxed in this upright position. Then start running slowly. On your days for form work, you may then accelerate for 50 to 150 meters, running as a lightly balanced puppet. Not only does the posture correct itself, but your chest is forward as are your hips, allowing for a quick touch-off with the feet. You may have to make little adjustments, but when you're lined up in a relaxed mode, running will be easier and you'll feel less effort in the legs.

BOUNCE

When in doubt, use less energy and stay lower to the ground, and you'll run smoother and quicker with better leg turnover. The energy spent in bouncing too high even by an inch is wasted—burned up in the air. The higher you lift yourself off the ground, the greater shock you have to absorb when landing and the longer it'll take for your feet and legs to recover from that run. Excess bounce also forces the legs to go through inefficient, extraneous motion during the extra time in the air. A higher back kick, for example, is the result of excess leg swing because your body is off the ground for an extra second or so. Such a kick produces early fatigue in the hamstring muscles.

You can correct bounce by keeping your feet close to the ground during sections of every run, especially when you feel the temptation to bounce (during the first mile and when going downhill). Instead of bouncing and spending energy, save your resources with a quick and light "lift-off" of the foot. You'll run about as fast by staying low to the ground with more steps per minute.

OVERSTRIDE

As the forward leg absorbs body weight, the lower leg should not be extended out in front of you.

CORRECTING OVERSTRIDE: Running easier

Our tendency to overstride is another attempt to counter slowing down with a quick fix. Unfortunately, our intuitive sense of pace gets us into trouble in this area. As runners get tired and realize that the main driving muscles are weakening due to fatigue, they subconsciously lengthen the stride to speed up. As in the case of other "quick fixes," this one will help for a short distance but is very counterproductive later.

Longer strides will over-stretch the muscles, causing them to tighten up later and weaken. If the stride is too long, it can put the knees or the muscles out of efficient mechanical range, increasing recovery time and causing injury. Everybody has "weak links," places where they tend to get injured most often. When the main driving muscles are tired, the knees wobble more and the "weak links" are likely to be pushed beyond their capacity. In other words, the damage will be greater.

When you feel tension in muscles which are at their limits – especially the calf and hamstring groups – you need to shorten the stride a bit more to relax them. Keep shortening the stride until the leg muscles relax. This may allow you to pick up the turnover of the feet and legs. But even if this increase doesn't happen, you'll reduce the chance of injury and speed up recovery due to the increased fatigue of overstriding. Often, the adjustment needed is a shortening of only an inch or two less than the overstride, but the relaxation it provides will allow the legs to go at a faster rhythm so that some runners can actually speed up at the end of the race.

As you pick up the turnover on form accelerations, be sure to keep the stride short enough so that the leg muscles are relaxed and can maintain a quick rhythm.

Turnover Drill

To correct overstride and keep feet low to the ground

The Research: Studies have clearly shown that as runners become faster, their stride length decreases. Therefore, the way to get faster is to increase turnover of feet and legs. Even those who lack a fast bone in their bodies will benefit from turnover drills because they teach the body to find a more efficient motion.

The Drill: After a slow mile warm-up, select a level and traffic-free stretch of road, trail or track. Without picking up your speed, count the number of times either your left foot or your right comes down. Jog or walk for a minute or so and run back, counting again, with the goal of increasing the count by one or two. Repeat this four to six times, with the same projected increase each time but without a significant increase in effort.

How Often? If you do this drill once a week, you'll intuitively learn to stay low to the ground with an increasingly lighter touch of the foot. You'll see more progress when doing it twice. But you'll lose two weeks of progress if you miss a week.

Faster A Year From Now...with no increase in effort if you do this drill at least once a week. The increased turnover and improved efficiency also makes running feel easier.

When in doubt, keep the stride short so that you can maintain a light, quick step on each of these pick-ups.

169

Efficiency Wins: The Battle of Running Form in Boston 1995

A classic confrontation occurred in the Boston Marathon between the efficiency of a marathoner and the strength and power of a 5K/10K runner. From the starting gun, Uta Pippig looked to be cutting her classic marathoner stride too short. Her closest competitor, Elena Meyer, appeared to be playing her cards right by going out slowly, forcing Uta to shoulder all of the pressure of pacesetting.

By the mid-point, Uta had built a modest lead and was running so smoothly that her quick turnover gave the appearance of weakness. With a tiny stride and no knee lift, she appeared to be jogging. This signaled to several experienced observers that it just wasn't her day. Elena, however, sensed this, and began her drive to overtake the leader. The South African's strong, athletic leg motion led many experts to say that it was only a matter of time before she would pull even with the German.

At 15, 17 and 19 miles, it continued to appear that Meyer's long and powerful stride must be taking big chunks out of Pippig's lead. The TV commentators noted how wimpy the German's turnover appeared. But to the surprise of all, a time check showed that Pippig's lead was *increasing* slightly.

By 22 miles, Meyer had dropped out with muscle cramps and Pippig had picked up her pace. But when the camera showed the leader, she still looked like a jogger. That short and wimpy stride with no knee lift resulted in a 2:26 marathon—one of the fastest woman's times of the year.

170

TROUBLESHOOTING FORM PROBLEMS

QUADS *too tired, sore or weak*

When the main running muscles get tired, your stride length shortens as you slow down. The best strategy in this situation is to shorten the stride a little more and allow for a slight slowdown. Many runners, however, will try to maintain the same pace by using other muscles. The quadriceps on the front of your leg above the knee can allow this (for a while) by lifting the leg and maintaining a longer stride length. But the quads are not designed to do this and will fatigue easily. Afterward, you can usually count on two to four days of soreness, at least.

Sometimes quad soreness is directly related to running more downhill than you are used to running. Even when using a short stride while running downhill, some effort is required of the quadricep muscles—especially on long downhills. Many runners aggravate this by overstriding as they go down. Yes, it is tempting, and it is easy to extend the lower leg out in front of the body too much to pick up speed. To keep the legs and body under control, the quads must then be used as brakes. Not only is this an inefficient use of muscle power, but your quads will complain for several days afterward, especially after a long run. The recommended technique is to maintain a short stride and let gravity move you down with little effort.

Light exercise every day (such as walking on flat terrain) will speed up the recovery of sore quads. It is not a good idea to massage them, stretch them or exercise them too hard while they are sore.

BEHIND THE KNEE: *Discomfort, pain, or weakness*

Another sign of overstriding is pain or increased discomfort behind the knee. When you reach out further than you should with the lower leg, you're out of the knee's efficient range of motion. The full impact of your body's weight must be supported by the knee and through a mechanical range in which it is weakened. This is a hinge joint and was designed only to support body weight in the act of moving forward, with the foot directly underneath.

When your main running muscles become tired, they cannot give the knee any protection from this repeated abuse. As the tendons behind the knee become more stretched out during the run, the knee is forced to assume body weight in a straight or "locked out" position. Downhill running and faster running tend to bring on this problem.

Always try to maintain some bend in each knee when running. A shorter stride length will reduce the chance of this overstride problem. Do not try to stretch the tendons behind the knee at any time. Light massage with a chunk of ice can help. (Get a doctor's permission before using anti-inflammatory drugs.)

"WOBBLY" RUNNING FORM *at the end of long runs*

Most runners feel great at the beginning of long runs. It's natural to be tired at the end, but when the legs aren't supporting you well, you've overdone it in the beginning. The greatest downside of this condition is that you can easily aggravate your "weak links": those areas where you tend to experience injury.

This condition is totally preventable. Start the long ones a lot slower—at a pace that is at least two minutes slower per mile than you could run that distance on that day. It is also wise to take one-minute walk breaks every three to eight minutes (from the beginning!).

SHOULDER AND NECK *muscles tired and tight*

If you're leaning forward as you run, you'll have a tendency to compensate by holding the head back, which uses the muscles of the shoulder and neck more and produces fatigue more rapidly. When the body is held upright, the head, neck and shoulders are in alignment and require little or no muscle power to keep them in position.

Those who hold their arms too far out from the body will also overextend the muscles of the shoulder and neck. The ideal arm motion is minimal, with the arms held in a relaxed position next to the body. When the lower arm goes through a small range of motion alongside the shorts and the upper part of the arm hardly moves, there is little fatigue in the arms, shoulders or neck muscles.

LOWER BACK *very tight and over-fatigued*

Another sign of too much forward lean is a tired and tight lower back. By maintaining an upright body posture, you'll avoid the tendency to overstress the back. If you think that your back muscles are weaker than they should be, talk to a physical therapist (etc.) about some strength exercises to compensate. One that has worked well for me is the back curl. Do not try this or any strength exercise, however, until you've been given clearance by a strength expert.

HAMSTRINGS *tired or sore*

You're lifting the foot behind you too far and/or extending stride too long. The

171

longer stride is particularly a problem at the
end of the long run as it overextends
muscles like the hamstring, which are
already tight and tired. Try to keep stride
short, especially at the end of the run. Your
back leg motion should have the lower part
of the leg parallel to the horizontal—at its
highest elevation.

KNEE PAIN

When the main driving muscles get tired,
they can no longer control your "safe" range
of motion, and the resulting wobble can
leave you in pain, sore or injured. A slower
early pace, and walk breaks, will help the
legs stay fresh.

SORE FEET AND LOWER LEGS

You're pushing off the ground too hard and
probably too high. Stay closer to the ground,
lightly touching it, and maintain a short
stride.

LOWER BACK *tired and sore*

You're leaning forward as you run.
Straighten up and shorten stride.

STRETCHING WARNING: Even if your legs
are tight after running, don't stretch at that
time. A gentle period of massage and
stretching before bed will give you the
benefits without as much risk of over-
stretching. Never try to "stretch out" a tight
leg muscle during a run—except for the I-T
Band.

Note: For more information on running
form, see Galloway's Book on Running, pp
146-157.

Marathon Cross Training (XT)

The XT days

On non-running days, cross training can give the attitude boost we need while it bestows additional conditioning. The best programs are those which are fun, and therefore draw you back to do them again and again. For this reason, many marathon runners do a variety of exercises in a single XT session to reduce the chance of boredom and burnout.

XT can maintain marathon conditioning while injured

Don't think that "it's over" if you come down with an injury during a marathon program. Over the years, I've met dozens of runners who, while injured, maintained conditioning through significant cross-training and were able to finish the marathon comfortably. During an eight-week injury, one runner ran in the water and came back to do the marathon in a personal best: under three hours!

The best exercises for running

As in any form of conditioning, the best exercises to get in shape as "back-ups" for the running muscles are those which best use the leg muscles in the running way.

Water running has produced the best effect for large numbers of marathoners. Cross-country ski machines have also produced a high level of running conditioning.

The best exercises for fat-burning

Exercises which elevate the body temperature, keep it up, and use lots of muscle cells are best. Cross-country ski machines, rowing machines, and then cycling and other indoor machines can help to increase the fat-burning effect.

Beware of the stair!

Stair machines use many of the muscles used in running. This means that they aren't the best choice for alternative exercise on a rest day from running. But they can simulate hill running, to some extent, if you use them occasionally to replace a running day (or as a second running session on a running day).

Gradually introduce the muscles to XT

- Ease into each new exercise.

- For the first few weeks, don't do the same exercise every day.

173

Mon	Tue	Wed	Thu	Fri	Sat	Sun
H2O run	cycle	H2O run	swim	H2O run	off	long H2O run
strength	swim	strength	X-C ski machine	strength	swim	

- You can, however, do several different exercises which can be alternated.

- To get the best effect for the marathon, it's better to use a slow continuous motion instead of quick, short bursts of high intensity.

EASING INTO NEW EXERCISES

- On the first day go five easy minutes, rest for 20 to 30 minutes, and then go for five more minutes.

- You could start with two to three different exercises, alternating them and gradually increasing the session to one hour.

- During each successive session, increase by three to five minutes on each of the two segments.

- For example:

Session #

1 5min/5min

2 8min/8min

3 12min/12min

4 15min/15min

5 18min/18min

6 22min/22min

- Exercise every day at first, if you wish, building up to two 30-minute sessions.

  - You may then combine the exercise into one continuous session with a frequency of every other day. On the off day, you may do a different exercise routine. For example, look at the schedule at the bottom of this page.

IF INJURED:

- Don't do any exercise which could aggravate the injured area.

- Try to simulate the same intensity and duration of your scheduled running session for that day. For example, if a long run were scheduled, estimate the length of the time you'd be running and spend that time continuously running in the water, on the cross-country ski machine, etc. As you're doing the alternative exercise, try to maintain about the same level of exertion as you would feel when running.

GRADUALLY WORK INTO NEW EXERCISES

- Build up to about the same duration and intensity of exercise you'd be doing if running.

- You can alternate back and forth between many exercises to keep the activity interesting.

- Never push the muscles to the point of tiredness or loss of strength in individual exercises or in the session as a whole.

IF YOU'RE NOT INJURED BUT ARE JUST ADDING EXTRA FITNESS TO YOUR PROGRAM...

- Choose a variety of exercises for your non-running days.

- You don't need to do any one of the exercises for more than about 10 minutes, if you don't want to. By alternating between activities, you'll tend to avoid boredom.

- Water running and cross-country ski machines are the best for runners.

175

BENEFITS OF WATER RUNNING

BENEFITS OF WATER RUNNING

- Legs must find the most efficient mechanical path through the water. Extraneous motions of the feet and legs are reduced or eliminated over time.

- The water's resistance strengthens muscles which can serve as back-up strength to the primary running muscles. By alternating off and on, the main running muscles will retain resiliency longer. These smaller "reserve" muscles will also be able to keep you going for a little while if you overuse the main running muscles and need some help to keep going during the last few miles in the marathon.

- You get a great cardiovascular training session without any pounding. Since the prime running muscles are not being used, most injuries can heal.

Water Running Techniques

THE MARATHON MOTION

This is the same running form one would use when running efficiently on land. The body should be upright, not stiff. A slight forward lean is okay, but don't lean too far. The ideal motion is a smooth one, getting quick turnover. Focus on finding the most efficient path through the water. In this way you'll be cutting out mechanical inefficiencies and encouraging an efficient stride on land.

- Knees don't come up very far.

- Lower legs and feet are kicked forward.

- The whole leg is brought behind you, with knee slightly bent.

- Back leg bends to a right angle and then returns forward.

- Arms can be moved through a range of motion similar to that of regular running. Don't exaggerate the arm swing.

CROSS COUNTRY (X-C) SKI MOTION

This strengthening exercise should be done in short segments of 10 seconds to a minute. By weaving segments into the marathon motion, you'll increase strength in the quadriceps (front of thigh), hamstrings, butt muscles, hip flexors, and lower back.

- The legs are almost completely straight.

- The range of motion is about 20 percent longer than the marathon motion.

- Move the legs like a scissors through the water.

Start each segment with a short range of motion, gradually extending it. Over time, you may increase both range of motion and speed, but be careful. Remember that you're building strength and not anaerobic performance. Never extend any motion to the point that you feel at your mechanical limits. And don't work too long in the X-C ski motion so that you're out of breath.

THE SPRINT

For those who have been doing speed play and don't want to risk injury while in a marathon program, the sprint motion can keep the speed components in good form without the risk of pounding or interval training injuries.

- Shorten your marathon motion to about half.

- Keep legs and feet directly underneath you.

- Pick up the turnover of your legs and feet so that you're going through the leg pattern about twice as fast as the marathon motion.

This shouldn't be a true sprint (going all out) because you want to go at a pace that you could continue for one to two minutes. You will be huffing and puffing through the second half of each of these, as they are anaerobic. Start each "sprint segment" by gradually increasing the turnover. The short range of motion directly underneath you will cause your head and shoulders to rise out of the water somewhat. The arm motion should also be a shortened version of the marathon motion to keep up with the legs.

CAUTIONS:

- Make sure that the water running motion is within efficient mechanical range.

- If you're injured, get clearance from your doctor that you're not aggravating the injury.

- Don't overtrain. Just going through an efficient water running motion will bestow benefits. You don't have to push it.

177

BREATHING

*B*y using an efficient breathing technique, you'll not only be capable of a higher level of performance in the marathon but also you'll teach yourself how to acquire a better supply of oxygen and improve almost every aspect of your exercise experience...as well as the way you feel doing the other things you do.

THE CONCEPT OF DEEP BREATHING (ALSO CALLED "BELLY BREATHING")

* You're filling up the lower part of the lungs first.

* Through practice you can quickly inhale and quickly exhale while deep breathing.

* You don't need to fill the upper part of your lungs to capacity.

ELIMINATING SIDE PAINS

The deep-breathing technique can help you reduce or eliminate those irritating side pains which often erupt just when you're getting into your exercise. Such pains seem to be primarily caused by shallow breathing—using the upper part of our lungs in a minimal way. This low energy expenditure method is adequate for our normal sedentary activities and seems to provide sufficient oxygen at the beginning of an exercise session. But it also minimizes the amount of oxygen which you could absorb during exertion and often puts you into debt. If you start your runs with shallow breathing, you'll probably get side pains during some of them. Since side pains are aggravated by going out faster than you should (even when the pace feels easy), slow down at the beginning of all of your runs if you've been experiencing these discomforts.

DEEP-BREATHING TECHNIQUE

* Quickly exhale as completely as possible every third or fourth breath.

* This almost guarantees a complete intake as you inhale immediately afterward.

* Breathe normally in between the deeper breaths.

* Don't do this deeper breathing more often because you could hyperventilate.

* You must start this technique from the beginning of your run to maximize its effect.

Some folks time their exhale to take place as they push off, every second or third step. If this sounds intriguing, try it two ways: 1) breathe out completely as you push off either the right or the left foot or 2) alternate between the left or right foot. To see which method works best, you should attempt one method only during a specific run.

You can practice this breathing method at any time—not just when exercising. Be sure to start each exercise session using this technique. After several weeks or months of regular breathing in this way, it will become your almost automatic breathing method.

For more information on breathing, see Galloway's Book On Running, pp. 152.

STRETCHING

THE GOOD NEWS:

When stretching is done regularly, in the correct way, it will reduce the tightening effect which naturally occurs as we age. Unfortunately, running increases the speed of this tightening. Regular stretching is a positive component of a marathon program when done carefully.

THE BAD NEWS:

Stretching is the third leading cause of injury among runners. While injuries are almost always the result of improper stretching, it is very easy to injure yourself while doing a stretch that seems perfectly safe.

STRETCHING DOES NOT WARM YOU UP FOR A RUN

The best warm-up for running has been the following: 1) walking, 2) very slow jogging or 3) gradually picking up your pace to "normal." Stretching before a run will not warm you up better or sooner, and it won't help you run faster in that run.

THE BEST TIME TO STRETCH:

Pick a time in the afternoon or evening when you're relaxed, when you don't have to rush through the stretch routine and when your muscles are warmed up from the activities of the day. Most folks find that the period just before getting into bed is the best time for stretching; indeed, stretching helps you relax for an earlier drift into dreamland.

DON'T!

* Stretch when you're in a hurry

* Stretch before running

* Push a muscle into tension or tightness

* Stretch a tight muscle during or immediately after a run

* Stretch immediately after running (wait at least 30 minutes)

DO!

* Take your time when stretching

* Move the muscle gently into a relaxed extension

* Hold it in that position for six to thirty seconds

* Back off gently

* Stretch at least twice a week

The areas of your body which need more stretching due to running: calf muscles, hamstrings, and lower back. Make sure that you choose safe exercises. For more information on stretching, with specific stretches, see Galloway's Book On Running, pp. 159-165, and Stretching, by Bob Anderson.

STRENGTH TRAINING

Strong and balanced postural muscles will keep you upright when you're fatigued, improving your breathing and oxygen intake, as you maintain running strength and efficiency.

I don't believe that we need to do any strength exercises to run a marathon. If you have any doubts, look at the "toothpick" legs of the winners of any major marathon. It's obvious that they don't spend time in the gym. The most important physics concept for running, in my opinion, is inertia. Running is easier and more fun when we spend a little energy to get moving and then fine-tune our movements to take advantage of our momentum. Read more about this in the form chapter in this book and in Galloway's Book on Running.

I do, however, recommend a couple of strength exercises for long-term postural support. I discovered this after my arms and shoulders were getting increasingly tired on long runs in the mid-1980's. By doing the exercises listed below, I've virtually eliminated that type of fatigue-even in marathons.

Legs can be strengthened most efficiently by doing regular hill training (see the chapter in this book). Running up an incline forces the leg muscles to perform against natural resistance in the act of running. By doing artificial weight exercises, you can upset the natural balance that has developed between the muscle groups. Such an imbalance can cause injury.

POSTURAL STRENGTH EXERCISES

I've found that a bare minimum of strength training can keep the postural muscles strong and balanced. These muscles maintain the upper body in a relaxed but upright position. When neglected, they slowly weaken. Over a ten-year period, individuals gradually slump and stoop a little more. Runners notice this sooner. On long or hard runs, those with weak postural muscles will lose their form more quickly, slowing down the pace and increasing recovery time. A slumping upper body also cuts down on the efficiency of breathing and reduces oxygen absorption. After starting with about 10 exercises in the late 1980's, I gradually evolved down to the two which are noted below. The "crunch" strengthens the front of the body, and "arm running" strengthens the muscles of the lower back, upper back, shoulders and neck. But if you're looking for beach muscles, this isn't the right program.

THE CRUNCH

This is the old sit-up, with the range of motion reduced significantly. By keeping the body near the floor and constantly using the muscles, you get a lot of good strengthening in a short amount of time.

This exercises the upper abdominal group (the "six-pack").

HERE'S HOW:

- Lie down on your back on a padded surface with your knees bent.

- Raise your upper torso very slightly off the floor (lower back still touching the surface). Lift and lower only three to five inches or so until the muscles fatigue.

- Don't continue until the muscles give out.

ARM RUNNING

This exercise is done in the standing position with legs spread about as wide as your shoulders (or less wide if this is not comfortable). You can experiment a little bit with the motion, but don't do anything which will put your back at risk. It's always safer when you use handheld weights to keep them close to the body.

HERE'S HOW:

- Stand upright and relaxed with your feet spread about the width of your shoulders.

- Use handheld weights in both hands. Use a weight that will give you a little challenge but is not a struggle.

- Move the arms through the motion you'd use when running, keeping the hands close to the body.

- Starting with two to three repetitions, increase by one rep each session until you get up to 10.

- To see results, you need to do this twice or three times a week

- I do several sets of 10, spread throughout the day, three days a week.

Note: If you want to develop strength, it helps to see a strength expert. The exercises and the advice above is only given as one runner to another. Never do any exercise that could pull or strain a muscle.

COLD WEATHER RUNNING

*E*xperts in extreme temperature research tell me that even when the temperature drops to minus 30 (without the wind) there's no reason to be concerned about lung damage. There are so many buffer zones in your respiratory system that prevent outside air from impacting any area deeper than your mouth—and masks can prevent problems there. By putting on the right combination of layers, fabrics, extremity protectors and skin care products, you can enjoy running on very cold days, like the runners of Alaska, Minnesota and the ice belt of Canada.

DRESSING: DON'T BE HELD HOSTAGE BY THE WEATHER. VISIT A GOOD RUNNING OR SKI STORE AND FIND OUT WHAT TO WEAR.

1. Wear a series of thin layers. Close to your skin, you'll want something warm. Polypro is one of a series of winter fibers that keep the warmth close to the skin but allow extra heat and perspiration to escape.

2. Continue to add external layers, adjusting to the temperature and wind conditions.

3. Cover up all extremities with extra layering: hands, ears, toes.

4. Men, wear an extra layer or two as underwear, as you need.

5. In extreme cold (when temperature or wind chill is below 10° Fahrenheit, -11° Centigrade), do not expose any skin, if possible. Even when there is minimal exposure, put Vaseline or other cold weather insulation/protection on any area which may incidentally be hit by the wind (eyelids, etc).

6. Be sure to coat your shoes or use socks that insulate your feet. Most running shoes are designed to let heat out and cold into your feet, which can cause frostbite on days colder than 32° F or 0° C. Remember that you generate a significant wind chill effect on your feet as you move them through the running motion.

7. As you warm up through running, peel off each layer before you start sweating. Too much sweat accumulation will freeze and cause problems.

WARM-UPS THAT TAKE THE STING OUT OF WINTER

1. On very cold days, bundle up and exercise for a very few minutes indoors. You may walk, jog in place, use an indoor track, or exercise on the ma-

chines (cycle, rowing, stair, etc.) Before you start sweating, go outdoors and you'll have a reservoir of warmth to get you down the road.

2. Start your run/walk going into the wind. This allows you to come back with the wind.

3. If you start to get very warm, remove an outside layer of clothing or unzip your outer layer, if applicable. A garment with long sleeves allows you to tie it around your waist or put it in your fanny pack—because you may need it later.

4. On cold days, pick environments where you could seek refuge for at least a few minutes if you need to.

5. On very cold or windy days, alternate between inside and out. If you have an indoors facility, it helps to come inside when you start to get cold. Exercise indoors only long enough to take the sting away—but head outdoors before you start sweating.

6. Don't let yourself sweat because it is likely to freeze and leave you very cold. Remove a layer or go outside before the sweat starts flowing.

Clothing Thermometer

What to wear as it gets colder (In Fahrenheit)

60° +	Tank top or singlet and shorts
50°-59°	T-shirt and shorts
40°-49°	Long sleeve T, shorts or tights or wind pants, socks or mittens or gloves
30°-39°	Long sleeve T and T-shirt, tights and shorts, socks or mittens or gloves and hat over ears
20°-29°	Polypro top or thick long sleeve T, another T-shirt layer, tights and shorts mittens or gloves, and hat over ears
10°-19°	Polypro top and thick long sleeve T, tights and shorts, wind suit (top and pants), thick mittens, thick hat over ears..
0°-9°	Two polypro tops, thick tights and shorts (and thick underwear or supporter for men), Goretex or similar thickness warm-up, gloves and thick mittens, ski mask and hat over ears, and Vaseline covering any exposed skin.
minus 15 to minus 1	Two thick polypro tops, tights and thick polypro tights and thick underwear (and supporter for men), thick warm-up, gloves, thick (arctic) ski mask and thick hat over ears, Vaseline covering any exposed skin, thicker socks on feet and other measures for feet, as needed.
minus 20 and below	Add layers as needed. Stay in touch with the outdoor and ski shops for the warmest clothing which is thin. Watch your feet. There are some socks which heat up...and other innovations.

Note: These are only recommendations; use the combination of layers which works best for you.

HOT WEATHER RUNNING

There's good and bad news about running in the heat. First, the bad news: when the temperature rises above 55° F (10° C), you're going to run slower and feel worse than you will at lower temperatures. But by gradually preparing yourself for increased temperatures and taking action from the beginning of hot weather runs, you'll get a welcome dose of the good news. You'll learn how to hydrate yourself, what to wear, and when and how much your body can take in hot weather, all of which will help you recover faster and run better than others of your ability on hot days. While even the most heat-trained runners won't run as fast on hot days as on cold ones, they won't slow down as much nor will they feel as much discomfort.

Note: Be sure to read the next section, Heat Disease Alert. Many runners get into serious trouble even on moderately warm days without knowing it. Mark this section and revisit it several times during the warm season of the year. Anyone who has heart disease risk factors or suspicions of these should talk to a doctor trained in exercise before continuing.

Until the temperature rises to about 65° F, most runners don't notice much heat buildup, even though it is already putting extra burdens on the system. It takes most folks about 30 to 45 minutes of running

(with or without walk breaks) to feel warm. But soon after that, if the temperature is above about 62° F, you're suddenly hot and sweating. On runs and especially races under those conditions, most runners have to force themselves to slow down. It's just too easy to start faster than you should when it's 60° to 69° F because it feels cool at first.

As the mercury rises above 65° F, your body can't get rid of the heat buildup. This causes a rise in core body temperature, leading to an early depletion of fluids through sweating. The internal temperature rise also triggers rapid dispersion of blood into the capillaries of the skin, reducing the amount of that vital fluid that is available to the exercising muscles. Just when these workhorses are being pushed to top capacity, they are receiving less oxygen and nutrients due to reduced blood flow. What used to be a river becomes a creek and can't remove the waste products of exercise (such as lactic acid). As these accumulate, your muscles slow down.

Even the most heat-conditioned athletes will record slower times in warm weather. The faster you run in hot weather, especially from the beginning, the longer it takes to recover. But it's also possible to take action from the start of the run to reduce muscle damage, speed recovery, and

How to stay cool (55° F or above)

- **Slow down early:** The later you wait to do this, the more dramatically you'll slow down at the end and the longer it will take to recover from the run. Walk breaks, early and often, help you lower the exertion level, which conserves resources for the end and reduces heat buildup.

- **Wear lighter garments and not cotton:** Loose-fitting clothes allow heat to escape. Don't wear cotton clothing. Sweat soaks into cotton, causing it to cling to your skin, increasing heat buildup. Several materials will wick the perspiration away from your skin: coolmax, polypro, etc. As the moisture leaves your skin area, you receive a cooling effect, and these types of materials allow this to happen.

- **Pour water over yourself.** You lose up to 70 percent of the heat you can lose through the top of your head so regularly pour water there (even if you're like me, "hair challenged"). Regularly pouring water on a light, polypro (or a similar material) singlet or tank top will keep you cooler.

- **Don't wear a hat!** Hats keep your heat from being released through the best vent you have, the top of your head. Don't cover it up.

- **Drink cold water.** Not only does cold water leave the stomach of a runner quicker than any type of fluid, it produces a slight physiological cooling effect—and an even greater psychological cooling effect. But don't drink too much either. Most of us do well with six to 10 ounces an hour during warm weather. Drink until you hear sloshing in your stomach, then stop. When the sloshing sound goes away, resume drinking.

- **Take a dip or a shower.** On hot days, you can significantly reduce heat buildup if you spend three to four minutes in a pool or cold shower every mile or two. Do this several times and even the hottest day's run becomes manageable. The break in your run will not cause you to get out of shape. Over the span of a month, most runners get in more training this way because they don't overheat early.

- **Don't eat a big meal.** Eating too much, particularly meals that are high in protein or fat, will put extra stress on your system when you exercise. Even worse is the probability that too much food loading will lead to unloading during the run. That can be embarrassing! Instead of big meals, eat light snacks, which you know will digest easily, every hour or two. Many runners find that they must not eat anything within two hours or so of their hot weather run (although PowerBars or PowerGel works well for most).

186

even lower your time in warm weather races.

Humidity. The higher the humidity, the quicker you'll feel the effect of the heat and the more difficult it will be to continue. Watch the weather reports and install a temperature and humidity gauge at your house. After a while, you'll learn the combination of the two which causes you

discomfort so that you can avoid the times of the day when those conditions arise.

Body Fat. The more body fat you have, the worse you'll feel as the temperature rises. I don't have any research on this, but my experience tells me that for every increase of five percent in body fat, the effects of heat and humidity are felt three to five minutes sooner. For example, if a runner with 12 percent body fat feels severe heat discomfort at 45 minutes of running, then a 22 percent runner feels it around 35 minutes, and a 32 percent runner feels it around 25 minutes. Body fat acts like a blanket to hold heat in. It does too good a job during the summer.

The best time for hot weather running is before the sun comes up. The more you can run before sunrise, the cooler you will feel, relative to how you'll feel later in the day. The second best time to run, by the way, is right after sunrise, unless the temperature cools off dramatically at sunset, then that time period would present a great opportunity. In humid areas, however, it usually doesn't cool down much after sunset.

TRAINING FOR HOT WEATHER

One day a week, you can train yourself to deal with the heat by inserting the hot segments below into your run, even if you are starting in the middle of winter. Of course, you need to run at least two other days per week, and you must do this heat training day every week. Before running each hot segment, read the page that follows this chapter on heat disease. At the first indication of symptoms, stop the run before you get into trouble. The process of heat training follows the same principles of conditioning for endurance and speed. By pushing yourself a little bit and then backing off, your body makes adaptations to better deal with heat the next time.

On each run, warm up for at least 10 minutes of easy running (and walking), and ease off with at least 10 minutes of easy running (and walking) after the heat phase. If the outdoor temperature is cool, you may put on one or more layers of clothes, especially on the upper body, during the hot segment. You may also do these segments indoors. Run very easy on

Week #	# of minutes of hot segment
1	5-7 minutes
2	7-9 minutes
3	9-12 minutes
4	12-16 minutes
5	16-22 minutes
6	22-26 minutes

Tallahassee Showers

To cope with the heat and humidity of Tallahassee, I discovered an outdoor shower beside the FSU track. Practically every afternoon during June, July and August, I'd structure my runs so that I looped by the track at least every two miles. If my body heat built up more quickly, I'd cut the loop short and head for the shower. For these runs, I used special shoes which would slip on and off quickly without unlacing. Without those regular dousings, I wouldn't have run half the distance I was able to cover.

these segments. You're only working on heat adaptation.

ADJUSTING FOR HEAT

As the weather gets hotter, you must slow down your pace from the beginning. For more information on hot weather running, see Galloway's Book On Running, pp. 77-78, 94-95, 101-102.

When it's	A 10 min/mile pace becomes:	with humidity over 60% the 10 min/mi becomes
55-60 degrees	10:06	10:10
60-65 degrees	10:18	10:25
65-70 degrees	10:30	10:50
70-75 degrees	10:42	11:10
75-80 degrees	11:12	11:48
80-85 degrees	12:00	13:00
Above 85	Forget it......take the day off or run for fun (with shower breaks)	

88

HEAT DISEASE ALERT

*T*he most common health problem among endurance exercisers is heat disease. This is a serious condition which has resulted in death in a high percentage of cases, even in highly trained, young athletes.

PREVENTION:

- During hot weather, exercise at the coolest time (usually before sunrise).

- Drink water all day long.

- Avoid caffeine, alcohol and other drugs.

- Wear clothing that is light and loose.

- Eat small, lowfat snacks which you know will not cause you distress (far enough ahead).

- Don't significantly increase duration or intensity.

- Slow down pace even more to adjust for heat, humidity and hills—especially in the beginning.

- Take walk-breaks more often on hot days.

SYMPTOMS:

- Intense heat buildup in the head, significant headache, general overheating of the body

- General confusion and loss of concentration and muscular control

- Over-sweating and then cessation of sweating, clammy skin and excessive breathing

- Extreme tiredness, upset stomach, muscle cramps, vomiting, feeling faint

RISK FACTORS:

- Sleep deprivation

- Infection (viral, bacterial, etc.)

- Dehydration (avoid alcohol and caffeine)

- Severe sunburn, skin irritation

- Unaccustomed to hot weather

- Overweight

- Untrained for specific training session

- Occurrence(s) of heat disease in the past

- Under medications—especially the following: cold medicines, diuretics, medicines for diarrhea, tranquilizers, antihistamines, atropine, and scopolamine

- The following medical conditions:

  High cholesterol, high blood pressure, under extreme stress, asthma, diabetes, epilepsy, drug use (including alcohol), cardiovascular disease, smoking, unfit lifestyle

SEE A PHYSICIAN WHO KNOWS THE BENEFICIAL EFFECTS OF RUNNING AND FITNESS

- Before beginning the program

- If you have any question about any of the above conditions

- If you notice any significant change in body functions, immune response, etc.

TAKE ACTION!

- Watch for heat disease in group members and take action if you think they are in trouble.

- Walk, cool off and get help immediately.

HEART RATE MONITORS IN A MARATHON PROGRAM

Note: Before using a heart rate monitor, you must be tested for maximum heart rate. The tables or formulas based on age are only averages and should not be used to determine whether you're overtraining or not. Testing should be done under the supervision of a trained professional. You don't need to go through a Maximum Oxygen Uptake test; the Max Heart Rate test is sufficient and not as involved.

+ If your estimate of max heart rate is too low, you'll not receive maximum benefit from using the heart monitor on speed sessions. You're wasting one of the primary sources of biofeedback which the heart monitor can give.

+ If your max heart rate estimate is too high, you'll overtrain on speed sessions and risk a long recovery time. It's also possible to overtrain on easy days and not recover between the harder sessions.

HOLDING YOU BACK ON A LONG RUN

Almost everyone is capable of running faster for three to six miles than they can run for 15 or more. If you wear your heart monitor on a long training run and try to stay close to 70 percent of maximum heart rate, you'll almost certainly run too hard at first, which will make the end of the run difficult and increase recovery time.

When Heart Monitors can help

1. To hold you back during a long run— especially at the end
2. To make sure that an easy day is really *easy*
3. To ensure that "form accelerations" are "easy gliders"
4. To help you improve marathon racing form—without overtraining
5. To keep you from having a long recovery after marathon speed sessions
6. To tell you when you have rested enough between mile repeats in a marathon speed session

7. To serve notice when you're overtrained and need to take some extra days off or easy
8. To make sure that you're not increasing tiredness on marathon pace miles (on Wednesday or Friday)

When Heart Monitors don't help

1. At the beginning of long runs (especially if you try to stay close to 70 percent max heart rate).
2. When you don't know your exact maximum heart rate.

The reason for this is as follows. At the start of a long run, you can run slower than you could race a 5K or 10K and feel very comfortable for the first few miles. Running close to 70 percent of max heart rate means that you're at 70 percent of your 5K or 10K pace, which is almost certainly too fast for a long run that exceeds 15 miles.

In other words, you can run too fast during the first part of a long run and still register a heart rate of less than 70 percent of maximum heart rate.

Use the two-minute rule instead of your heart monitor during the first part of the long ones: Run at least two minutes per mile slower than you could run that distance on that day. This means that you must adjust for heat, humidity, hills, etc. If your pace is slower than this, you'll only benefit from a faster recovery, while receiving the same endurance value as a fast run of the same distance.

The heart monitor can help you regulate subconscious increases in effort between pace checks. I recommend staying below 65 percent of max heart rate for the first half of the long run, during which period you'll probably notice an elevated rate on the hills (telling you to slow down). During the second half, the gradual onset of fatigue will cause the heart rate to naturally rise at the same effort level. Adjust pace to keep the rate below 70 percent during the second half.

MAKING SURE THAT AN EASY DAY IS REALLY AN EASY DAY

The easy runs during the week merely maintain the conditioning you gained on the weekend long run (or repeat miles). To ensure that you're running slowly enough, wear your heart monitor, and stay below 65 percent of max. This conservative plan will limit the possibility of going too hard when you need to be recovering.

SHOULD I RUN MARATHON PACE MILES DURING THE WEEK?

If you've recovered from the weekend long or hard runs, it's beneficial for time goal marathoners to run at marathon pace on the Wednesday and Friday easy runs. Here are some heart monitor guidelines for running parts of the easy day runs at goal pace:

1. Run a slow warm-up, ensuring that heart rate is significantly below 70 percent of max heart rate. If there are any signs of tiredness, just run slowly for the rest of the session.

2. After one to two slow miles, do four to eight acceleration-GLIDERS. These will help your running form to become smoother while you become comfortable running at a faster rhythm.

3. As you start the first mile at marathon pace, monitor your heart rate. Ideally, the rate will stay around 70 percent of maximum, but it's okay if it creeps a bit higher. If the rate reaches 75 percent of max, and you're not running faster than goal pace, just run slowly for the rest of the session. This is a sign that you're still fatigued from earlier sessions.

KEEPING YOUR "FORM ACCELERATIONS" FROM BECOMING SPRINTS

The purpose of gliding fast during some of your easy weekday runs is to work on more efficient form. You want these quicker turnover "glides" of 100 meters or so to be at a faster pace than you would run normally but without a significant increase in effort or heart rate. The heart monitor can give you this check on reality. If the rate rises above 75 percent on an acceleration, shorten stride, keep feet lower to the ground, avoid pushing off hard, and glide fast. This should keep the heart rate from getting out of bounds.

TO HELP YOU IMPROVE MARATHON RACING FORM

Your speed sessions of mile repeats can not only develop the endurance-speed needed for the marathon, but with the help of the heart monitor, you have the biofeedback necessary to improve form at the same time. [See the section in this book on mile repeats.]

Each mile repeat should be run only about 20 seconds faster per mile than your goal marathon pace. By using a heart monitor, you can teach yourself to run more efficiently by finding form innovations which help you run smoother. Let's say that during the first two mile repeats, your heart rate goes up to between 75 and 80 percent of max heart rate. On the remaining mile repeats, you maintain the same pace and try to keep the heart rate from going beyond 75 percent by running more efficiently. [See the chapter on form for suggestions for improvement.]

MONITORS WILL TELL YOU WHEN YOU CAN START ANOTHER MILE REPEAT——AND HELP SPEED RECOVERY.

By keeping your monitor on during the rest interval, you can tell when you have recovered enough to run another one. You should wait until the heart rate has gone below 70 percent and then walk for at least another 100 meters or so. It is better to let the heart rate drop to below 65 percent of

max, if possible. This extra rest will improve recovery.

MONITORS TELL YOU WHETHER YOU'VE OVERTRAINED

Pick a time of the day when you're less likely to be influenced by psychological or emotional items which would influence heart rate. For example, many find that the time right after waking is ideal. Each day, put on your monitor at this time and note your heart rate over a five to 10-minute time frame. If you have less time, then shorten this test period. After a few weeks, you'll establish a base line which tells you what your heart rate averages. Over the span of six to12 months, you will learn what the level is when you're rested, when you're training moderately hard, and when you've overtrained.

193

- When your resting heart rate (taken under the same conditions, day after day) is five percent higher than the low baseline, take an easy day.

- When the rate climbs to 10 percent or more higher than your low baseline, take the day off from running. You may do some non-pounding exercise if desired.

Heart Monitors: Limiting workout damage by limiting the time above 80 percent

Your heart rate is an excellent indicator of the level of your exercise, provided that you don't dramatically extend the length of the workout beyond the level to which you're currently trained. When you're running below 70 percent of maximum heart rate, you are unlikely to overtrain in intensity. (You can still overtrain by going farther than you've trained to go.) By keeping the heart rate between 70 and 80 percent of max heart rate, you can assume that your effort will normally produce a creative stress on the system, causing it to improve. This is the range you want to see during most of your speed workouts. But even the time spent in this 70 to 80 percent range must be managed so that you gradually increase.

But when you push the effort beyond 80 percent of max heart rate, you increase the recovery time of that workout. For those looking for top performance, incursions into the 80 and even occasional 90 percent bouts are fine (provided your doctor is fine with this). Because your recovery time and injury risk increase with the amount of time spent above 80 percent, the heart monitor can act as a damage control device.

Hard workouts like these should only be done once a week, and you should ease into the hard stuff. At first, make sure that you're only spending a few seconds at a time in the over-80 percent range. As the workouts progress, you can increase the length of the 80-percent-plus a little and also increase their frequency. Monitor your increase as follows: track the total number of minutes above 70 percent, above 80 percent, and above 90 percent in each speed workout, and don't let the increase in any segment of any one workout exceed 25 percent above that of the week before.

Remember that overwork can be cumulative. Too many days per month of racing, speedwork and long runs which are too fast (easy days should be run at least two minutes per mile slower than you could run that distance on that day) can add up

194

Improving form and efficiency by staying below 81 percent

The heart rate monitor is one of the best biofeedback devices for improving form through efficiency. As always, the best environment for change is managed stress, and the monitor can tell you when to back off.

If you haven't been doing speedwork, once a week is as often as you should do this workout. Veteran speed trainers may do a second speed workout (or a race) during and leading up to racing season, but it should be less than the original. Again, be sure to monitor total workload and recovery from races, speed and long runs.

Distance

This should start at the distance of an average run during the week.

Warmup

Go for at least one mile of easy jogging and one-half mile of accelerations.

Venue

The best place for this workout is at a track where you can monitor speed at a variety of short and longer intervals.

Workout

Run repetitions of 800 to 1600 meters. Start each at (or slightly below) current race pace for the distance trained for. Increase intensity until you are at 70 percent of max heart rate until that feels natural and comfortable. Increase very gradually to 80 percent of max. Now you're ready for the workout. Your goal is to find form improvements that will allow you to run faster yet stay at 80 percent of max heart rate (or below).

Techniques

Shorten stride an inch or two and increase turnover of feet and legs. Keep the push-off short and quick and directly under the body. Shift between different muscle groups as necessary so that one group doesn't get tired.

Monitor

While you are monitoring your heart rate, time segments on the track of 200 to 400 meters at a time. When the distance of the repetition gets too long (often 800 to 1200 meters), your heart rate will increase. This is a sign for you to take a break. Jog or walk for recovery and start again.

Warmdown

This should involve at least one mile of slow jogging and one-half mile of walking.

195

THE POWER OF THE GROUP

You may not be able to find a group, but marathon training will be more fun if you do.

- As a team, you can share the challenges, the laughs, the struggles and the exhilaration.

- No one needs to go through a tough day without being bolstered by the others.

- As you give support, you'll receive much more in return.

- Every year, in just about every pace group, lifelong friendships are formed.

I'm very proud of the over 98 percent marathon completion rate among those who go through the Galloway Training Program. I can't take credit for this rate of success, however. It's the fun and the bonding that occurs in each pace group as individuals become a team. In a group, individuals who have trouble getting motivated get on track. Competitors who tend to get injured from pushing too hard by themselves stay back with the group and stay healthy.

Much of the credit for the upsurge in marathon completion goes to the groups that are springing up across North America. Individuals training alone usually reach a plateau of fatigue, injury, lack of motivation or complications in other areas of life and drop out of the program. As the members of the group share the anxiety of the marathon challenge, they respond in interesting ways by becoming a closer group and inspiring one another.

If there's not a group in your area, you can start one by running together with just one other person. See the marathon training program flyer at the end of this book. Many lone runners will call friends and talk until they're motivated to get out the door. Some have simulated group runs by talking on cell phones during runs. Any innovation, modern or otherwise, which allows you to share motivation, will keep you moving down the road.

It's interesting to watch the groups come together. On the first day together, most are feeling a bit shy, reluctant to say much more than polite conversation. But after another group run or two, each member develops a sense of belonging and trust for the others. Over the next few months, often without realizing it, each will need to pull at least a little support from teammates, and each will give the same to the others. Through the joking and the gut-level respect generated through meeting challenges together, bonds are established which last a lifetime. Starting as ordinary fitness people, you'll rise to the extraordinary challenge of the marathon.

BACK TO OUR ROOTS

The primitive satisfaction we feel in group runs brings us directly back to our roots. Our ancestors migrated in small gatherings and developed a lot of human social skills along the way. In many cases, survival depended upon the successful completion of the migration and the ability to work together physically, mentally and spiritually. In a different way, our cardiovascular survival depends upon our weekly migrations.

Certainly, the varied and significant rewards of the migration are programmed into our being by these hearty ancestors. When we reach the finish line of each long one, we experience an unusual sense of genuine accomplishment, which is the same type experienced by Phidippides and a continuous stream of ancestors before him, going back at least a million years.

Some companies are discovering that the power of marathon team-building improves the bottom line as it reduces the waistline. I've seen how this experience breaks down barriers between divisions within a corporation as even the non-exercisers pull for the trainees to meet the challenge. You can't buy the productivity and attitude benefits that come from such a program.

BONDING WITH OTHERS...AND SELF

The most successful groups are those composed of folks at the same conditioning level. Together, this team of fitness equals will share the challenges, the exhilaration and the human moments. Because of the group, no one will go through a tough day without begin bolstered by the others. All will share the uplifting successes of each, in training and the other areas of life. As you give support, you'll receive much more in return.

Lifelong friendships are molded here. You'll receive help on some outings and give support on others. You'll learn more about the others in your group than you could ever imagine. And you'll give strength to others without realizing it. Everyone becomes a real person here, and everyone improves in often-unnoticed dimensions.

GROUP FUN

The primary goal of each group is to have fun as the distance is covered. I'm not saying that every step is wonderful or every hill bestows joy, but as you exchange jokes and stories and let the chemistry of your personalities create a unique group identity, the fun will emerge. At first you may have to search for it and use your imagination. Soon you'll enjoy a continuous stream of very short but very significant moments of gutter humor which bring the marathon experience to life.

197

HOMEWORK ASSIGNMENT: A JOKE, A JUICY STORY AND A CONTROVERSIAL ISSUE

If everyone brings each of these to every run, group entertainment is guaranteed. Sometimes it takes only one issue, and you can't believe that you're at the end of your run. Many groups give awards at breakfast after the run: the juiciest story wins a big orange juice.

KEEP THE GROUP TOGETHER— USING THE "HUFF & PUFF" RULE

In each of the Galloway training locations, we subdivide into pace groups based upon current conditioning and background. But even in the most "equal" groupings, one or two individuals will often struggle on each long run. It doesn't hurt a faster runner to slow down for the endurance is based on the distance covered, not the pace. So the group adjusts the pace to accommodate the members who just aren't having a good day (more frequent walk breaks, slower pace, etc.).

If someone is huffing and puffing during the first half of the run, slow the pace down at that time, even if the slower person says to leave him or her behind. During the last two to three miles, huffing is going to occur, but it shouldn't keep the individual from carrying on a conversation. If this occurs, not only does the group need to slow down for the last few miles, but on the next long one, the pace should be adjusted from the beginning.

ADJUSTING

During the first few weeks the groups will be a bit fluid, and some of you will want to move up or down. Please take the advice of your group leader if he or she suggests that another group's pace would be more comfortable for you. The first group priority is that everyone feel comfortable so that the "team" can stay together. Those who are faster must slow down to keep from producing injury or severe fatigue in the slower members. It doesn't hurt anyone to slow down. Faster runners who "throttle back" receive the same endurance and will recover faster. If you're not sure that you're in the correct group, consult your group leader. The best time to change groups, should this be necessary, is during the first three to four weeks, but it's okay to change after that.

GROUP RULES

1. Help the Group Leader by supporting the walk breaks and keeping the pace slow. Also, help with water, refreshments, etc.

2. Everyone in the group should be able to carry on a conversation, even at the end of the run. If anyone is huffing and puffing at all in the first half of the run, slow the pace down and/or take more frequent walk breaks.

3. Take all of the walk breaks, early and often. As the long ones get longer, the walk breaks should be taken more frequently.

4. If you're feeling tired (or you sense that someone else is struggling), tell the Group Leader so that the pace can be slowed.

5. When you're feeling great, slow down and stay with the group—don't lead them astray!

6. Each member of the group is responsible for his or her own safety. Never assume that others are looking out for you.

7. Your health is your responsibility. Get checked out by a doctor who knows about endurance exercise; confer with him or her when needed. Get help before medical problems occur.

8. Wear the shirt of your group in case you get separated.

9. Drink water all the time until you hear sloshing in your stomach.

10. Keep it fun. Bring a joke, a juicy story and a controversial issue to every run and share.

DON'T CUT OUT ANY WALK BREAKS

In every group, there are a few macho folks who push for eliminating the first few walk breaks. Hey, these are the most important ones! By starting early and doing each one, you'll speed up the recovery for every person in the group.

YOU'RE IN THE PROCESS OF BECOMING A MEMBER OF AN ELITE GROUP

About one tenth of one percent of the population completes a marathon each year. At the same time that most of the population is decreasing exercise and getting obese, your group is getting fitter. The dropout rate among individuals training on their own is about 10 times as high as those who join groups with pace groups. While most individual runners become injured or drop out of their marathon training during the last six weeks, pace group programs have almost no dropout during this same period. Group energy and support creates a bonding and level of respect experienced by few groups in today's world.

GROUP LEADERS NEED YOUR SUPPORT

It's not an easy job to try to keep everyone in a group from going too fast. On any given run, there are usually one or two individuals who are feeling good and want to increase the pace. By restraining these exuberant individuals at the beginning, the Leader will not only help those who aren't feeling good, but all members of the group will benefit from the chemistry of keeping the whole group together. Even the frisky ones will benefit. Instead of slowing down later and suffering due to the fast early pace, they will feel strong to the end and will have the best chance of recovering quickly. Don't argue with your Group

Leader when asked to slow down and stay together...even if it's a bad hair day or your blood sugar is low.

DESIGNATED SWEEPER

Even when the pacing is perfect, there are rare occasions when individuals cannot keep up with the group due to injury, sickness, etc. In each group, each week, a designated sweeper should drop back and stay with that person, providing support or transportation as needed. This assignment will rotate each week and is seldom needed with proper pacing for the group as a whole.

THE VICTORY CELEBRATION

One of the highlights of our Galloway group training is the celebration after the marathon medals have been won. This gathering is filled with the exuberance of group victory, fun awards, and war stories (some of them actually true). This one event brings together the positive emotions and collective respect into an experience that reinforces the great marathon accomplishment.

Be prepared to share stories and to laugh. Your homework is to take notes on each group run. Bring your disposable camera. There are always a few interesting things that happen, experiences shared, and statements made. Just a few of those details, photos and quotes will spice up a great event.

199

BIG RUNNERS

*T*all and heavy runners take more stress on every step and find it harder to run continuously. Carrying around extra weight is like fast-forwarding the time line 10 to 30 years.

There's good news, however. By putting in more walk breaks, early and often, running becomes easier and much more fun. You'll recover much more quickly while enjoying the end of the run more than ever.

The chapter on the "Age Issues" is a great guide for heavy runners. To interpret how to apply the rest guidelines, here are my suggestions:

Age	fitness level	pounds overweight	Your legs feel like you are:
20-29	very fit	10-20	30-39
20-29	average	10-20	35-45
20-29	unfit	10-20	40-50
20-29	very fit	over 20	35-45
20-29	average	over 20	40-50
20-29	unfit	over 20	45-55
30-39	very fit	10-20	40-49
30-39	average	10-20	45-55
30-39	unfit	10-20	50-60
30-39	very fit	over 20	45-55
30-39	average	over 20	50-60
30-39	unfit	over 20	55-65
40-49	very fit	10-20	50-60
40-49	average	10-20	55-65
40-49	unfit	10-20	60-70
40-49	very fit	over 20	55-65
40-49	average	over 20	60-70
40-49	unfit	over 20	65-75
50-59	very fit	10-20	60-69
50-59	average	10-20	65-75
50-59	unfit	10-20	70-80
50-59	very fit	over 20	65-75
50-59	average	over 20	70-80
50-59	unfit	over 20	75-85

HOW TO PREDICT YOUR MARATHON PERFORMANCE

By running several 5K races during your marathon training, you can predict how fast you're capable of going in the marathon itself. This was designed by Gerry Purdy and reprinted, in part, from information supplied for Galloway's Book On Running. More extensive charts are offered in Gerry's Computerized Running Training Programs, published by Track & Field News.

1. If you're running your first marathon, use this chart only to see what you could run if you were running to capacity. Then set your goal about two minutes per mile slower than that time. If your first one is slow and enjoyable (and the two are related), you'll continue to enjoy exercise and benefit from it. You'll have the opportunity to run faster in the next marathon... or the one after that.

2. Run several 5K's on non-long-run weekends. Make sure that they are run on certified courses (which have been accurately measured). See what your 5K predicts in the marathon. The more 5K's you run, the better your prediction potential.

3. This prediction is only valid if you have run the 26 to 28 mile-training run (two minutes per mile slower than you could run it) three weeks before the marathon itself. Those with goals of 3:40 and faster need to have also done the mile repeats as prescribed on the schedules in the front of this book.

4. If the marathon course is hilly or marathon day weather is above 50 degrees F and above 50 percent humidity, your time will not be as fast as it would be under ideal conditions. As the heat and humidity rise, you must adjust your pace to be more conservative from the first mile of the marathon. Be aware of heat disease symptoms and get help at the first sign of these.

5. Adjustment: Since this table is based upon ideal conditions that never occur together, you must adjust. Also, don't use your best 5K time to predict your marathon performance. Take an average of your best three times, and then add 10 to 20 minutes to the prediction. A conservative pace in the beginning will conserve your resources, allowing you to run faster at the end if you're ready to do so.

PREDICTING RACE PERFORMANCE

5KTIME	MARTIME	HALF MARTIME	5KTIME	MARTIME	HALF MARTIME
13:20	2:10:00	1:01:24	16:08	2:38:44	1:14:45
13:25	2:10:46	1:01:45	16:15	2:39:53	1:15:17
13:29	2:11:32	1:02:06	16:22	2:41:02	1:15:49
13:34	2:12:19	1:02:28	16:29	2:42:13	1:16:22
13:38	2:13:06	1:02:50	16:36	2:43:24	1:16:54
13:43	2:13:54	1:03:13	16:43	2:44:37	1:17:28
13:48	2:14:43	1:03:35	16:50	2:45:50	1:18:03
13:53	2:15:32	1:03:58	16:57	2:47:05	1:18:37
13:58	2:16:22	1:04:22	17:04	2:48:21	1:19:12
14:03	2:17:12	1:04:46	17:12	2:49:38	1:19:48
14:08	2:18:04	1:05:09	17:19	2:50:56	1:20:24
14:13	2:18:55	1:05:33	17:27	2:52:15	1:21:01
14:18	2:19:48	1:05:57	17:35	2:53:36	1:21:38
14:23	2:20:41	1:06:22	17:43	2:54:58	1:22:16
14:28	2:21:34	1:06:47	17:51	2:56:21	1:22:54
14:34	2:22:29	1:07:13	17:59	2:57:45	1:23:33
14:39	2:23:24	1:07:38	18:07	2:59:11	1:24:13
14:44	2:24:20	1:08:04	18:15	3:00:39	1:24:53
14:50	2:25:16	1:08:30	18:24	3:02:07	1:25:34
14:56	2:26:13	1:08:57	18:32	3:03:37	1:26:16
15:01	2:27:11	1:09:24	18:41	3:05:09	1:26:58
15:07	2:28:10	1:09:51	18:50	3:06:42	1:27:41
15:13	2:29:10	1:10:18	18:59	3:08:17	1:28:24
15:19	2:30:10	1:10:47	19:08	3:09:53	1:29:09
15:25	2:31:11	1:11:15	19:18	3:11:32	1:29:54
15:31	2:32:13	1:11:44	19:27	3:13:11	1:30:40
15:37	2:33:16	1:12:13	19:37	3:14:53	1:31:27
15:43	2:34:20	1:12:42	19:47	3:16:36	1:32:14
15:49	2:35:25	1:13:13	19:57	3:18:21	1:33:02
15:55	2:36:30	1:13:43	20:07	3:20:08	1:33:52
16:02	2:37:37	1:14:14	20:17	3:21:57	1:34:42

5KTIME	MARTIME	HALFMARTIME	5KTIME	MARTIME	HALFMARTIME
20:27	3:23:48	1:35:33	28:15	4:48:17	2:14:02
20:38	3:25:41	1:36:25	28:35	4:52:04	2:15:44
20:49	3:27:36	1:37:18	28:56	4:55:57	2:17:29
21:00	3:29:34	1:38:11	29:18	4:59:56	2:19:18
21:11	3:31:33	1:39:07	29:39	5:04:02	2:21:08
21:23	3:33:35	1:40:02	30:02	5:08:15	2:23:01
21:34	3:35:39	1:40:59	30:25	5:12:34	2:24:59
21:46	3:37:46	1:41:57	30:49	5:17:01	2:26:59
21:58	3:39:55	1:42:56	31:13	5:21:36	2:29:01
22:10	3:42:06	1:43:57	31:38	5:26:19	2:31:08
22:23	3:44:21	1:44:57	32:05	5:31:12	2:33:30
22:36	3:46:38	1:46:00	32:31	5:36:17	2:36:00
22:49	3:48:58	1:47:05	32:59	5:41:23	2:38:30
23:02	3:51:21	1:48:10	33:28	5:46:50	2:41:00
23:16	3:53:46	1:49:17	33:55	5:51:58	2:43:30
23:30	3:56:15	1:50:24	34:19	5:56:01	2:46:00
23:44	3:58:47	1:51:33	34:48	6:01:24	2:48:00
23:58	4:01:23	1:52:45	35:05	6:05:00	2:49:00
24:13	4:04:02	1:53:57	35:30	6:10:00	2:51:00
24:28	4:06:44	1:55:11	35:55	6:15:00	2:53:00
24:43	4:09:30	1:56:26	36:20	6:20:00	2:55:00
24:59	4:12:20	1:57:44	36:45	6:25:00	2:57:00
25:15	4:15:13	1:59:03	37:10	6:30:00	2:59:00
25:31	4:18:11	2:00:24	37:35	6:35:00	3:01:00
25:47	4:21:13	2:01:47	38:00	6:40:00	3:03:00
26:04	4:24:19	2:03:11	38:25	6:45:00	3:05:00
26:22	4:27:29	2:04:37	38:50	6:50:00	3:07:00
26:40	4:30:45	2:06:06	39:15	6:55:00	3:09:00
26:58	4:34:05	2:07:36	39:45	7:00:00	3:11:00
27:16	4:37:30	2:09:09			
27:35	4:41:00	2:10:44			
27:55	4:44:36	2:12:22			

203

PACE CHART

Mile Pace	2 mile	5 mile	10 mile	13 mile	half marathon	15 mile	20 mile	Marathon
5:00	10:00	25:00	50:00:00	1:05:00	1:05:30	1:15:00	1:40:00	2:11:00
5:20	10:40	26:40	53:20:00	1:09:20	1:09:52	1:20:00	1:46:40	2:19:44
5:40	11:20	28:20	56:40:00	1:13:40	1:14:14	1:25:00	1:53:20	2:28:28
6:00	12:00	30:00	60:00:00	1:18:00	1:18:36	1:30:00	2:00:00	2:37:12
6:20	12:40	31:40	1:03:20	1:22:20	1:22:58	1:35:00	2:06:40	2:45:56
6:40	13:20	33:20	1:06:40	1:26:40	1:27:20	1:40:00	2:13:20	2:54:40
7:00	14:00	35:00	1:10:00	1:31:00	1:31:42	1:45:00	2:20:00	3:03:24
7:20	14:40	36:40	1:13:20	1:35:20	1:36:04	1:50:00	2:26:40	3:12:08
7:40	15:20	38:20	1:16:40	1:39:40	1:40:26	1:55:00	2:33:20	3:20:52
8:00	16:00	40:00	1:20:00	1:44:00	1:44:48	2:00:00	2:40:00	3:29:36
8:20	16:40	41:40	1:23:20	1:48:20	1:49:10	2:05:00	2:46:40	3:38:20
8:40	17:20	43:20	1:26:40	1:52:40	1:53:32	2:10:00	2:53:20	3:47:04
9:00	18:00	45:00	1:30:00	1:57:00	1:57:54	2:15:00	3:00:00	3:55:48
9:20	18:40	46:40	1:33:20	2:01:20	2:02:16	2:20:00	3:06:40	4:04:32
9:40	19:20	48:20	1:36:40	2:05:40	2:06:38	2:25:00	3:13:20	4:13:16
10:00	20:00	50:00	1:40:00	2:10:00	2:11:00	2:30:00	3:20:00	4:22:00
10:20	20:40	51:40	1:43:20	2:14:20	2:15:22	2:35:00	3:26:40	4:30:44
10:40	21:20	53:20	1:46:40	2:18:40	2:19:44	2:40:00	3:33:20	4:39:28
11:00	22:00	55:00	1:50:00	2:23:00	2:24:06	2:45:00	3:40:00	4:48:12
11:20	22:40	56:40	1:53:20	2:27:20	2:28:28	2:50:00	3:46:40	4:56:56
11:40	23:20	58:20	1:56:40	2:31:40	2:32:50	2:55:00	3:53:20	5:05:40
12:00	24:00	1:00:00	2:00:00	2:36:00	2:37:12	3:00:00	4:00:00	5:14:24
12:20	24:40	1:01:40	2:03:20	2:40:20	2:41:34	3:05:00	4:06:40	5:23:08
12:40	25:20	1:03:20	2:06:40	2:44:40	2:45:56	3:10:00	4:13:20	5:31:52
13:00	26:00	1:05:00	2:10:00	2:49:00	2:50:18	3:15:00	4:20:00	5:40:36
13:20	26:40	1:06:40	2:13:20	2:53:20	2:54:40	3:20:00	4:26:40	5:49:20
13:40	27:20	1:08:20	2:16:40	2:57:40	2:59:02	3:25:00	4:33:20	5:58:04
14:00	28:00	1:10:00	2:20:00	3:02:00	3:03:24	3:30:00	4:40:00	6:06:48
14:20	28:40	1:11:40	2:23:20	3:06:20	3:07:46	3:35:00	4:46:40	6:15:32
14:40	29:20	1:13:20	2:26:40	3:10:40	3:12:08	3:40:00	4:53:20	6:24:16
15:00	30:00	1:15:00	2:30:00	3:15:00	3:16:30	3:45:00	5:00:00	6:33:00
15:20	30:40	1:16:40	2:33:20	3:19:20	3:20:52	3:50:00	5:06:40	6:41:44
15:40	31:20	1:18:20	2:36:40	3:23:40	3:25:14	3:55:00	5:13:20	6:50:28
16:00	32:00	1:20:00	2:40:00	3:28:00	3:29:36	4:00:00	5:20:00	6:59:12
16:20	32:40	1:21:40	2:43:20	3:32:20	3:33:58	4:05:00	5:26:40	7:07:56
16:40	33:20	1:23:20	2:46:40	3:36:40	3:38:20	4:10:00	5:33:20	7:16:40
17:00	34:00	1:25:00	2:50:00	3:41:00	3:42:42	4:15:00	5:40:00	7:25:24
17:20	34:40	1:26:40	2:53:20	3:45:20	3:47:04	4:20:00	5:46:40	7:34:08
17:40	35:20	1:28:20	2:56:40	3:49:40	3:51:26	4:25:00	5:53:20	7:42:52
18:00	36:00	1:30:00	3:00:00	3:54:00	3:55:48	4:30:00	6:00:00	7:51:36

204

RESOURCES

206

What To Look For In A Marathon Training Program

As the marathon has become a lifestyle change project, marathon training groups are springing up all over North America. Because of the group support, training can become fun and your chance of completing the marathon are greatly increased. Because there are a wide range of groups, look for programs which offer the following:

- Running Groups, based upon fitness level

- A leader in each pace group who enforces a slow pace and the walk breaks

- A schedule which gradually increases the long run past "the wall" (@ 23 miles)

- Long runs every other weekend (every third weekend when long one reaches 18 to 20 miles)

- Lots of laughs on every run

- For information on marathon training groups in many North American cities, call 1-800-200-2771.

Athens Marathon

Jeff Galloway announced that he will be joining the Apostolos Travel Group as they travel back to the marathoner's mecca: the original run from the seaside village of Marathon to the original Olympic Stadium of the modern games in Athens. This celebration of Phidippides' journey (almost 2500 years ago) and more than one century of organized marathon racing will be offered in a full tour or an extended weekend package. "So much of the experience of Greece depends upon where you stay and how your arrangements are made. Apostolos Travel professionals are Greek and provide cultural and local opportunities which normally wouldn't be available. Their choice of accommodations is superb: a small resort seacost town with scenic trails that Phidippides could have run. Several visits to inspiring ancient sites, most meals and all tour direction are included. This is an entirely different experience than you'd receive if you stayed in downtown Athens." For information, please call 303/755-2888. www.jeffgalloway.com

www.jeffgalloway.com

Stay in touch with training, fat-burning, and marathon gatherings, and read our weekly tips and monthly newsletter.

Sign up for this FREE Newsletter. Just call 1-800-200-2771 and leave your name and address for updates, fitness opportunities, trends.

What is a fitness vacation?

A growing number of people each year are choosing to spend some of their vacation time in a positive environment, enjoying hiking, running and just *being* in a beautiful area. This is one of the very few ways to really get away from the stress and become invigorated. It's tough to have to go to places like Lake Tahoe, Athens and the Alps, but somebody has to do it!

- Record holders don't attend. These are folks who are getting started or want to do more.

- You can learn techniques directly from the people who developed them.

- In a relaxed environment, lifelong friendships are made.

- Motivation, commitment and mental breakthroughs are covered.

- Your specific questions can be addressed, training program modified, etc.

- This fun time will be remembered for life!

- For more information on the various types of fitness vacations, call 800-200-2771.

Fat-Burning Tip: *"Increase the length of all of your runs to more than 45 minutes."*

Slow your pace down, and add a few more one-minute walk breaks early in the run, if necessary. Once you reach the magic 45-minute barrier, those who are running (and walking) within themselves will be burning mostly body fat as fuel. By continuing to do this regularly and extending the distance and time, you'll help the exercising muscle cells to become fat-burners.

Energizing Tip: *"Eat before you get really hungry."*

If you wait until you're significantly hungry, you'll almost certainly overeat. By eating small snacks at the first sign of hunger, you'll maintain the energy you need for job or school, sustain concentration, and avoid building up extra calories which will be converted into fat. Avoid snacks which have sugar (including fruit and fruit juices) and those with more than 15 percent of the calories in fat.

What about supplements?

Jeff: I don't see any harm in taking minimal doses of the anti-oxidants, and I take 500 mg of vitamin C and 400 iu of vitamin E daily.

One of the few products on the market that has excellent research to back it up is Endurox. This supplement has been shown to speed recovery between exercise sessions and to encourage fat burning. I've noticed that while taking it for the last year and a half, I'm able to run four or five days in a row without getting tired legs – versus fatigue after three days BE (before Endurox).

It's unlikely that taking vitamins will cut out the lulls or doldrums during the day. This is usually due to low blood sugar and can be corrected by regular doses of PowerBars. After six years and about 100 competitive products, I have found that PowerBar delivers the best sustained energy level for exercise and for life in general.

For further information, visit the Endurox website at www.endurox.com

Jeff Galloway's Weekend Retreat

Join us for a few days of hiking, running, walking and learning with the man who literally wrote the book on running. Olympian Jeff Galloway (*Galloway's Book On Running*), will help you set up an injury-free exercise routine, as you enjoy the support of others who want to get started, become more motivated, or energize their commitment to exercise.

Ski Lodge accomodations

The hotel has a fitness center, two hot tubs, beautiful pool, kitchenettes, and tennis courts nestled at the end of Squaw Valley. Meals will be all-you-care to eat, with choices, including low-fat options.

All abilities, all levels

Adult runners and walkers, especially novice and intermediate folks, will enjoy the information, the support of the group, and gentle but satisfying exercise. There will be hikes and time to socialize.

Fatburning, Motivation, Form and technique, Nutrition, Injury-free Exercise

Jeff will help you cut through the overwhelming mass of conflicting information so that you can set up a time-sensitive program for fatburning, racing, or just finishing (a 5K, 10K or marathon). Jeff's motivational style will keep you fired up for months to come.

Meet such guests as

- ♦ **Joe Henderson** - running's most prolific writer who knows just about everything that's going on in our sport
- ♦ **Bob Anderson** – the expert who literally wrote the book on *Stretching*
- ♦ **Sister Marion Irvine** – the humorous and inspiring nun who qualified for the Olympic Trials at age 50
- ♦ **Dr. Gary Moran** – physiologist and expert in biomechanics, strength, etc.
- ♦ **Dr. David Hannaford** – sports podiatrist specializing in running injuries
- ♦ **John Bingham** – the Penguin from *Runner's World*!

For more information: Call 1-800-200-2771 x 10.
www.jeffgalloway.com

Jeff Galloway's Fitness Vacations

LAKE TAHOE

Imagine yourself on a hike or a run along a crystal clear lake, surrounded by beautiful mountains, with an endless series of trails and other recreational opportunities. Even when the temperature goes above 85 degrees F, you'll be comfortable in the 10-30 percent humidity. Jeff has averaged 20 days per summer at Tahoe for 21 years and has experienced only about 15 cloudy or rainy days, total.

If you'd like to explore this beautiful area on the south shore of the lake with a group, look into Galloway's vacation at Tahoe. After a morning run along scenic paths in national forests or on the Truckee River bike path, you'll have breakfast. Jeff and staff will then present seminars on the topics listed below. Most afternoons are spent hiking some of the most beautiful areas you'll ever experience or in other fun activities, such as swapping T-shirts, etc.

You'll meet inspiring and friendly experts such as Bob Anderson (the expert who literally wrote the book on Stretching), Sister Marion Irvine (a humorous and inspiring nun who qualified for the Olympic Trials at age 50), Joe Henderson (running's most prolific writer who knows just about everything that's going on in our sport), Dr. Gary Moran (physiologist and expert in biomechanics, strength, etc.), Dr. David Hannaford (sports podiatrist specializing in running injuries). and John Bingham (the Penguin from Runner's World).

SWISS ALPS

A "Sound of Music" Running Experience

Join Jeff Galloway for a delightful running tour of the Swiss Alps and run or walk 30K trail event. During 11 days, you'll enjoy some of the most beautiful scenery you'll ever experience. Home base will be the beautiful alpine resort town of Davos. The Swiss Alps is a fairytale area of sparkling lakes and lush green valleys surrounded by rugged peaks that live up to the beauty and appeal of their promotional literature. Besides excursions to scenic Swiss towns, we'll spend a day in Zurich, and you'll have an option to visit Lucerne.

For more information, call 1-303-755-2888 or email: apostolos@athensmarathon.com

TYPICAL CAMP SCHEDULE:

7:00	Group run/walk/stroll
8:00	Breakfast
9:00-12:00	Clinic Sessions
12:00	Lunch
1:00-6:00	Hiking, Sightseeing, Exploring
6:00	Dinner

CLINIC SESSIONS:

Nutrition   Mental Strength   Stretching
Getting Better As We Get Older
Motivation   Water Running   Cross Training
Marathon Training   Running Faster
Fatburning   Strengthening

Athens Marathon

October-November

Join us for the
Athens Marathon Tour

In 490 B.C., Phidippides ran from the battlefield of Marathon to Athens bringing news of victory. You can run the original route in his very footsteps.

Apostolos Greek Tours would like to be your host in Greece for the Marathon. Tour packages include:

- All Marathon entry paperwork and fees

- Round-trip airfare from our gateway city to Athens plus all ground transportation, all lodging and most meals in Greece

- Organized tours of ancient sites and museums including the Acropolis, Mycenae, Delphi and others

- Lots of activity and fun for non-runners too!

- Custom packages fit to your exact needs

- And much, much more!

For a free information packet, contact
Apostolos Greek Tours
3145 S. Akron Street, Denver, CO 80231
voice: 303/755-2888
fax: 303/755-4888
email: apostolos@athensmarathon.com
website: www.athensmarathon.com

Ask about our upcoming Switzerland tour too!

FURTHER READING......
OR VIEWING....

Galloway's Book On Running (GBR)

Experts have called this book "the standard among running books" and "the complete running information resource, written so you can understand it." In its 287 pages, you'll find just about everything you wanted to know about running: training, nutrition, injuries, shoes, stretching and strengthening, running form, 10K programs by time goal, racing, beginning, women's running, and much more. Organized so that you can easily find the segment in which you're interested, this has become the best-selling running book in North America.

"Breaking The Tape"

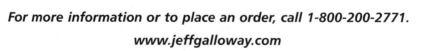

In two 30-minute VHS videotapes and a 30-minute motivational audiocassette, Jeff Galloway talks you through the world of running information. The first 30-minute segment includes tips on nutrition, stretching, choosing the right shoes, running injury free, and cross training. Tape Two covers form, pacing, peaking, setting realistic goals, building an interval speedwork plan for the 5K and 10K, and Jeff's six-month marathon training program. This is great for individual instruction or for group clinics and exercise reinforcement.

Jeff Galloway's Training Journal

In this spiral-bound training tool, Jeff will lead you through the process of setting up a training program, step by step. Not only can you set up and record your progress for a year at a time, you'll be able to analyze the data in tables: logs for shoes, injuries, speed sessions. Graphs for morning pulse will help you monitor overtraining.

For more information or to place an order, call 1-800-200-2771.

www.jeffgalloway.com

Let Jeff Galloway coach you at home!

proudly presents

Jeff Galloway's Training Software

for Marathon and Half Marathon

Renowned runner, author and lecturer Jeff Galloway, whose best selling books have helped hundreds of thousands of runners, has now made his acclaimed training program available through the PC Coach software training system.

Based on the techniques Jeff uses in his Marathon programs across the country, this program will set you on the path to success, whatever your goals!

The Galloway Plan creates exciting training programs for all ability levels from beginner on up. The plan sets up a detailed training schedule for you based on:

- **Your running history and experience**
- **Your race distance (Marathon or Half-Marathon)**
- **Your personal goals (Race goal time, Train to finish, Fat burning)**
- **Your race date**

Week by week, throughout your training, Jeff is there on your computer screen to monitor your progress, adjust the training schedule, and give you tips and training advice that will keep you motivated each day, right up to your race. Whatever your running experience, Jeff's program can give you the best program for your special situation.

For more information, or to receive a free demo of the Galloway software, visit the PC Coach web site at http://www.pccoach.com or call 1-800-522-6224.

MAJOR MARATHONS

JANUARY

Walt Disney World Marathon

P.O. Box 10,000
Lake Buena Vista, FL 32830-1000
407)939-7810
www.runningnetwork.com
generally held on the first or second weekend
in January
course open 7 hours

Houston Marathon

720 North Post Oak Road, Ste. 335
Houston, TX 77024
713-957-3453
www.houstonmarathon.com
generally held on Martin Luther King Day
holiday weekend
course open 5 ½ hours

214

San Diego Marathon

511 S. Cedros Avenue, Suite B
Solana Beach, CA 92075
619-792-2900
www.sdmarathon.com
course open 4 ½ hours

FEBRUARY

Las Vegas International Marathon

P.O. Box 81262
Las Vegas, NV 89180
702-876-3870
www.lvmarathon.com
generally held on the first weekend in February
course open 5 hours

Motorola Austin Marathon

P.O. Box 684587
Austin, TX 78768-4587
512-505-8304
www.motorolamarathon.com
course open 6 hours

Official All Star Cafe Myrtle Beach Marathon

P.O. Box 8780
Myrtle Beach, SC 29578-8780
843-293-RACE
www.coastal.edu/mbmarathon
course open 7 hours

MARCH

Sutter Home Napa Valley Marathon

P.O. Box 4307
Napa, CA 94558-0430
707-255-2609
email: shnvm@napanet.net
generally held on the first weekend in March
course open 5 ½ hours

Los Angeles Marathon

11110 W. Ohio Avenue, Suite 100
Los Angeles, CA 90025
310-444-5544
www.lamarathon.com
over 15,000 participants in 1998

Shamrock Sportsfest Marathon

2308 Maple Street
Virginia Beach, VA 23451
757-481-5090
www.shamrock.sportsfest.com
course open 6 hours

Maui Marathon

Valley Isle Road Runners Association
P.O. Box 330099
Kahuli, Maui HI 96733
808-871-6441
www.mauimarathon.com
course open 8 hours

APRIL

Boston Marathon

Boston Athletic Association
131 Clarendon Street
Boston, MA 02116
617-236-1652
www.bostonmarathon.org

This is a qualifying race. You can qualify between January 1st of the year prior to the race year and mid-March that race year. The qualifying times are as follows:

Age	Men	Women
18-34	3:10	3:40
35-39	3:15	3:45
40-44	3:20	3:50
45-49	3:25	3:55
50-54	3:30	4:00
55-59	3:35	4:05
60-64	3:40	4:10
65-69	3:45	4:15
70+	3:50	4:20

Big Sur International Marathon

P.O. Box 222620
Carmel, CA 93922-26200
831-625-6226
www.bsim.org/
generally held at the end of April
one of the most beautiful marathon courses in the world
course open 5 ½ hours

Country Music Marathon

Nashville Sports Council
401 Church Street, Suite 2700
Nashville, TN 37219
858-450-6510
www.cmmarathon.com
the county music capitol of the world
course open 7 hours

London Marathon

www.london-marathon.co.uk/
Sports Tours International 44 (0) 161 703 8161
lottery system

MAY

Vancouver International Marathon

P.O. Box 3213
Vancouver, B.C., Canada, V6B 3X8
604-872-2928
www.wi.bc.ca
one of the most scenic marathons in the world
course open 5 hours

Cincinnati Flying Pig Marathon

644 Linn St. Ste. 626
Cincinnati, Ohio 45203
513-721-PIGS
www.flyingpigmarathon.com

Pittsburgh Marathon

200 Lothrop Street
Pittsburgh, PA 15213-2582
412-647-7866
www.upmc.edu/pghmarathon
course open 6 hours
generally held during the first weekend in May

CVS- Cleveland Marathon

29525 Chagrin Blvd., Suite 316
Pepper Pike, OH 44122
216-378-0141
course open 5 ½ hours

Avenue of the Giants Marathon

281 Hidden Valley Road
Bayside, CA 95524
707-443-1226
www.humboldt1.com/~avenue
natural beauty in Humboldt Redwoods State Park
no time limit

National Capitol Marathon

P.O. Box 426 Station A
Ottawa, Ontario, Canada, K1N 8V5
613-234-2221
www.sirus.on.ca/running/ncm.html

215

Rock and Roll Marathon

C/O Elite Racing
5452 Oberlin Drive. Ste. B
San Diego, CA 92121
619-450-6510
www.rnrmarathon.com

over 15,000 participants in 1998
finish line open for 8 hours

Key Bank Vermont City Marathon

P.O. Box 152
Burlington, VT 05402
802-863-8412
email: RUNVT@together.net
www.vcm.org/

course open 6 hours
limited number of participants (fills up early)

JUNE

Grandma's Marathon

P.O. Box 16234
Duluth, MN 55816
218-727-0947
www.grandmasmarathon.com

course open 6 hours
generally held in mid-June
registration generally closes early

Mayors' Midnight Sun Marathon

Anchorage Sports and Recreation
P.O. Box 196650
Anchorage, AK 99519
907-343-4474

course open 8 hours
trademark Alaskan scenery

JULY

Providian San Francisco Marathon

120 Ponderosa Court
Folsom, CA 95630
916-983-4622
www.sfmarathon.com

the ultimate tour of San Francisco
course open 6 hours

Calgary Marathon

Stampede Run-Off
P.O. Box 296, Station M
Calgary, Alberta, Canada T2P 2H9
403-264-2996

a marathon with a cowboy flavor
course open 5 ½ hours
generally held during the first weekend of July

AUGUST

Pike's Peak Marathon

P.O. Box 38235
Colorado Springs, CO 80937
719-473-2625
www.pikespeakmarathon.org

one of the most difficult marathons in the world
must have completed either the Pikes Peak Ascent, an ultramarathon, or a marathon
usually fills early

Marathon By The Sea

C/O Canada Games Aquatic Centre
50 Union Street
Saint John, New Brunswick, Canada
E2L 1A1
506-658-4715
www.aquatics.nb.ca

Silver State Marathon

2358 Camelot Way
Reno, NV 89509
702-849-0419
http://silverstatemarathon.com

generally held in late August

SEPTEMBER

U.S. Air Force Marathon

88 SPTG/SV
5215 Thurlow Street, Suite 2
Wright-Patterson AFB, OH 45433
800-467-1823 or 937-787-4350
http://afmarathon.wpafb.af.mil

generally held at the end of September
course open 8 hours

Clarence DeMar Marathon

P.O. Box 6257
Keene, NH 03431
877-526-2379

course open 5 hours
known as a wonderful small marathon

216

Community First Fox City Marathon

P.O. Box 1315
Appleton, WI 54913
920-830-7529
www.runningzone.com/
foxcitiesmarathon
course open 8 hours

OCTOBER

St. George Marathon

Leisure Services
86 South Main Street
St. George, UT 84770
801-634-5850
www.stgeorgemarathon.com
generally held during the first weekend of
October
reaches its participant limit very quickly
course open 6 hours

Portland Marathon

P.O. Box 4040
Beaverton, OR 97076
503-226-1111
www.portlandmarathon.org
generally held during the first weekend of
October

Twin Cities Marathon

708 North First Street, Ste. CR-33
Minneapolis, MN 55401
612-673-0778
www.doitsports.com/marathons/
twincities
beautiful and well organized marathon
generally held during the first weekend of
October
reaches it's 7,600 participant limit very quickly
course open 6 hours

Wineglass Marathon

Greater Corning Area Chamber of
Commerce
P.O. Box 117
Corning, NY 14830-0900
607-936-4686
www.pennynet.org/wineglass.htm
Runner's World has ranked it as "one of the
most scenic marathons"
course open 6 hours

Hartford Marathon

119 Hebron Ave.
Glastonbury, CT 06033
860-652-8866
www.hartfordmarathon.com
course open 6 hours

The Lasalle Banks Chicago Marathon

P.O. Box 10597
Chicago, IL 60610-0597
888-243-3344 or 312-243-3274
www.ChicagoMarathon.com
generally held towards the end of October
over 18,000 participants in 1999
one of the fastest marathon courses in the
world

Marine Corps Marathon

P.O. Box 188
Quantico, VA 22134-0188
800-RUN-USMC or 703-784-2225
www.marinemarathon.com
generally held towards the end of October
over 15,000 participants in 1999
course open 7 hours

Detroit International Marathon

Detroit Free Press/Flagstar Bank
P.O. Box 44405
Detroit, MI 48244-0405
313-393-7749

NOVEMBER

New York City Marathon

New York Road Runners Club
9 E. 89th Street
New York, NY 10128
212-423-2249
www.nyrrc.org/mar.htm
over 30,000 finishers
entries are accepted in a lottery system

Columbus Marathon

P.O. Box 26806
Columbus, Ohio 43226
614-433-0395
www.columbusmarathon.com
course open 5 ½ hours

217

Philadelphia Marathon

P.O. Box 21601
Philadelphia, PA 19131-0901
215-685-0054
www.philadelphiamarathon.com
course open 5 ½ hours

Atlanta Marathon

C/O Atlanta Track Club
3097 East Shadowlawn Avenue, NE
Atlanta, GA 30305
404-231-9064
held on Thanksgiving Day
course open 5 hours

Seattle Marathon

P.O. Box 31849
Seattle, WA 98103-1849
206-729-3660
www.seattlemarathon.org

DECEMBER

California International Marathon

P.O. Box 161149
Sacramento, CA 95816
916-983-4622
www.runcim.org
generally held during the first weekend of
December
course open 5 ½ hours

Dallas White Rock Marathon

3607 Oak Lawn
Dallas, TX 75219
214-528-2962
www.whiterock-marathon.com

Tucson Marathon

1643 N. Alvernon Way, Suite 108
Tucson, AZ 85712
520-320-0667
course open 6 hours

Honolulu Marathon

3435 Waialae Avenue, Room 208
Honolulu, HI 96816
808-734-7200
www.honolulumarathon.org/
no course limit

*For other marathon information, please see
The Ultimate Guide to Marathons by Dennis
Craythorn and Rich Hanna, Marathon
Publishers, Inc., 1996.*

218

RUNNING RESOURCES AND CONTACTS

California

JEFF GALLOWAY'S MARATHON TRAINING PROGRAM
Getting you to the finish line injury-free
Sacramento, San Francisco
1-800-200-2771 x12
www.jeffgalloway.com

AIDS MARATHON TRAINING PROGRAM
1313 N. Vine Street, 4th floor
Los Angeles, CA 90028
323-993-1400
lainfo@aidsmarathon.com
www.aidsmarathon.com

THE L.A. LEGGERS
P.O. Box 761
Santa Monica, CA 90406
310-577-8000
laleggers@earthlink.net
www.laleggers.org

A SNAIL'S PACE RUNNING SHOP
8780 Warner Avenue, Ste. 12
Fountain Valley, CA 92708
714-842-2337

A SNAIL'S PACE RUNNING SHOP
24741 Alicia Pkwy, Ste. K
Laguna Hills, CA 92653
949-707-1460

FLEET FEET
1730 Santa Clara #D3
Roseville, CA 95661
916-783-4558

FLEET FEET
8128 Madison
Fair Oaks, CA 95628-3756
916-965-8326

FLEET FEET
2311 J. Street
Sacramento, CA 95816
916-442-3338

FLEET FEET
310 C Main St.
Pleasanton, CA 94566
925-426-5576

FLEET FEET
2086 Chestnut St.
San Francisco, CA 94123
415-921-7188

PERSONAL BEST
2587-J Chino Hills Pkwy
Chino Hills, CA 91709
909-393-2000

PHIDIPPIDES- ENCINO
16545 Ventura Blvd.
Encino, CA 91436
818-986-8686

RUNNERS HIGH
6416 East Stearns
Long Beach, CA 90815
562-430-7833

RUNNERS HIGH
5375 East Second Street
Long Beach, CA 90803
562-433-7825

RUNNER'S FACTORY
51 University Ave.
Los Gatos, CA 95030
408-395-4311

STEVENS CREEK SOFTWARE/
THE ATHLETE'S BOOKSTORE
www.stevenscreek.com

TRANSPORTS
6022 College Avenue
Oakland, CA 94618
510-655-4809

Colorado

JEFF GALLOWAY'S MARATHON TRAINING PROGRAM
Getting you to the finish line injury-free
Denver, Boulder
1-800-200-2771 x12
www.jeffgalloway.com

BOULDER RUNNING COMPANY
2775 Pearl Street
Unit 103
Boulder, CO 80302
303-786-9255

RUNNER'S ROOST
1685 S. Colorado Blvd.
Denver, CO 80222
303-759-8455

RUNNER'S ROOST
6554 South Parker Road
Aurora, CO 80016
303-766-3411

RUNNER'S ROOST
107 E. Bijou
Colorado Springs, CO 80903
719-632-2633

P.C. COACH
Software training programs
303-494-9155

TATTERED COVER BOOK STORE
1628 16th Street
Denver, CO 80202
303-436-1070

219

Connecticut

JEFF GALLOWAY'S MARATHON TRAINING PROGRAM
Getting you to the finish line injury-free
Hartford
1-800-200-2771 x12
www.jeffgalloway.com

THE RUN-IN
2172 Silas Deane Highway
Rocky Hill, CT 06067
860-563-6136

D.C.

JEFF GALLOWAY'S MARATHON TRAINING PROGRAM
Getting you to the finish line injury-free
Washington D.C/Northern Virginia, Bethesda MD
1-800-200-2771 x12
www.jeffgalloway.com

AIDS MARATHON TRAINING PROGRAM
730 11th Street, NW #200
Washington, DC 20001
202-543-2RUN
dcinfo@aidsmarathon.com
www.aidsmarathon.com

Florida

JEFF GALLOWAY'S MARATHON TRAINING PROGRAM
Getting you to the finish line injury-free
Orlando, Miami, Daytona, Jacksonville, West Palm, Tampa
1-800-200-2771 x12
www.jeffgalloway.com

FOOTWORKS
5724 Sunset Dr.
S. Miami, FL 33143
305-666-7223

THE TRACK SHACK
1104 N. Mills Ave.
Orlando, FL 32803
407-898-1313

RUNNING WILD
5437 North Federal Hwy.
Ft. Lauderdale, FL 33308
954-492-0077

RUNNERS EDGE
3195 N. Federal Hwy.
Boca Raton, FL 33431
561-361-1950

Georgia

JEFF GALLOWAY'S MARATHON TRAINING PROGRAM
Getting you to the finish line injury-free
Atlanta, Gwinnett County, Augusta
1-800-200-2771 x12
www.jeffgalloway.com

ATLANTA TRACK CLUB
3097 East Shadowlawn
Atlanta, GA 30305
404-231-9064

PHIDIPPIDES
220 Sandy Springs Circle
Atlanta, GA 30328
404-255-6149

PHIDIPPIDES
Ansley Mall
1544 Piedmont Road, NE
Atlanta, GA 30324
404-875-4268

Idaho

THE ATHLETE'S FOOT
1752 West State Street
Boise, ID 83702
208-338-6661

Illinois

JEFF GALLOWAY'S MARATHON TRAINING PROGRAM
Getting you to the finish line injury-free
Chicago, Rockford
1-800-200-2771 x12
www.jeffgalloway.com

FLEET FEET
210 West North Avenue
Chicago, IL 60610
312-587-3338

RUNNERS HIGH
7 S. Dunton
Arlington Heights, IL 60005-1401
847-670-9255

RUNNERS EDGE
1211 Wilmette Avenue
Wilmette, IL 60091
847-853-8531

SPRINGFIELD RUNNING CENTER
2943 W White Oak Dr.
Springfield, IL 62704
217-787-4400

Indiana

ATHLETIC ANNEX RUNNING CENTRE
1411 W. 86th Street
Indianapolis, Indiana 46260
317-872-0000

Kansas

GARY GRIBBLE'S RUNNING STORE
Stoll Park Center
11932 W 119th
Overland Park, KS 66213
913-469-4090

ELITE FEET, INC.
11934 Roe Avenue
Overland Park, KS 66209
913-498-3338

Kentucky

KEN COMBS RUNNING CENTER
4137 Shelbyville Rd.
Louisville, KY 40207
502-895-3410

220

Louisiana

JEFF GALLOWAY'S MARATHON TRAINING PROGRAM
Getting you to the finish line injury-free
New Orleans
1-800-200-2771 x12
www.jeffgalloway.com

PHIDIPPIDES
6601 Veterans Blvd.
Metairie, LA 70003
504-887-8900

Maryland

JEFF GALLOWAY'S MARATHON TRAINING PROGRAM
Getting you to the finish line injury-free
Bethesda, Northern Virginia
1-800-200-2771 x12
www.jeffgalloway.com

AMERICAN RUNNING ASSOCIATION
4405 E-W Hwy, Ste. 405
Bethesda, MD 20814
301-913-9517

AIDS MARATHON TRAINING PROGRAM
730 11th Street, NW #200
Washington, DC 20001
202-543-2RUN
DC, Northern Virginia, Maryland
dcinfo@aidsmarathon.com
www.aidsmarathon.com

FEET FIRST
10451 Twin Rivers Rd.
Wildlake Village Green
Columbia, MD 21044
410-992-5800

Massachusetts

JEFF GALLOWAY'S MARATHON TRAINING PROGRAM
Getting you to the finish line injury-free
Boston
1-800-200-2771 x12
www.jeffgalloway.com

BILL RODGER'S RUNNING CENTER
353-T N. Market Place
Boston, MA 02109
617-723-5612
www.billrodgers.com

Michigan

COMPLETE RUNNER
915 South Dort Hwy.
Flint, MI 48503
810-233-8851

GAZELLE SPORTS
3930 28th St.
Grand Rapids, MI 49512
616-940-9888

GAZELLE SPORTS
214 S. Kalamazoo Mall
Kalamazoo, MI 49007
616-342-5996

GAZELLE SPORTS
24 West 8th Street
Holland, MI 49423
616-392-2282

HANSON'S RUNNING SHOP
20641 Mack Ave.
Grosse Pointe Woods, MI 48236
313-882-1325

HANSON'S RUNNING SHOP
3407 Rochester Rd.
Royal Oak, MI 48073
248-616-9665

HANSON'S RUNNING SHOP
8409 Hall Rd.
Utica, MI 48317
810-323-9683

TOTAL RUNNER
29207 Northwestern Hwy
Southfield, MI 48034
248-354-1177

TOTAL RUNNER
15355 Dix-Toledo Rd.
Southgate, MI 48195
734-282-1101

BAUMAN'S RUNNING CENTER
1453 West Hill Rd.
Flint, MI 48507
810-238-5981

Missouri

GARY GRIBBLE'S RUNNING STORE
8600 State Line
Ward Pkwy Mall
Kansas City, MO 64114
816-363-4800

New Jersey

MILES AHEAD
2241 Meetinghouse Road
Manasquan, NJ 08736
732-223-0444

New Mexico

FLEET FEET
8238 Menaul Blvd. NE
Albuquerque, NM 87110
505-299-8922

221

New York

JEFF GALLOWAY'S MARATHON TRAINING PROGRAM
Getting you to the finish line injury-free
New York City
1-800-200-2771 x12
www.jeffgalloway.com

North Carolina

JEFF GALLOWAY'S MARATHON TRAINING PROGRAM
Getting you to the finish line injury-free
Charlotte, Raleigh
1-800-200-2771 x12
www.jeffgalloway.com

FLEET FEET
102-A E Main St.
Carrboro, NC 27510
919-968-3338

RUN FOR YOUR LIFE
2422 Park Road
Charlotte, NC 28203
704-358-0713

9TH ST. ACTIVE FEET, INC.
705 Ninth Street
Durham, NC 27705
919-286-5101

Ohio

BOB RONCKER'S RUNNING
SPOT
1993 Madison Road
Cincinnati, Ohio 45208
513-321-3006

THE RUNNING SPOT- EAST
106 Main St.
Milford, Ohio 45150
513-831-2378

DAVE'S RUNNING SHOP, INC.
5577 Monroe St.
Sylvania, OH 43560
419-882-8524

OHIO RIVER ROAD RUNNERS
Bill Mercer
2061 Dane Lane
Bellbrook, OH 45305
513/848-2576

CEDARWINDS
Runners Books and Smartware
P.O. Box 351
Medway, Ohio 45341
1-800-548-2388

Oregon
South Carolina

**JEFF GALLOWAY'S MARATHON
TRAINING PROGRAM**
Getting you to the finish line
injury-free
Salem
1-800-200-2771 x12
www.jeffgalloway.com

GALLAGHER FITNESS
233 Commercial Street. NE
Salem, OR 97301
503-364-4198

Pennsylvania

AARDVARK SPORTS SHOP
571 Main Street
Bethlehem, PA 18018
610-866-8300

RITTENHOUSE SPORTS
SPECIALTIES
126 S. 18th St.
Philadelphia, PA 19103
215-569-9957

NATIONAL RUNNING CENTER
117 Mill Street
Dalton, PA 18414
1-800-541-1773
www.nationalrunningcenter.com

South Carolina

**JEFF GALLOWAY'S MARATHON
TRAINING PROGRAM**
Getting you to the finish line
injury-free
Greenville
1-800-200-2771 x12
www.jeffgalloway.com

PERSONAL BEST SPORTS
1922 Augusta Road, Ste. 110
Greenville, SC 29605
864-370-9721

THE EXTRA MILE
4711-18 Forest Drive
Columbia, SC 29206
803-782-8555

Tennessee

**JEFF GALLOWAY'S MARATHON
TRAINING PROGRAM**
Getting you to the finish line
injury-free
Nashville
1-800-200-2771 x12
www.jeffgalloway.com

BREAKAWAY ATHLETICS
9245 Poplar Avenue
Germantown, TN 38138
901-755-5789

BREAKAWAY ATLETICS
1708 Union Ave.
Memphis, TN 38104
901-722-8797

FLEET FEET
597 Erin Dr.
Memphis, TN 38117
901-761-0078

KNOXVILLE TRACK CLUB
3530 Talahi Gardens
Knoxville, TN 37919
423-673-8020

RUNNER'S MARKET
4443 Kingston Pike
Knoxville, TN 37919
423-588-1650

Texas

**JEFF GALLOWAY'S MARATHON
TRAINING PROGRAM**
Getting you to the finish line
injury-free
Dallas, Fort Worth, Houston
1-800-200-2771 x12
www.jeffgalloway.com

RUN-ON!
5400 East Mockingbird Ln.
Ste. 114
Dallas, TX 75206
214-821-0909

FLEET FEET
6590 Woodway
Houston, TX 77057
713-465-0033

FLEET FEET
5950 FM 1960 West
Houston, TX 77069
281-440-8783

FLEET FEET
2408 Rice Blvd.
Houston, TX 77005
713-520-6353

FLEET FEET
514 Everhard Road
Corpus Christi, TX 78411
361-225-3338

FLEET FEET
6408 North New Braunfless
San Antonio, TX 78209
210-805-0845

LUKE'S LOCKER
1540 South University
University Park Village
Fort Worth, TX 76107
817-877-1448

LUKE'S LOCKER
3607 Oak Lawn
Dallas, TX 75219
214-528-1290

Virginia

**JEFF GALLOWAY'S MARATHON
TRAINING PROGRAM**
Getting you to the finish line
injury-free
Northern Virginia, Richmond
1-800-200-2771 x12
www.jeffgalloway.com

AIDS MARATHON TRAINING
PROGRAM
730 11th Street, NW #200
Washington, DC 20001
202-543-2RUN
DC, Northern Virginia,
Maryland
dcinfo@aidsmarathon.com
www.aidsmarathon.com

PACERS
1301 King St.
Alexandria, VA 22314
703-836-1463

Washington

**JEFF GALLOWAY'S MARATHON
TRAINING PROGRAM**
Getting you to the finish line
injury-free
Seattle
1-800-200-2771 x12
www.jeffgalloway.com

Wisconsin

RODIEZ RUNNING STORE
10903 West Lincoln Avenue
West Allis, WI 53227
414-321-1154

Canada

THE RUNNING ROOM
LOCATIONS
The Running Room network
allows you to connect with
community running groups,
events, and clinics. I have
visited most of the locations
listed and am impressed with
the staff, the selection, and the
information resources.
www.runningroom.com

Alberta
Edmonton

EDMONTON ADMINISTRATIVE
OFFICE AND WAREHOUSE
9750-47 Avenue, Edmonton,
AB T6E 5P3
403-439-3099

TEAM SPORTS, 9750-47 AVE.
Edmonton, AB T6E 5P3
403-439-3099

8537-109 STREET
Edmonton, AB T6G 1E4
403-433-6062

KINSMEN SPORTS CENTRE
9100 Walterdale Hill
Edmonton, AB T6E 2V3
403-433-5901

CALLINGWOOD MARKETPLACE
#236 6655-178 Street
Edmonton, AB T5T 4J5
403-483-1516

#17 ST. ANNE ST.,
St. Albert, AB T8H 1E8
780-460-1102

Calgary

321A- 10TH ST. N.W.,
Calgary, AB T2N 1V7
403-270-7317

GLENMORE LANDING
SHOPPING CENTRE
#118, 1600-90 Ave., SW
Calgary, AB T2V 5A8
403-252-3388

UNIT #435, CROWFOOT
VILLAGE
20 Crowfoot Crescnet, NW,
Calgary, AB T36 2P6
403-239-2991

British Columbia
Vancouver

SUITE 103, 679 DENMAN
STREET
Vancouver, BC V6G 2L3
604-684-9771

#001 CITY SQUARE
555 West 12th Ave.
Vancouver, BC V5Z 3X7
604-879-9271

SUITE 738, 2601 WESTVIEW
DRIVE
North Vancouver, BC V7N 3W9
604-983-9761

#235, 2083 ALMA STREET
4th and Alma Shopping Ctr,
Vancouver, BC V6R 4N6
604-225-0222

WESTWOOD CENTRE, #202
2748 Longheed Hwy.,
Port Coquitlam, BC V3B 6P2
604-945-1810

UNIT 410, 7380 KING GEORGE
HIGHWAY,
Surrey, BC V3W 5A5
604-599-6001

Kelowna

#115 2463 HIGHWAY 97
NORTH,
Kelowna, BC V1X 4J2
250-862-3511

Victoria

1008 DOUGLAS ST.
Victoria, BC V8W 2C3
250-383-4224

223

Manitoba
Winnipeg
KENASTON VILLAGE MALL,
1875 Grant Avenue,
Winnipeg, MB R3N 1Z2
204-487-7582

2095 PEMBINA HWY.
Pembina Village Shopping Ctr.,
Winnipeg, MB R3T 5L1
204-489-8888

Saskatchewan
Regina
2118 ALBERT ST.,
Regina, SK S4P 2T9
306-790-8480

Ontario
Toronto
2629 YONGE ST.
Toronto, ON M4P 2J6
416-322-7100

UNIT #3, 2100 BLOOR ST.
WEST
Toronto, ON M6S 1M7
416-762-4478

1977 QUEEN ST.
East Toronto, ON M4L 1J1
416-693-1530

COMMERCE COURT, #30
Wellington Street West
Toronto, ON M5L IE8
416-867-7575

RICHMOND HILL
Unit 1, 8900 Yonge St.
Richmond Hill, ON L4C 0L7
905-764-7255

HAMILTON
1457 Main St.- West
Hamilton, ON L8S 1C9
905-528-7444

MISSISSAUGA
Sussex Centre, #70
Burnhamthorpe Road West
Mississauga, ON L5B 3C2
905-279-6486

BARRIE
151A Dunlop Street East
Barrie, ON L4M 1B2
705-726-2550

LONDON
620 Richmond St.
London, ON N6A 5J9
519-438-8550

Ottawa
911 BANK ST.
Ottawa, ON K1S 3W5
613-233-5617

160 SLATER ST.
Ottawa, ON K1P 5H8
613-233-5165

UNIT 13, 1568 MERIVALE
ROAD
Merivale Shopping Fair
Nepean, ON K2G 3J9
613-228-3100

Nova Scotia
HALIFAX
5514 Spring Garden Road
Halifax, NS B3J 1G6
902-420-0774

- Jeff's books can also be found at www.Amazon.com and www.Bordersbooks.com.

- Look for Jeff's articles at www.runnerworld.com.

- Look for more schedules and tips at www.asimba.com.

- We work closely with John Bingham, the Penguin, Runner's World columnist. For information on any of his programs, including Team Penguin, visit his website at www.WaddleOn.com.

- Tawni Gomes, an on-line support group, www.connectingconnectors.com, 650/991-4200, inspired by Oprah Winfrey and Bob Greene, author of Making the Connection

INDEX

225

229

NOTES

NOTES

NOTES

NOTES

NOTES